MW00748327

Fifty Years of Families, Friends and Memories

Pinawa

Chris Saunders and Louise Daymond

2017

Copyright © 2017 by the Pinawa Foundation

All rights reserved. This book or any portion thereof may not be reproduced or used in any manner whatsoever without the express written permission of the publisher except for the use of brief quotations in a book review or scholarly journal.

First Printing: 2017

ISBN 978-0-9950984-3-5

Pinawa Foundation
Post Office Box 100
Pinawa, Manitoba R0E 1L0

Illustrations and photographs are courtesy of Atomic Energy of Canada Limited or from public sources unless otherwise indicated. Cover photograph courtesy of Richard Allen Everitt.

Contents

Foreword

This book is Pinawa's story from an idea in 1962 to the thriving community of today. As the first federal government-planned community in Canada, Pinawa will be forever linked to Atomic Energy of Canada Limited and the impressive nuclear science and engineering accomplishments at Whiteshell Laboratories.

Most of us believe our community is special; usually because of the people, the setting or the clubs and special events that happen in our home town. Pinawa is no exception. This book is a record to the place that we have experienced both the routine and the extraordinary events of our lives: births and funerals, the first day of school and graduations, a wedding, a first job, a retirement celebration, and walking along our river trail.

We would like to acknowledge and thank authors Pat Roy and Louise Daymond for their 20th Anniversary History Book of Pinawa, and Chris Gilbert and the Centennial Committee for their 1967 history book. They were the inspiration for this 50th Anniversary edition. We would also like to thank all of you who contributed information, articles and photographs. Your contributions have helped make this book possible.

We dedicate this book to the thousands of people that have been part of the Pinawa story – 50 years of families, friends and memories.

Pinawa's Suspension Bridge

Chapter 1
Introduction

Pinawa, derived from the aboriginal word "pinnowok", meaning "calm, gentle water", has been the name of only two communities around the world, both in Manitoba.

Pinawa was first used in 1903 when the Winnipeg Electric Company set out to do something unique; build a year round hydroelectric generating station in Manitoba's wilderness. New immigrants, many from Scandinavia and England, came to find work. They arrived in Lac du Bonnet by train, then walked or hitched a wagon ride, crossing the Winnipeg River by ferry. Tents and crude shanties sprang up around the construction site.

As work progressed and men began to bring their families out, the first permanent houses were built and the village of Pinawa was born.

The company store was a busy place, especially on payday or when the mail arrived because it was also the post office. In the beginning, this tiny store carried all the staples, including things like flour, sugar, salt and canned goods. The company gardens and animals supplied a lot for the store. The cows provided meat, milk, butter and cheese; chickens provided meat, eggs and feathers for pillows; and sheep provided meat and wool. As the community grew around Pinawa, local farmers also brought in produce and meat to sell at the store.

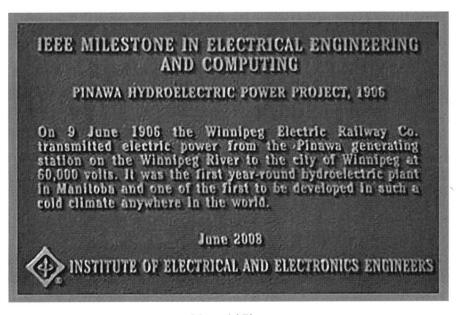

Memorial Plaque

Dam Crew - 1907

Pinawa hydroelectric plant and town site in the 1920s

The town hall became the meeting place, movie theatre, church and dance hall for the town. Holidays were big events, featuring picnics and entertainment. At the Christmas concert, everyone, young and old, played a part. People who had moved away came back to attend the Halloween Dance. Everyone in town brought home-cooked food from their country of origin. The Winnipeg Electric Company made sure there were many recreational facilities for the people of Pinawa. These included tennis courts, two hockey rinks, a baseball diamond and a curling rink.

The first school, built in 1913, was a one-room log structure with a big potbelly stove that the nine students gathered around for warmth on a cold day. A second school was built farther from the town. Some say the reason was to keep the town quiet so shift workers could sleep during the day. The new location was also more accessible for children from the growing farm community around Pinawa. Grades one to eight were taught. School lessons included going to the movies. The children had to learn to read the subtitles of silent movies. Teachers also took advantage of the outdoor classroom around them. There were plenty of field trips to identify trees, animal tracks and plants.

Old Pinawa dam

Pinawa was home and the memories were many. In 1951, Mrs. Bernard, who wrote the monthly article "Pinawa Pointers" for the Winnipeg Electric Employees Magazine, wrote in her column:

"I often wonder what it will be like here in years to come… if this place is ever a ghost town, I'll bet there will be nothing but friendly spirits here. If, years hence, someone comes to Pinawa on a summer's evening, I'm sure if one listens carefully, there will be strange sounds carried on the twilight breeze. The echo of the laughter of all the children who have played here from the beginning, the voices of the women discussing gardening and recipes and calling the small fry in at night and the raillery of the men coming home from work at five o'clock. Though Pinawa may be deserted, I'm sure it will never be lonely."

Pinawa's second school, c. 1940
(Photograph courtesy of L. Bruce)

On September 21, 1951, after 45 years of service, the first year-round hydroelectric plant in Manitoba switched off the power. By then the town of Pinawa was almost deserted. Only a few employees remained to decommission the power plant.

In the late 1950s scientists and engineers at Atomic Energy of Canada Limited (AECL) began examining alternate types of nuclear reactor designs. To support this work, AECL proposed that a new research laboratory be established in Manitoba. AECL president J.L. Gray journeyed to Manitoba to meet with premier Duff Roblin. The new research centre would not be costless for the province. It would have to look after some of the infrastructure, such as roads and a bridge across the Winnipeg River, as well as housekeeping details. By the summer of 1960 agreement seemed far away. With help from the federal government, however, an agreement was approved by cabinet on July 21, 1960 and the Whiteshell Nuclear Research Establishment (WNRE) was born.

The plan was to build a plant site along the Winnipeg River, and a town site to house the employees and their families was to be carved from the wilderness along the water some 15 km from the plant. The province would do their part by building a bridge across the river. The highways leading into the town and the plant site were also under their jurisdiction.

Several communities in the economically depressed region welcomed the government's announcement, and many town councils held out hope that their communities would suit the needs of the new facility, which included a plentiful supply of water, and at least 11,000 square acres of undeveloped land for the plant site. On October 1, 1959, the front page of the Winnipeg Free Press heralded the news of an "atomic site" to be built somewhere in Manitoba on its front page.

In Lac du Bonnet, MLA Oscar Bjornson wasn't shy about pressing the premier to locate the facility in his riding. Bjornson told the Springfield Leader, in an interview one week following the announcement that "no effort should be spared to inform the Manitoba government that the people in this constituency want this project for our area. It is almost beyond the imagination of the residents what this will do, not only for the whole of Manitoba, but also the eastern portion of the province." The siting announcement was made October 18, 1960.

The research centre and the town site were both to be on the edge of Whiteshell Provincial Park. A town site was selected and designed by Central Mortgage and Housing. The name Pinawa was accepted after the AECL board was told about its aboriginal meaning. Pinawa was formally re-established about 10 km from the original Hydro town in 1963 when the first residents arrived.

This book tells the story of taking the new community of Pinawa from a concept in 1960 to the thriving community of today. It is also a record of many of the memories and extraordinary events you may have experienced if you have been part of the Pinawa family over the past 50 years.

Whiteshell Nuclear Research Establishment in 1965

Chapter 2
Building Our Home

In 1961 the community of Pinawa started taking shape, after a year of surveyors and engineers scanning for suitable water and sewer lines, drilling test holes and marking out the town. W.L. Wardrop and Associates, in collaboration with Central Mortgage and Housing Corporation (CMHC), laid the plans for the upcoming construction. Of course, land purchases had to be made. Many stories abound regarding the farm which is now occupied by Whiteshell Laboratories. Farmer Peter Manisto was in no hurry to sell nor was he hesitant to express himself forcefully. However, after several meetings, the right conditions were found and terms agreed to.

Access to all the activity was indirect and often inconvenient. In summer, a water route from Seven Sisters was used, as was a roundabout road through Lac du Bonnet. During the winter, old logging routes were used, along with a direct crossing of the Winnipeg River northwest of Lac du Bonnet.

Winnipeg River Bridge

Built in 1961 by Con-Bridge of Canada, McNamara Construction, F. Lamb and Associates and Western Bridge and Tank, the bridge across the Winnipeg River on what is now Highway 211, was the first of its kind in Manitoba. What set it apart was the anchoring of the supporting piers into the bedrock of the river. It had to be built to withstand the rigors of transporting the loads of steel and construction materials for the plant site and the town site, along with the 16-ton stainless steel calandria, the nucleus of WNRE's WR-1 nuclear reactor. The total cost of the project was $850,000.

Construction began in 1960, and was completed in January 1962. In early June, the bridge was formally opened and dedicated by Honorable Gordon Churchill, Chairman of the Privy Council on Scientific and Industrial Research, the Honorable Duff Roblin, Premier of Manitoba, AECL's J.L. Gray and MLA Walter Weir.

F.W. Gilbert (1910-1966)

Fred Gilbert is the forefather of Pinawa. He was responsible for creating the town site for the employees of the first nuclear research establishment west of Chalk River, Ontario. His vision created a community unlike any other in the province. He was also first manager at the WNRE, arriving in 1961.

Fred Gilbert was born in 1910 in Winnipeg, where he attended school. He obtained his B.Sc. in Engineering Physics from Queen's University in Kingston in 1936. He was at the forefront of nuclear industry when he became the first manager of the nuclear facility at Chalk River, Ontario. He oversaw the construction and criticality of the first reactors at the Chalk River site, as well as a reactor in India in 1960.

Gilbert was involved in every facet of Pinawa's origins and was a key member of several of the town's first organizations, including the Pinawa Club. He was a member of the Professional Engineers of Ontario and the United Church of Canada.

News footage at the time portrays a busload of dignitaries and news people piling out of a smoke-filled bus into the muck and mire of the road at the entrance to the bridge. Some had umbrellas; many did not, and there were rueful smiles from the construction workers as they waited for the speeches to be made and the curtain pulled on the dedication plaque, which reads:

This bridge was built jointly by the Manitoba Department of Public Works and the Atomic Energy of Canada Limited to serve the WNRE and the town site of Pinawa, unveiled jointly by the Hon. Gordon Churchill, Q.C., P.C., D.S.O., L.L.B., Chairman of the Privy Council on Scientific and Industrial Research and the Hon. Duff Roblin, Premier of Manitoba."

The bridge has served the residents and visitors of Eastern Manitoba well for over 50 years. Rehabilitation work was completed in the fall of 2013, extending the expected life of the bridge until at least 2040.

Mike Tomlinson and Ed Lundman receiving tachometer from Unit #1 of Pinawa Dam; Donated to New Pinawa by Manitoba Hydro - 1965

Bridge piers anchored to the bedrock

W.B. Lewis (1908-1987)

Wilfrid Bennett Lewis, a physicist, dominated nuclear research and the development of nuclear power in Canada for nearly three decades, from the end of World War II until his retirement in 1973. The development of the Canadian Deuterium Uranium (CANDU) reactor was his most stunning achievement.

Born in England, Lewis earned a doctorate at Cavendish Laboratory in 1934 and continued his research on nuclear physics there until 1939. During the war he worked on the development of radar and in 1945 became chief superintendent of the Telecommunications Research Establishment at Malvern. A year later he agreed to head Canada's fledgling nuclear research facility at Chalk River, Ontario, where he made his professional home for the next twenty-seven years.

Lewis's drive, intelligence, and remarkable organizational skills placed him at the forefront of Canada's nuclear program, including establishing Pinawa. Lewis's influence on the development of science, technology, and industry in Canada and abroad was unique and profound. His story sheds new light on Canada's postwar science history, debates concerning national science policy, and growing international scientific collaborations.

As the bridge was being completed, the road to Pinawa was chopped out of the dense spruce forests to the east. The road hastened work at the town site and as 1961 ended there was an air of expectancy about the new town as it awaited the first resident.

An Order in Council in the spring of 1962 established Pinawa as a Local Government District (LGD), with C.G. Kirby as Administrator. A few months later, Ed Lundman was appointed as first Resident Administrator. Construction continued. The sounds of machinery, men and tools prevailed, warning the surrounding countryside that the changes were here to stay. Row houses on McGregor Crescent and Athlone Crescent were constructed and approximately 100 other residential units began to rise among the trees; an elementary school was also started.

Building Highway 211

Many AECL employees living at Deep River, Ontario were excited about the prospect of moving to the new town in Manitoba. For others, there was doubt; many questions needed answering about new homes, new work and a new province. The *Whiteshell Gazette* appeared at Chalk River. Mimeographed and put together by a group of enthusiastic volunteers, the newsletter was designed to answer some of the questions for employees who would soon be moving.

The first issue rolled off the presses at Deep River, Ontario in January, 1963 under the guiding hand of John Leng. Publication was later taken over by Dorothy Robertson, Bunny Putnam and Gladys Guthrie. The publication continued sporadically after the move to Pinawa and late in 1964, began a continuous monthly publication run until 1966 with an editorial staff of Doug Badger, Bob Hollies, Eric Graham and Fjola Davidson.

Dorothy Robertson and Bunny Putnam (Photograph courtesy of the Putnam family)

Ara Mooradian (1922 – 1996)

Born in Hamilton, Ontario, Ara Mooradian gained his early training as an engineer and scientist at the University of Saskatchewan and the University of Missouri. His career began at the Consolidated Mining and Smelting Company before joining the staff at the Chalk River Nuclear Laboratories. At Chalk River he was Head of the Development Engineering and Fuel Development Branches.

In 1964 Ara became the Managing Director of the Whiteshell Nuclear Research Establishment and later the Vice-President. He became Vice-President of the Chalk River Nuclear Laboratories in 1971 before taking up the position of Executive Vice-president for Research and Development at AECL (1977) and then Corporate Vice-president (1978).

Ara Mooradian is noted for his contributions to the development of low cost fuel for CANDU nuclear power generating stations. His honours have included the Canada Medal, the W.B. Lewis Award and Fellowships of the Royal Society of Canada and the Chemical Institute of Canada. His extra-curricular activities have included being the first mayor of the Town of Deep River. He was noted for his furniture design and construction, and his enthusiasm for the outdoors.

Robert (Bob) Hart (1927 – 1998)

Bob Hart arrived to Chalk River Laboratories in 1948. After working on various projects including purification of heavy water in a reactor system, reprocessing of nuclear fuels and studying the physical properties of these fuels, he moved to Whiteshell Laboratories in 1965 as head of the Reactor Core Technology Branch. He was appointed director of the Applied Science Division in 1969, managing director of the Whiteshell Site in 1973 and a vice president of AECL in 1974. In 1978 he became executive vice-president in charge of the Research Company, AECL. Bob was awarded the W.B. Lewis medal by the Canadian Nuclear Association in 1981, with the following citation: "For giving the Whiteshell Nuclear Research Establishment world recognition in such fields as organic heat transport technology, thermal hydraulic technology for nuclear safety technology analysis, radioactive waste management."

He was the beloved husband of Yvonne (nee Wemp). Bob will be fondly remembered as a respected colleague and a caring manager. He was a faithful member of Emmanuel United Church and exhibited his commitment through his involvement in church worship and council activities in Social Outreach Projects, and as class grandparent and counsellor at Vincent Massey and Hillcrest Schools.

After retiring in 1991, he contributed to the 1997 book on the history of AECL, "Canada Enters the Nuclear Age."

Landscaping on Devonshire

Alexander Avenue

Construction on Athlone

Patterson Crescent

Jack Remington (1935-2002)

Jack Remington was born on a small farm in the Swan River Valley near Durban, MB. Jack spent his youth in the valley until he moved to Flin Flon to finish his high school. He worked for Hudson Bay Mining and Smelting before continuing on to university. He met Barbara and they were married in Winnipeg in 1957. He graduated from the University of Manitoba in 1960, with a degree in Mechanical Engineering. Jack served nine years in the Canadian Armed Forces, first as an officer cadet while in university, then Lieutenant, and finally Captain. Four of his years were with Royal Canadian Electrical and Mechanical Engineers (RCEME) stationed in Kingston, ON and Calgary. He joined AECL, Whiteshell Laboratories, in 1964 as an Operations Engineer. He worked as Mechanical Engineering section head and then branch manager of Design and Project Engineering. He retired in 1991. In his retirement, Jack held a number of committee positions both on the Pinawa Club, Curling and Golf sections for many years and was also an active player in both areas. He was heavily involved in the expansion of the Pinawa Golf Course from nine to eighteen holes, as secretary treasurer and his years of engineering project management at Whiteshell Labs ensured things stayed on budget. He later led the ad-hoc committee for the redrafting of the club constitution. Jack also served ten years as Campaign Manager for the Canadian Diabetic Association organizing local fundraising. Jack enjoyed life to the fullest and made the most of time spent with family and special friends, including his golf buddies.

Other organizations took shape in Deep River in preparation for the communal efforts that would be required in Pinawa. Protestant communicants formed the Pinawa Christian Fellowship (PCF). Leaders in the organization, Dorothy Robertson, Jock Guthrie, Jim Putnam and Dr. Abe Petkau, satisfied that they had a satisfactory arrangement, waited until the move to Pinawa for further organization. Information on Roman Catholic services was also obtained and reported faithfully by the Gazette. Recognition was given to the need for a library and again, a group met to plan for the necessities. Marg Smith, Bunny Putnam, Helen Tomlinson, Mari-Ann Weeks, Bea Mathers and Marion Stewart spearheaded the collection of books which formed a foundation for the Pinawa Library.

Teams of horses were necessary to move construction materials to the housing site. Eventually the quagmire would be replaced by wide, curving cemented roadways.

Often, the most memorable events came spontaneously; 1963 might be called *"The Year of the Big Bonspiel."* A one-sheet rink, open to the elements from above and protected only skimpily from the sides by bales of hay, somehow appeared at the plant site and a bonspiel was indeed held.

Pinawa truly began to grow 1963. The first family - the Ben Banhams, arrived. Between mid-July and the end of 1963, 83 families and a number of single people took up residence in new homes smelling of fresh paint and surrounded for the most part by sticky Manitoba gumbo. With the new residents came the demand for services, for shopping, for the conveniences expected of all towns. The construction of the shopping centre, service station and the L.G.D. offices began, but needs were immediate and had to be met.

Robert Jones (1927-2010)

Robert Jones was born in St. James, Manitoba. He received several scholarships in High School and University. He graduated with an Honours degree in Chemistry from the University of Manitoba in 1950. He joined A.E.C.L. after graduation and went to work at the Chalk River facility. Shortly after beginning his career, he met Barb in Deep River where they were married in 1952. In 1963 his work with A.E.C.L. took him back home to Manitoba (Pinawa). Through his career he worked in a number of areas for A.E.C.L. including analytical chemistry, fuel development, R D, and in his later years the commercial office. Bob had a strong work ethic and was a highly motivated man, working hard to provide for his family. His greatest passion was the outdoors and travelling. He spent many hours in the winters cross country skiing with his friends, developing trails and shelters throughout the back country surrounding Pinawa where a trail named Jones-Graham-Gauthier Freeway was established. He loved hiking in the Canadian Rockies and the entire family would travel to the Rockies for summer vacations. Bob retired from A.E.C.L. in 1985 and had a long list of countries to visit in the coming years. Bob and Barb travelled the world together including Europe, Russia, Mexico, New Zealand, Australia, and Hawaii.

New road

Curling in Pinawa in 1963

The Bay manager, Cal Jewison, filled his obligation as storekeeper to the town from a two-car garage at his residence. The Bank of Montreal manager from Lac du Bonnet, Jim Gormican, arrived twice weekly with a trailer bank and parked on Willis Drive in front of the present Pinawa Club, to transact the monetary business of the town. The L.G.D. set up a post office at 17 McGregor Crescent with Don Graham in charge, and AECL's town office started operations at 19 McGregor, later to move to 10 McGregor. Bill McKeown handled housing problems, untangling the many snarls that came to be a way of life as more and more arrived in town. A hospital, too, was of course needed. Dr. Henry Beaumont and five nurses took over mending the sick at 6 McDiarmid Road with Drs. Weeks and Petkau on call.

The town was even provided with telephone service. A pay phone was located outside 17 McGregor on a lamp post. And what a tale could be told by that telephone. The one about the new resident who desperately wanted to make a call in pouring rain and cleverly decided to track the location down by following the overhead wires; about his perseverance in pushing his car out of the mud after getting stuck because he was watching the wire instead of the road; and about how he finally tracked down the elusive instrument, made his call and as he turned to walk to his car realized that it was across the road from where he lived.

Roger Smith (1918-2007)

Born in Winnipeg, Roger Smith graduated in Physics from the University of Manitoba before joining the Canadian Army in 1940. He was transferred to the British Army in 1944 until 1946, achieving the rank of Major. In 1947 he joined Atomic Energy of Canada in Chalk River where he became the Supervisor of NRX Reactor. In 1958 he moved his family to Vienna, Austria to work at the International Atomic Energy Agency as the head of the Safeguards division. Subsequently he played a major role in the planning and development of Whiteshell Nuclear Research Establishment and the town of Pinawa, moving there in 1963.

He volunteered with various organizations including Boy Scouts of Canada, Canadian Executive Services Organization, Pan Am Games and Manitoba Summer Games. He was inducted into the Order of Manitoba in 2000 based on his work as a nuclear scientist, volunteer and efforts in the planning of Whiteshell Nuclear Research Establishment and the town of Pinawa.

Several times people who expected a call, waited at the phone only to be put on the run when a bear appeared about the same time the phone rang. Then there was the one about the visitor to Pinawa who left the town shaking his head because he could hear a phone ringing when his company had made him make the trip to town in person because there were "definitely" no phones there. Despite the stories, the shortcomings, the trials and the hard work, significant advancement in the town's growth came in 1963.

Recent arrivals, a term which could have applied at this stage to almost everyone, were disconcerted to find that bears that had made their homes in the area seemed to want to continue to do so. Many "bear" experts soon developed. One at least learned that when giving chase to these beasts, pyjama drawstrings should be drawn tightly, particularly so in the vicinity of the nurses' residence.

Lynne Kobold – Duty nurse at clinic in 1964

Anton (Tony) Sawatzky (1923-2005)

Tony Sawatzky was born in Altona, MB and spent the latter half of his childhood in Steinbach, MB. He earned his B.Sc.-Honors at the University of Manitoba in 1950. He went on to Temple University in Philadelphia to complete his PhD in Physics in 1957. He worked at the AECL in Chalk River, ON for six years. He and his family were amongst the first settlers in the newly formed town of Pinawa in 1963. He greatly enjoyed his career as a metallurgist at the Whiteshell Labs until his retirement in 1985. Tony was a devoted family man who cherished being surrounded by his loved ones. He was very involved in his church and was a man of many interests and talents including gliding, woodworking, and golf, as well as building and flying model airplanes. He enjoyed travelling and was an avid reader.

Living as the new residents were on the shore of a lake, boating soon became a major recreation. The first boat dock, where the canoe launching area is now located, was completed by volunteers, and guided by the forceful Harry Smith. It served well until the present marina was completed in 1967. The boat club was, of course, most active. The unknown waters were explored and charted and the information mapped by Walter Litvinsky. The charts still serve well.

Throughout the remainder of 1963, the plans for the organization of the PCF, the library, school, Women's Club and the Roman Catholic congregation came to fruition. A youth group too became active, as did the Volunteer Fire Brigade. Curlers from Pinawa journeyed to Seven Sisters and to Lac du Bonnet to take part in league and bonspiel activities; open air dances on the sub-floors of homes under construction were popular. The first dancer to walk over the edge was guaranteed a big round of jibes and applause. The end of the eventful year was celebrated in grand style with a masquerade at the plant site dining hall. A freezing rain greeted the celebrants at its finish, but all reached Pinawa safely.

The beginning of 1964 was marked by the formation of an organization which did much to make newcomers to Canada's "instant town" welcome and at home. The Women's Club had their first formal meeting directed by Joy McKeown. Their interest lay in providing the necessities for new families, and electricians particularly received attention from the organization in their efforts for the conveniences of home. Commercial installations held the spotlight in this year. Permanent quarters were occupied by John Cronin's service station; Cal Jewison began operations at the new Hudson's Bay store; Eyfe Walterson began to serve patrons in his drugstore; George Bonney looked to the cosmetic needs of the ladies and the gentlemen at the Barber Shop and Beauty Salon; Ed

McWilliams Place

Ingersoll and staff looked after the town's money needs from the Bank of Montreal; Jack McLeod handled the Royal Mail.

The Pinawa Club, under President F.W. Gilbert, opened their two sheet curling rink and clubhouse. It was a welcome night for proponents of the roaring game when Max Allan sent the first rock on its way over the new ice.

The Kelsey House Staff Hotel also went into operation late in the year.

In August of 1964, 27 families arrived from Deep River to renew acquaintance and make new friends. The opening of the Pinawa Hospital, long anticipated, was formalized in December. The last occupant of the temporary hospital's nursery and the first in the new one was Jason, the son of Jerry

Pinawa Shopping Centre - 1964

and Sheila Martino. The occasion was reported in the press: *"Jason was accompanied by Sheila Martino, a close relative."*

Thespians in Pinawa were also active in this year. More and more space of the faithful Gazette was being devoted to the activities of the Pinawa Players, along with reports of the Pinawa Up-n-Atoms, a square dancing group, and the Pinawa Lions under Torchy Torresan, Charter President. The Gazette also reported amending restrictions dealing with construction of exterior TV antennae along with some comments about the shortcomings of the inescapable government. The inevitable reconciliations followed, however.

Pinawa was indeed growing. Vigorous participation in all community affairs indicated that the growth was healthy, well directed and boding even better things ahead.

Elna Grant (1922 – 2011)

Elna Grant was born in Winnipeg Beach, MB. She received her entire education in Winnipeg, graduating from St. James Collegiate in 1938. After a post-secondary education, she entered the work force. Her career spanned many enjoyable years with the Provincial Government in Winnipeg, with the Bank of Montreal in Souris and with Atomic Energy of Canada Ltd. in Pinawa. Her places of employment gave her the opportunity to meet many interesting and wonderful people, many of whom have remained friends to this day.

She and Ross were married in 1948 and moved to Souris in 1950 to run the drugstore. They were very involved in the community and Ross especially enjoyed working with the high school football team. Elna thought of the team as her team too. In 1970 they bought the drugstore in Pinawa and quickly became very heavily involved in their new community.

Her love of dancing never waned. She was a very accomplished dancer having won many contests. Jitterbug was her "signature" dance back in the day. One summer in Clear Lake she attended 14 dances in 14 nights. It was no wonder that she was always so eager to start working on organizing the AECL R&D Christmas Dance every year. She wanted to get out there and dance.

After retirement her love of books led to many volunteer hours with the Pinawa Public Library. She spent several years actively participating in and enjoying curling and golf. She was an avid spectator of all sports but especially of football and baseball. A love of travel took her and Ross to many exciting places, including several return visits to Hawaii and some rollicking times in Las Vegas. After Ross's passing she enjoyed many fantastic adventures with great friends.

Friendship was highly valued by Elna. She was adored by her neighbours. She had very special relationships with young people. From the neighborhood kids, to the students who worked at the drugstore, to the Ward boys who lived with them while going to school – she truly admired them all and took great pride in their accomplishments. The town of Pinawa will never have as great an ambassador as Elna. She loved the town and was very boastful about it wherever she travelled.

First Bank of Montreal

Pinawa Pharmacy – Eyfe Walterson Doreen Thompson and customer Ron Wiggins

Alice Chambers (1937-1999)

Born at Elkhorn, Manitoba, Alice Chambers attended the University of Manitoba and by the early 1960s had completed an Honours BSc in microbiology and was working in Ottawa at the National Research Council. In 1968, she and her husband Keith moved to Pinawa, from Leeds, England with their infant daughter Anna. There, the family would grow to include two sons, Andrew and Paul.

Alice was fast involved in her new community. Among other things, she served 14 years on the local school board, was a founding member of the recycling committee, worked in the public and school libraries, and volunteered as a Guide leader. In May 1992, her career as an environmental activist took shape when Alice noticed an ad in the Winnipeg Free Press regarding an environmental license for an old pulp mill downstream from where she lived. Discovering that the mill was discharging 38 million litres of lethal effluent every day was her wake-up call to the true state of "environmental protection" in Manitoba.

Alice put her science background to use and became a virtual one-woman research institute. She was well known for her vast knowledge of environmental issues and the supporting science behind them. Her opinion was valued by many local, regional and international organizations. Alice often received "unofficial" calls from government sources for "hard to find" documents as well as requests for information from university students and numerous environmental networks. Her way was not the stump speech or noisy demonstration, but meticulous digging. She was not afraid to wade into the deepest, thickest bureaucratic mire and hold governments to their word.

It was a credit to this small, gentle woman with the twinkle in her eye and the devastatingly accurate facts that those on both sides of the table grew to respect her. These qualities inspired appointments to a number of advisory boards such the Manitoba Environmental Council. Former Premier Gary Filmon said of her: "She has been the voice of the people, and a strong clear voice for nature."

Alice's activism was set against the backdrop of personal tragedy. Her husband died suddenly in 1993, and three years later, she contracted cancer. But far from slowing down, she redoubled her efforts and, between treatments, Alice put all her energy into furthering the cause of conservation. She remained passionate about nature, family and life. She died on 13 December 1999, at Pinawa, Manitoba.

First Hudson Bay store

Tracy McCallister - First baby born in Pinawa

Kelsey House construction - 1964

Pinawa Service Station - 1964

The Bay - 1964

A Proud Pinawa Pioneer

Back in 1962, Edward Lundman, a civil engineer working for Harper Construction in Winnipeg, heard of an exciting position in the soon to be built town of Pinawa, Manitoba, as the first resident administrator.

Having worked as town engineer in Yellowknife, NWT, and Dauphin, MB, he was well suited to the job of managing the growth of a brand new town. It would be an adventure for him, his wife Rowena, and their three children, Brenda, Marta and Patricia.

The first building in town was the sewage lift station, which was built by Harper Construction. He was proud to have built the first building and kept a small model of it on his desk for the rest of his life.

Pinawa officially opened for business in July 1963. The first 'settler' was F.W. Gilbert, and the Lundman family was not far behind as the 5th family to move in. New families in town

Ed Lundman - 1964

moved into temporary housing in the row houses near the then unfinished beach until their homes were ready. The roads were not paved and the Manitoba gumbo was everywhere. Children walked out of their boots which stuck in the mud. Mosquitoes and black flies were voracious and some mothers made little children wear nylon stockings over their heads for some protection from the bites. Bears wandered through the town site, especially after they discovered the joys of free meals from garbage cans. Skunks, frogs and garter snakes were common, but deer were not.

Pinawa was a rapidly growing community, with new young families moving in almost every day. Paper carriers for the Winnipeg Free Press (Brenda) and the rival Winnipeg Tribune (Billy Graham) kept an eye out for moving vans, hoping to be the one to snag a new subscriber. When school opened in September 1963, there were insufficient numbers of pupils for individual classes for each grade, and the few high school students had to attend school in Lac du Bonnet. That situation changed rapidly and within a few years there were two busy elementary schools and a high school with the best of resources and 150 students.

Ed Lundman was an impressively tall man who at 6' 7" towered over most people. He wore many 'hats' in his position. Not only was he the town's resident administrator, he was the official school trustee (in lieu of a school board), town engineer, building inspector, dog catcher (or so he once said), and safety backup to the RCMP officer when he had to patrol the town site to scare bears away. A prized possession was a head carved by his close friend Roger Smith with five bumps which each sported a different hat, representing all his diverse responsibilities. He was also a strong supporter of the Pinawa Christian Fellowship and many other community activities.

Ed Lundman, Ara Mooradian, Fred Anderson, Roger Smith at opening of the Pinawa Rifle Range, located beneath F.W. Gilbert School

Ed loved Pinawa, as did the entire family. Where else could you be part of the creation of a beautiful riverside community, surrounded by nature, with many indoor and outdoor activities and potential new friends moving in as the town grew?

Over the next five years the town matured. Roads were paved, new schools went up, houses and gardens were built, the shopping centre replaced the store in the manager's garage, the hospital replaced the townhouse-based clinic, a teen centre was established and the golf course, curling club and tennis courts were created. With over 2000 people living in the town, you no longer recognized everybody. But everybody recognized Ed Lundman.

In 1968, after 5 busy and fulfilling years, Ed decided it was time for a new adventure and he left Pinawa to study for his Masters of Science in Management at MIT in Boston, Mass. After graduation he continued his career in administration and the management of change with positions in Ontario (Fonthill, Hamilton, Stouffville and Toronto), until he and Rowena finally retired to Ottawa, where all three daughters had settled.

No other job, no other town, brought him the satisfaction and happiness he had in guiding the initial growth of Pinawa. Therefore, when he was determining his final resting place, he decided that Pinawa was where he would prefer to be buried. He died at the age of 85 on January 1, 2011 in Ottawa, and was interred in the Pinawa Cemetery on August 7, 2011.

Early Years

From 1959 to 1963, the idea for Pinawa was conceived, surveyed, planned and constructed. In 1963, the first residents of Pinawa arrived, and with them came new ideas and support for the growth of this community. Our first administrator was C.G. Kirby, although he was not the resident administrator. Ed Lundman was appointed Resident Administrator in 1963, and held the position until his departure in 1968.

The beginnings of commercial necessities were formulated in 1963. Don Graham handled the mail, housing was the responsibility of Bill McKeown, and the local RCMP personnel were Nick Searle and Torchy Torresan. The elementary school opened with Mr. Peter. Thiessen, Principal. Religious ceremonies were

Ed Lundman, Roger Smith and Ara Mooradian check their targets

held in the school auditorium, with all denominations using the facility. Hospital care was set up under Dr. Henry Beaumont. Among the first social clubs in Pinawa were the Pinawa Up 'n'Atoms, the Lions Club, Hi-C Youth Group, Guiding and Scouting movements, a Volunteer Fire Brigade, the Library (located at the Elementary School), the Curling Club (with games played in Lac du Bonnet and Seven Sisters up until the time of the rink completion here), skating and hockey on a rink at the Elementary School prepared by volunteers, and the Pinawa Players amateur theatre group. A local Women's Club was also organized.

Sewer, waterlines and pavement moved into Stage 2 in 1965. Stage 1, already being referred to as the "old section", filled in with residences. The high school and community centre were completed, with the teenage group taking over the old hospital building for their own.

Already in 1965, 23 organizations were active and open to membership. Most in the town looked anxiously at construction of the golf course. Two more sheets of ice were added to the curling rink as membership continued to grow and competition tightened for the trophies that began appearing in the club's cases. Other sporting events appeared. The record books indicated that the speediest wood tick at the running of the Pinawa Plate dashed over a nine and one quarter inch track in the astounding time of 38 seconds.

But things more serious were also being attended to. The town's first election named Dick Tuxworth Chairman of the Library Board and selected a committee comprising Eva Sutherland, Mari-Ann Weeks, Helen Tomlinson, Eyfe Walterson, John Minton and Resident Administrator Ed Lundman.

The first Pinawa Birthday Party was celebrated in July, 1964 coordinated by the Volunteer Fire Department and supported by other community organizations. As the result of collaboration between AECL and the U.S. Atomic Energy Commission, several families from the U.S. moved to Pinawa in 1965, adding to the international flavour of the town and contributing as only people of a different background can.

The growing maturity of the town was emphasized when the Pinawa Christian Fellowship came under the ministry of its first full-time pastor, Reverend Donald Ross of the United Church. The year ended with 62 families having moved to Pinawa, bringing with them new ideas and energies for further development of the town.

November 1, 1965 – Manitoba History

The Whiteshell Reactor-1 (WR-1), WNRE's signature facility, was built starting in 1962. The reactor was designed and built by Canadian General Electric for $14.5 million. Shawinigan Engineering was responsible for constructing for the building that housed the reactor. WR-1 would to test the concept of using an organic fluid to remove the heat generated by the reactor. Organic fluids can operate hotter temperatures and at lower pressures than water-cooled reactors.

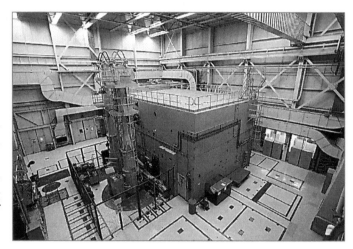

Whiteshell Reactor #1

WR-1 went critical on November 1, 1965. Pinawa shared in this historic milestone. WR-1 was a useful research facility for 20 years, testing experimental fuels, reactor materials, and other coolants. It was the centre piece of a thriving research community - 567 employees by 1967. The reactor was a busy place, usually working around the clock. It had an availability of 85% over its lifetime, which was exceptionally high for a research reactor.

WR-1 was shut down for the last time on May 17, 1985, its place in history secured as the world's only operating heavy water-moderated reactor cooled by an organic fluid. The legacy of WR-1 is that organic coolants are still being considered for future reactor designs. Design features of WR-1 have found their way into the nuclear reactors of today; instrument triplication, parameter duplication and frequent testing; transfer systems to move irradiated fuel, fuel channels and equipment safely from the reactor to water-filled storage facilities; and long-term dry storage of fuel.

Growing the Town

The Pinawa Club was completed, and the Pinawa Collegiate opened, with Mr. G.W. Hanna, Principal, in 1966. Kelsey House was completed to its present size and work was begun on the proposed Pinawa Motor Inn. The two elementary schools were named for F.W. Gilbert and W.B. Lewis, and excavation began for the addition of the Junior High to the Collegiate.

Homes in the Stage 2 area south of Burrows Road were for the most part completed in 1966. The year is still remembered for the violent March blizzard which left the town snowbound. Although services were quickly restored, the roads remained blocked for several days, requiring a helicopter airlift of milk and bread from Winnipeg, arranged by Bay manager Garth Cowie.

Pinawa's First Family, the Banhams, left in 1969, giving Mr. Banham the distinction of being the first retired employee of WNRE. Mr. Banham was Security and Fire Chief at WNRE, and worked at AECL for a total of twelve years.

A new minister arrived to take over the leadership of the PCF, and the Pinawa Dental Clinic opened with Drs. Cross and Derksen accepting patients in April of 1969. Along with these "firsts", the first Horticultural Society flower show was held, along with the first Sailing Regatta.

The year of 1966 is remembered sadly too, for the passing of F.W. Gilbert. His vision created a community unlike any other in the province. He was also first manager at the WNRE. The community was shocked, for in a very real sense, he had been identified with the conception, planning and growth of Pinawa. His wise counsel and sincere friendship were to be keenly missed by all who had been associated with him.

AECL's WR-1 Commissioning and Operations Team - Frank Oravec, Del Tegart, Jim Biggs, Bernie Gordon, Bernie Pannell, Vinny McCarthy, Grant Unsworth, Mickey Donnelly, Art Summach, Dick Meeker, Roy Barnsdale, Mike Berry, Al Nelson, Wilf Campbell, and Larry Gauthier

Two of the town's major recreational facilities were completed in 1967. The marina and the nine hole golf course were welcomed by enthusiasts of both sports. Recreation activities continued in other directions as well. A new teen centre was established behind the high school in remodelled trailers, complete with a snack bar operated under the direction of the PCF Bible Study Group. The centre became known as the Inner Sanctum, then the Psychedelic Pearl, but whatever it was called, its popularity remained high.

A number of events, most of them unrelated, were noted in 1967. The Canada Centennial Voyageurs stopped to visit, happily enough, during the town's birthday celebrations and were treated to a community barbecue. Exchange students from Vancouver spent some days in town, also as part of the Centennial celebrations.

Pinawa welcomed 64 new families during 1967, and the town seemed to mature during the year; perhaps losing some of its roughness and pioneering atmosphere. Many of the signs of construction had disappeared beneath the hand of eager landscapers. Although still bright and new in appearance, Pinawa was more and more acquiring the atmosphere of suburbia.

Residential construction continued during 1968, primarily in Stage 2, north of Burrows Road and on Prescott Crescent. Pinawa's pioneering town administrator, Ed Lundman, his wife Rowena and their three children also left in 1968. Ed Lundman had assumed duties late in 1962 and moved to Pinawa in the following year. His duties were taken over by Doug Spray who came from the Yukon with his wife, Carol and two sons. Other administrative positions in the town were also filled. Bob Dale assumed duties as Superintendent of Schools in July, serving education needs of the town with Pinawa's first elected School Board of Bob Hart, Alex Mayman, Chairman Ed Olchowy, Art Summach and Helen Tomlinson.

Stanley Hatcher (1932-2014)

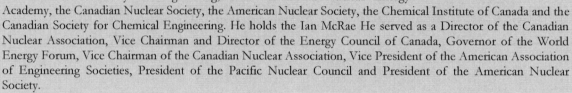

After graduating from the University of Birmingham in England and obtaining a M.Sc. in Chemical Engineering, Stanley Hatcher taught at the University of Toronto and obtained a PhD. He joined AECL's national nuclear R&D program at Chalk River Nuclear Laboratories.

In 1963 he headed the Chemical Technology Branch at the start-up of AECL's new Whiteshell Nuclear Research Establishment at Pinawa, Manitoba. He became site head in 1979. In 1985, Dr. Hatcher became President of AECL Research. He became President of AECL in 1989 and for three years led the restructuring of the corporation towards its new emphasis on support of CANDU.

Dr. Hatcher was a registered Professional Engineer of Ontario and a Fellow of the Canadian Academy of Engineering, the International Nuclear Energy Academy, the Canadian Nuclear Society, the American Nuclear Society, the Chemical Institute of Canada and the Canadian Society for Chemical Engineering. He holds the Ian McRae He served as a Director of the Canadian Nuclear Association, Vice Chairman and Director of the Energy Council of Canada, Governor of the World Energy Forum, Vice Chairman of the Canadian Nuclear Association, Vice President of the American Association of Engineering Societies, President of the Pacific Nuclear Council and President of the American Nuclear Society.

A large project undertaken under the sponsorship of the PCF was completed at Fort Hope, an Ojibway reserve northwest of Sioux Lookout in Ontario. A number of Pinawa's youth, directed by four or five adults, canoed to the site in two parties and constructed a rectory for the resident priest.

Pinawa welcomed another 73 new families in 1968. They enjoyed the benefits of Bill Chyzzy's newly-completed Pinawa Motor Inn, which added considerably to the town's attractions.

Mrs. Mooradian at grand opening of the Pinawa Motor Inn – 1968

Pinawa counted 2,031 residents as of June 1969, and looked back in some wonderment at the growth from 330 only five years earlier. The town's growth was reflected in the formation of a Recreation Complex Advisory Committee reporting to the town administrator in their planning for future recreational needs of the community. The committee consisted of Lloyd Dreger, Larry Gauthier, Ed McDonald, Jim Putnam, Lorne Swanson and Ted Thexton, under the chairmanship of Len Williams.

A major charity effort was organized and carried through by the town in 1969. More than two hundred residents took part in a Miles for Millions Walk, organized by the high school students, raising, in addition to blisters, a total of $2,400 for the Cancer Society and Care of Canada. Work afield by the PCF continued, involving financial aid, painting, decorating and landscaping at selected sites. A long-awaited announcement was made in November, 1969 that an indoor skating rink would be constructed over the next year. Behind the announcement was a story of widespread, enthusiastic support by local service groups, the high school, unions at the plant and many community organizations. Again the town looked to the future knowing that another project which they had organized and supported would soon be realized.

Pinawa Housing

Early on in Pinawa's development, virtually every home was owned by AECL, and managed by the company. The Pinawa Housing guide provided some insight to what a renter could expect in the 60s and 70s. The policy of the Company was to provide good quality housing constructed to National Building Standards. An effort was made to provide a fairly wide range of house sizes. As the rent was directly related to the cost of the houses, this also provided a range of rentals. AECL invited proposals from builders in the area. These houses were not personalized for obvious reasons. If an employee wished a personalized house it was recommended that the family purchase a lot from the AECL and build their own.

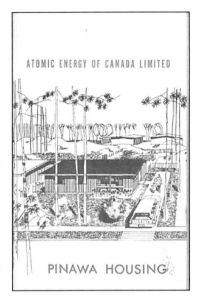

"Eligibility for Housing" – AECL tried to house all employees wishing to live in Pinawa. The Personnel Office at WNRE provided information on availability and rental structure at the time of hiring or transfer. The employee's selection was made known to the branch in which the employee worked and the branch submitted the request to the Housing Committee.

The Housing Committee had a representative from all AECL Divisions, and met about once a month. The availability of a house was based on a formula which took into account the position of the employee, length of service and income. An employee who had been residing in a house for one year or more could apply to the Housing Committee for a different allocation.

Rent was collected through payroll deductions, twice monthly. Renters were able to purchase their homes provided they had resided in Pinawa for at least 12 months, and that the home was at least 1 year old. The company required 10% down payment on a mortgage of up to 30 years.

The following services were free to tenants:

- annual conditioning service on the furnace and part replacement;
- repairs and adjustments of the furnace as required; chimney cleaning; electrical repairs; repairs to the building where negligence was not a consideration;
- interior redecoration on a four year cycle;
- exterior painting;
- fertilizer for application to the turf on the lot by the tenant;
- installation of a clothes line (choice of umbrella or line).

Living in Pinawa – Gerry and Joyce Hampton, with their children Karen and Allan

Pinawa Housing also provided information on Municipal Services, including Protection, Hospital, Shopping Centre, Manitoba Hydro, Manitoba Telephone Service, Metro Videon Television Cable, Fuel, Domestic Service, Hotel, Liquor Commission, School District, Community Centre, Library, Pinawa Club, and Church Service.

Chapter 3
Serving Pinawa

Pinawa, like all communities, has a dedicated group of people who work to serve our community and improve the lives of our residents. Starting in 1961, key individuals took leadership roles to push the town forward and help develop our own identity. With the first family in 1963, the need for a local government, healthcare, schools and other services became a focus, along with housing. Over the next several years the town matured and key services were started.

Local Government

An Order in Council in early 1962 established Pinawa as a Local Government District, with C.G. Kirby as the first Administrator. In 1963, Ed Lundman was appointed as first Resident Administrator. The Lundman family was the 5th family to move into town. In 1964, permanent office space was allocated to the LGD. In 1965, an Advisory Town Planning Committee was formed to review by-laws. In 1966, the sale of homes from AECL commenced. The first mill rate was set to cover the LGD operating expenditure of $400,000. Typical home assessments were from $6,000 to $10,000, with the tax rate ranging from $240 to $390 per year.

As with all new communities, the LGD dealt with both the routine and the extraordinary as the town developed and matured through the 60s and 70s. Services were expanded and improved; new facilities were added to the town infrastructure. The LGD also had the challenges of being a company town, with a large federal crown corporation overseeing their activities. The Master Agreement between AECL and the province brought additional issues and procedures that needed to be followed. By-laws were written; committees were formed to focus on specific topics; debate and varying opinions made to town a dynamic and interesting place to live and work.

From 1963 to 1973, the community was managed by the Resident Administrator. Starting in 1973, the town named an Advisory Committee to assist the Administrator. Howard Gilmour, Bob Dale, Gib Drynan, Edna Graham and Ross Grant sat on the first Advisory Committee. Martha Owen and Bob Reimer joined the committee in late 1974

Resident Administrators:
C. G. Kirby: 1962
E. A. W. Lundman: 1963-67
H. D. Spray: 1968-74
R. A. Dale: 1974 -88
G. Hanna: 1989-2012
J. Petersen - 2012

Mayors:
Howard Gilmour: 1975-86
Marvin Ryz: 1986-95
Lorne Swanson: 1995-98
Leonard Simpson: 1998-2006
Blair Skinner: 2006-13

Pinawa's First Elected Council in 1975: Bob Reimer, Gib Drynan, Mayor Howard Gilmour, Martha Owen; Front Row: Resident Administrator Bob Dale, Ross Grant

when Bob Dale moved into the Resident Administrator position for the community.

Pinawa's first elected council was formed in November 1975, with Howard Gilmour as mayor, with councillors Martha Owen, Gib Drynan, Bob Reimer and Ross Grant. Over the next 38 years, Pinawa has had five mayors and 29 councillors. Edith Kidner (1983-92) Dave Studham (1986-95) and Lloyd Rattai (1980-86; 1995-98) have the distinction of being the longest serving Councillors, each in office for 9 years.

LGD Office

Combining both terms as a Councillor and Mayor, Blair Skinner has served the community the longest, a total of 15 years to the end of 2013. The longest serving Resident Administrator was Gary Hanna, who filled the position for 23 years until his retirement in 2012.

The LGD of Pinawa began transitioning to allow it to be governed by a mayor and council in the mid-1980s. By the 1990s, 30-year-old infrastructure needed to be replaced. These financial challenges dominated the councillors of the time, along with economic development initiatives and the stability of AECL. Highlights included the Pinawa Community Development Corporation and W.B. Lewis Business Centre. In 2013, the town budget was over $3.4 million, with about $1 million being provided from AECL as a grant in lieu of taxes. Another $1 million is also provided by AECL to the Whiteshell School District each year.

James Howard Gilmour (1930 – 1997)

Howard Gilmour was born in western Manitoba in 1930. In 1958 he married Gail Nicholls and they moved to Winnipeg. In 1963 they moved to Pinawa.

Howard Gilmour held various positions, particularly at MacDonald's Sheet Metal (12 years) and Atomic Energy of Canada (28 years). He served on Council in Pinawa and was the first mayor, holding that position from 1975 to 1986.

He was a lifetime member of Manitoba Association of Urban Municipalities, a board member for the Manitoba Hazardous Waste Council and for the Manitoba Medical Board, along with many more boards too numerous to mention. His latest serving was for the Manitoba Society of Seniors. Howard was also a Charter member of the Lions Club of Pinawa

Howard was an avid sports fan and enjoyed his weekly curling games. Special times were spent in his motor home and through his travels many friendships were made. He treasured his family and many friends. Howard will always be remembered for his gentle nature and his ability to see the good in everyone.

AECL announced they were proceeding to close the site in 1998. The loss of the primary employer has become the LGD's focal point since this announcement. Provincial governments have formed economic development groups and provided funding. The LGD continues to fight for a larger role in determining Pinawa's future and to diversify further and lessen our dependence on a single company. Success has been slow but steady.

Over the past 15 years, the various councils have continued to address the routine issues of our community and pushed to consider new ideas. Highlights have included support for the Tim Horton's Camp, the development of new campgrounds and the industrial park, new sources of revenue, options to provide the needed services in different, more cost-effective ways, development of the Ironwood Seniors' Facility, and improvements and expansion at the hospital. The LGD has also taken an active role in addressing the need for more doctors in the region and the expected shutdown of AECL facilities.

Pinawa Councillors
Martha Owen (1975-83)
Bob Reimer (1975-77)
Gib Drynan (1975-77)
Ross Grant (1975-77)
Bob Dixon (1977-80)
Milt Holowchuk (1977-83)
Edna Graham (1977-83)
Lloyd Rattai (1980-86; 1995-98)
Edith Kidner (1983-92)
Gerald Hampton (1983-85)
Marvin Ryz (1985-86)
Bill Kovacs (1985-86)
Lorne Swanson (1986-92)
David Studham (1986-95)
Carole Edwards (1992-95)
Lorne Kiely (1992-98)
Scott Fraser (1992-95)
Don Daymond (1995-98; 2012-present)
Robert Brudy (1995-98)
Blair Skinner (1998-2006)
Allan Cassidy (1998-2001)
Tom Barnsdale (1998-2006)
Brian Wilcox (2001-02)
Karla Elcock (2002-10)
Lynn Patterson (2002-10)
Clayton McMurren (2006- present)
Rhonda Henschell (2010 to present)
Ron Drabyk (2010-12)
Dorothy Wilken (2010 to present)

Pinawa's Mayors: Marvin Ryz (86-95), Len Simpson (99-06), Lorne Swanson (96-98), and current Mayor Blair Skinner (2006). Pinawa's first mayor was Howard Gilmour (75-86; deceased). Photo by Don Daymond

Pinawa's Council for our 50th Birthday: Clayton McMurren, Rhonda Henschell, Donald Daymond, Dorothy Wilken; Front Row: Mayor Blair Skinner, Resident Administrator Jenny Petersen

Gary Hanna – Pinawa's longest serving Resident Administrator – 23 years

Reflections on the LGD of Pinawa from 1983-1995
By Marvin A. Ryz

The period in the history of the LGD of Pinawa from 1983 to 1995 was an interesting one of change. We were transitioning from a period where the town was run predominantly by a Resident Administrator, to a period where Pinawa was attempting to become a "normal" town and allow itself to be governed by a mayor and council, still however, under the watchful eye of a Resident Administrator. These were times of struggle for recognition of the mayor and council as having any real authority. Administrative responsibility did not easily evolve from a provincially appointed Resident Administrator to the mayor and council and that evolution is ongoing to this day. Attempts to become incorporated as a "normal" town or municipality were impeded by the Provincial/AECL Agreement. This Agreement signed on the 21st of June 1960 led to the establishment of the LGD of Pinawa in 1963. The Agreement provided for the essential and recreational services believed necessary at the time and which we enjoy to this day. The Agreement provided for a Resident Administrator and Official Trustee (Superintendent) of the School District, positions that were both filled by one individual for a period of time. Under the Agreement, instead of taxes based on assessment, AECL paid a "Grant in Lieu" of taxes to the LGD and the School District. The distribution of this GIL provided for many interesting discussions between Council and the School Board over the years. The Agreement did provide a clause that allowed for incorporation, however any new agreement would have to be negotiated between AECL, the District, the School District, the Municipality and the

Mayor Marvin Ryz
1986 to 1995

Province. Any change in status however would also have to be negotiated between AECL and the School District, the Municipality and the Province. Any change in status however would also have opened up the whole question of funding from the Province and AECL. Incorporation was a task so insurmountable that it has yet to be accomplished. As a result we are now only one of two Local Government Districts still in existence in Manitoba.

Being a member of Council requires that one attend countless meetings and being mayor means that you are an ex-officio member for all committees. During my three years as Councilor and nine more as Mayor of Pinawa, I kept a record of every meeting attended, both long and short. In the twelve years that number totaled a staggering 1700 meetings.

During this period, we developed Pinawa's first Council Chambers. I cannot help but chuckle as I recall my first years in Office. Without permanent Council Chambers, one was never quite certain where a scheduled Council meeting would take place even when an office was supposedly booked. On several occasions we were bumped and had to unceremoniously pick up our meeting material and move to one of the school classrooms or even to one of our homes. Good thing this was before the use of computers became so popular. Even then, when we were able to modify the LGD building to create the first small Council Chambers, Council was quickly criticized in the local paper for wasting money on new chairs and a table!

There were many highlights during this period. Together with the town of Beausejour, Pinawa was able to co-host the 1988 Manitoba Summer Games bringing nearly 1,700 athletes to our communities. Through the combined efforts of both communities and several hundred volunteers we were able to host a very successful Summer Games.

This period, with the support of the Manitoba Emergency Measures Program, saw the development of Pinawa's first Emergency Plan. The Plan clearly outlines the actions to be taken in the event of any foreseeable emergency arising in or near the LGD of Pinawa.

This period also brought with it challenging financial burdens resulting from an aging infrastructure. Our water lines were corroding at an alarming rate and many of the water lines along several entire streets had to be re-done. The placement of sacrificial anodes on the water lines and the use of different pipe materials have greatly alleviated this problem (now if we could only eliminate frost and ground movement). The water treatment plant and sewage lift station both required their first retrofit during these years. Additionally municipal equipment such as the fire truck, grader, street sweeper, garbage truck and many other essential pieces of equipment had to be replaced for the first time, all a drain on our limited resources. Through the benefit of a Federal and Provincial Government infrastructure program, Council was able to asphalt Vanier extension and the Arena Road, the first paving in town since the town was built.

Numerous ambitious attempts to encourage economic development were initiated during these years, and while many interesting possibilities were identified none came to fruition. Some of the more memorable ones were a Resort and Conference Centre, a Provincial Hazardous Waste Management Facility, Expanded Marina Complex and various manufacturing opportunities.

Another highlight was the co-operation received from all LGD staff, both in the office and at the town yard. They had to endure a new mayor and slate of councillors every few years with probably the same old questions about this and that. It is a steep learning curve for inexperienced members of Council and the LGD personnel were both patient and understanding in helping us during our first years. Similarly, working with the many Council members over the years was a rewarding experience. The talents and dedication each of them brought allowed for positive progressive change for our community.

One of the more positive aspects of being involved with Council is that as a Council member you have access to the facts (rather than rumors) of most of the issues around town. Rumors could quickly be addressed and dealt with.

From a health perspective I recall vividly when smoking in Council Chambers was finally prohibited. No more coming home with red and burning eyes after a three hour meeting in a small room where most people smoked.

The latter years of this period saw additional worries about the future stability of Pinawa as the looming threat of AECL's downsizing came ever nearer. These were very difficult times emotionally for the townsfolk as many had to decide whether to relocate or to stay in the region. The talk of becoming a ghost town fortunately never materialized and Pinawa has now rebounded to be stronger and more vibrant than ever. The influx of people not aligned with the nuclear industry has given the community the diversity it sorely needed and has ensured its survival.

This time also saw the entrepreneurial spirit of the community begin to flourish with the development of a very successful campground by one of Pinawa's own residents. This development has indeed been a huge asset to Pinawa and this success has encouraged others to follow similar endeavors. This entrepreneurial spirit and the return of "second generation" people to Pinawa to make it their home will guarantee the future of our community.

Pinawa Town Council – October 1995 to October 1998
By Lorne Swanson

Pinawa is a resilient community and its residents have adapted and thrived in trying times. For example, in 1995 Atomic Energy of Canada chose a date roughly one month after the Manitoba municipal elections to leak information to the Winnipeg Free Press of their plans to consolidate their R & D operations at Chalk River Laboratories and close Whiteshell Laboratories. At that time Agnes and I had been in Pinawa for 30 years and our family was grown up and independent but we were shocked by this news, as were our neighbours, and very anxious about the future. Rumours of cutbacks had preceded this event but we were stunned at the potentially devastating effect on our community. Was it possible that a world-renowned facility of such stature would be demolished? Pinawa homeowners worried about their investment in Pinawa with the major industrial taxpayer threatening departure.

Following this announcement, more jobs were threatened and many were lost. Council took ownership of the lands required for town operation. Other town site lands owned by AECL were purchased by entrepreneurs, including the former staff hotel which has survived as a functioning business.

A proposal to develop several cottage sites on Carter and Hind Islands was brought to Council by the Ministry of Natural Resources. Sites were identified which would have had only natural views across the water (no developed properties in sight) as in the currently developed areas in Whiteshell Park. Council rejected this proposal although it may have helped develop a busier and more functional marina. At the time of this proposal the future of the staff hotel was not yet resolved.

Mayor Lorne Swanson
1996 to 1998

While it was necessary to continue to deal with the normal business of a mayor and council, it was now also necessary to interact with a Federal Crown Corporation, Federal and Provincial governments and members of the business community. I was invited to serve on the Federally-sponsored Whiteshell Task Force (WTF), and represented the town in dealing with people and issues outside the normal scope of a town mayor.

As one can imagine, emotions ran high and there was a lot of confusion at the outset of the WTF meetings. For example, initially the AECL President set the task force at rest by announcing their intention to maintain the Reactor Safety Research Division intact at Whiteshell Laboratories. This was a huge relief to members of the task force who were desperate for good news but upon his return his position was different. When faced with the stunned protests of WTF members, he said "I misspoke", and that was the end of the issue for him. A former Cabinet Minister had told me that a Task Force established by the Federal Government in this type of situation is merely a stall to divert media attention.

In spite of these additional demands, the town under Gary Hanna with his staff was efficiently operated and progress was made on many fronts. Staff of Public Works was reduced by 2½ persons through attrition and yet the town was maintained in beautiful condition. A major waterline replacement was completed on Vanier. Mud jacking of concrete on Aberdeen reduced the oversized speed bumps. Installation of a large underwater impeller by the beach resulted in a significant improvement in water quality. The problem of bacterial accumulation was eliminated and cloudy water in the swimming area was cleared up. This made lifeguarding easier and significantly improved safety at our summer playground!

Provincial regulations made the development of a new Landfill site compulsory. Improvements were made to our recycling facility. A large section of Willis Drive was paved. The town office was brought up to date in office equipment and computer software applications. We created a functional Arena Board which has netted substantial savings for the town at that popular facility.

Pinawa Council created the Pinawa Community Development Corporation and W.B. Lewis Business Centre became operational. North Eastman Regional Health Association was successfully obtained as a major tenant at the Centre. We created the Pinawa Implementation Committee at the urging of Provincial authorities to help coordinate and focus the various organized groups in Pinawa and bring detailed opportunities to Council. This committee was possible only because of funding which was available to single-industry towns, such as Pinawa, faced with significant downsizing. This committee was seen as a very positive development for our town.

The mayor and council cooperated in development of "trails" in and around Pinawa, and we worked with the volunteers who have helped improve and beautify our community and those who initiated the popular street markets

This was a volatile period in Pinawa's evolution, as we took our first steps as a "normal" town. Council worked cooperatively and effectively throughout the term, as they must, to be successful and all of this was accomplished within our annual budgets, which is a significant accomplishment in the best of times.

The Tumultuous Years – 1998 to 2006
By Len Simpson

Whiteshell to Close!

"Pinawa waits for the worst!" This was one of the many front page headlines in the Winnipeg Free Press during the month of November, 1995. What followed were months of confusion, panic, demonstrations, and denials by AECL that a decision to close Whiteshell had been made.   However, when the dust finally settled, it was confirmed that AECL would be discontinuing support for the Nuclear Waste Management Program, and moving Reactor Safety Research, and other core programs supporting the CANDU product, to Chalk River. This began a long period of anxiety, rumours and false hopes. By 1997, steps were underway to close down programs and move those necessary for the CANDU business to Chalk River Labs. My Safety Division was scheduled to move east and if I wanted to continue to lead it I had to go with it. I was made an offer of a package if I chose to retire, and my love for Pinawa, plus the fact that some of my actions had made me unpopular with our new CEO, made retiring an easy choice.

Mayor Len Simpson
1998 to 2006

About 8 months after my retirement, my former secretary told me I was running for mayor in October '98 and showed me a filled out list of nominations. This was a surprise but after a short pause I realized this was an opportunity to lead the reinvention of the town. I won the election winning 60% of the vote from an 80% turnout of voters

Early Events

The Economic Development Authority of Whiteshell (EDAW), led by Peter Siemens, was established to find new occupants for the AECL site and new businesses for Pinawa. The first one of these was British Nuclear Fuels Limited (BNFL), who attached a VP to the site to reach an agreement with AECL. The three years from 1996 to 1998 were filled with confusion and mixed messages. While AECL claimed they supported these activities their actions showed that they had no interest in another nuclear operator moving to the site. There was considerable conflict between Siemens and AECL. At least one Division Director forbade his staff to talk to EDAW and BNFL; an instruction that was mostly ignored. In April 1998, frustrated by an inability to engage AECL in serious negotiations, the BNFL group pulled out. By November 1998, AECL announced they were proceeding to close the site and move core programs to Chalk River.

A $20 million EDAW loan was established to help entrepreneurs start businesses but whenever government funding is available, all sorts of people turn up including bottom feeders, looking for free land and with no money of their own to invest. It soon became clear that AECL was only interested in protecting their business and were not serious about privatizing Whiteshell.

Council Takes Action

Shortly after my election I was summoned to the office of our MLA and Minister of Health, Darren Praznik to discuss AECL's announcement to close Whiteshell.   We decided to form a Leaders Group, consisting of four provincial ministers and the reeves and mayors of the communities affected by AECL's action, and develop a report on our situation.   Darren, I, and several municipal leaders took a report to Ottawa and met with several ministries, AECL and the Auditor General's Office. We expressed our concerns about the delays in commercialization of Whiteshell, and also the emerging inadequate decommissioning plans which were being prepared for the site.

Up until the municipal election in December 1998, the high level discussions that affected our future were carried out by EDAW, the federal government, AECL and the various companies that were interested in the site. Pinawa council was excluded from the negotiations. The new council, supported by the general population, were determined to get more involved in our future. In a community workshop, we established that Pinawa needed to lessen our strong dependence on AECL and, to do this, the community had to grow. We decided not to wait for outcomes that may arise from EDAW's efforts to bring new businesses to the AECL site, but to act in areas where we had total control.

It was clear from day one that AECL's original plan to close the site and leave it with a skeleton staff, deferring major decommissioning for decades, was unacceptable; a position shared by the Manitoba government. This intention was reflected in AECL's first report on decommissioning Whiteshell Labs. We also felt that the Whiteshell site was a valuable resource and every effort should be made to bring in another federal program, as they had done in similar situations elsewhere. With the establishment of the Leaders Group, we had built a strong relationship with the Province and maintained this when Gary Doer's NDP government won power in September, 1999. Following our first visit to Ottawa with Darren Praznik, I continued to lobby Ottawa on an annual basis, taking advantage of the annual Canadian Nuclear Association Conference each year in Ottawa to meet with federal ministers, the nuclear regulator and AECL executives. I also continued to write reports challenging the AECL decommissioning plans and sending them to federal ministers, the nuclear regulator and Natural Resources Canada. My background in the industry was a great advantage. One acting AECL CEO indicated that much of their difficulty occurred because I knew too much about AECL and their corporate policies (secrets). We reminded the federal government at every opportunity that they had an obligation to leave Pinawa in a stable condition.

Decommissioning was a serious issue. Shortly after becoming mayor, EDAW identified decommissioning as a potential new business for Whiteshell to develop. Up until then it appeared that AECL viewed decommissioning as superficial decontamination followed by mothballing a facility until proper disposal facilities were built to take care of the decommissioning wastes. It apparently was not part of their mission to build such facilities so we went after Natural Resources Canada to provide them. Even though NR Can's motto at the time was "polluter pays", there was an extended period of buck passing over who had the financial responsibility. Shortly after I retired from AECL, Peter Siemens asked me to attend a workshop at Cambridge University on decommissioning and report back on the current practices. That was an eye opener and Canada was clearly far behind in the decommissioning field.

As I was visiting Paris in the spring of 1999, I invited Peter and the Assistant Deputy Minister of Manitoba Environment (Dave Wotton) to meet me in the UK and visit several sites where they could witness serious decommissioning in progress. We visited the UK Atomic Energy Authority sites at Harwell near Oxford and Winfrith in Dorset. Winfrith was the site of the Decommissioned Steam Generating Heavy Water Reactor, where they proudly showed us their spent-fuel bay that was now so clean that they actually served a lunch there when the decommissioning job was complete. Finally we visited the Sellafield complex in the north of England, where they have a low level waste disposal facility and a number of facilities undergoing full decommissioning. They also showed us the brand new state-of-the-art fuel reprocessing facility. Our visits made us realize the value of a site licensed for nuclear activities. They didn't just discard a site when they had no use for it, but were ready to bring in new nuclear activities to a community that is comfortable with the nuclear business. This is common practise around the world.

We returned to Pinawa envious of what other countries were doing and frustrated with our own nuclear industry. Dave Wotton and I each wrote trip reports. Soon after, when AECL presented its Decommissioning plan to the Canadian Nuclear Regulator in November 2002, we both made presentations protesting the AECL plan to defer decommissioning. We stressed the safety issue of deferring decommissioning and losing the expertise of workers familiar with the site, and the moral issue of deferring the decommissioning costs to future generations.

Later, I began to notice subtle changes in AECL's attitude to decommissioning and changes to AECL's relationship with the town. The Liberal government in Ottawa still had not responded to our many proposals, but in the summer of 2006 following a change in federal government, the new minister of NR Canada, Gary Lunn, announced a five year budget of over $500 million to address Canada's nuclear legacies. One quarter of that money was targeted for Whiteshell decommissioning. AECL now employs about 400 persons in Pinawa and expects to be continuously decommissioning for the next 20 or more years. We will never know exactly how much our lobbying led to this decision, but we had certainly stayed in the face of the federal government, and with the Conservatives coming to power we made sure our new MP, Vic Toews, was well aware of our situation.

Things began to improve after that. At a meeting between Council and the new CEO of AECL, we agreed to put the past behind us and move forward. When our community centre needed a new heating system and roof, AECL contributed $800,000. The Economic Development Committee of Council merged with the PCDC and, following some strategic planning sessions, set out to market the community as a good place to live and work. Success was slow but steady. Real estate values increased. The first $100,000 house sale occurred and a year later one sold for over $300,000. Every year sees an increase in building permit purchases, not just for new houses, but also for property improvements as people see the value of their property rise.

Having achieved proper funding for prompt decommissioning, and with the town attracting new residents, it was a good time to retire and I endorsed Blair Skinner for mayor in the 2006 election.

Summary

AECL continues to be a vital part of our community. They are hiring again and expect to be decommissioning the Whiteshell site for at least the next twenty years. The relationship between the company and the town is solid again, but we are no longer seen as being a company town. AECL is once again participating in town events such as the Pinawa parade and sponsoring our website. It remains our goal to diversify further and grow to lessen our dependence on a single company. We believe that having a site that is licensed for nuclear activities and situated on a transmission line corridor to Winnipeg is a real asset, especially with the nuclear renaissance in progress and the interest in Western Canada in going nuclear.

It was an incredible experience being Mayor of Pinawa from 1998 to 2006. The early years were frustrating but with the strong support of the Filmon and Doer provincial governments we survived that period and learned many lessons. The EDAW concept seemed like a good idea at the time, but required the cooperation of two levels of government (including at least two ministries on the federal side) and AECL, and the goals were not always focused on the same outcome. Accessing the loan fund was incredibly complex and negotiations were difficult. The absence of the town from the top level meetings left us unable to bring our desires directly to the table. The demise of the EDAW left the council fully in control of our future and we took control with a passion.

Our community's greatest asset is its volunteers. Early on they designed and built the Pinawa Suspension Bridge across the Pinawa Channel. It was part of the Pinawa section of the Trans Canada Trail, the first section to be completed in Manitoba. At the town centre, they designed and erected the Pinawa Heritage Sundial, which has become our most familiar land mark and is a must-see for visitors to Pinawa. They also organize our annual events such as the Manitoba Loppet, the Pinawa Triathlon, Art in the Gardens and the Pinawa Birthday Celebrations, all of which attract outside visitors and participants.

What was once seen as a company town located at the end of a 12 km road is changed forever. In 1998 we took over the AECL highway signs and developed the slogan "Discover the Secret". We now have a growing and diverse population, and an expanding business community. The future looks bright. We have recently changed our slogan to "Imagine Yourself in a Place". The *secret* has been discovered and Pinawa is on the map.

Reflections on Being Mayor of Pinawa
By Blair Skinner (Current Mayor; Elected October 2006)

It has been my honour to serve the residents of the Local Government District (LGD) of Pinawa, first on Council for 8 years (1998 to 2006) and then the following 10+ years as mayor. I never dreamed when I ran for Council in 1998, that I would still be involved 18 years later. The simple reason is that it has been a very positive experience. We have had many successes that provide incentive for a person to keep going. But ultimately, it starts with acknowledging that I have had full support of my family over those 18 years and that has been an important part of making the experience a very satisfying part of my life.

It has been a fantastic experience working with the various Councils. In 1998, I recognized that due to the closure of the Whiteshell Laboratories, Pinawa was going to change and I wanted to be part of that process.

I was considering running for Council when I received a phone call from Len Simpson who was planning to run for mayor. He had heard that I was thinking of running for Council, and encouraged me to do so. The voters evidently thought it was a good plan as we both got elected. That led to 8 very rewarding years of working under the leadership of His Worship, Mayor Len Simpson. The rest of those Councils were also excellent people to work with and included Lorne Kiely, Tom Barnsdale, Allan Cassidy, Brian Wilcox, Lynn Patterson, and Karla Elcock. Of course, we didn't always agree on everything, but there was mutual respect, constructive discussion, and more often than not, consensus. Major events of those first 8 years included:

Mayor Blair Skinner
Elected 2006

The Battle with AECL over funding the roof repairs and the upgrades to the HVAC system of the Community Centre. AECL eventually conceded that it was their responsibility and funded accordingly.

Efforts made by Council and the Economic Development Authority of Whiteshell to develop other opportunities for the Whiteshell Laboratories site. However, this was an exercise in frustration as we would get partially along the road with AECL, only to have them say, "It is not our mandate." This led to a formal decision by Council in June, 2001 to essentially abandon economic development at the Whiteshell Laboratories site and focus on development in Pinawa.

Discussion over a regional hospital in the area. This idea was pitched by the Regional Health Authority and immediately created a significant amount of animosity amongst our neighbouring municipalities who naturally thought that it should be located in their area. I suggested that, since we all agree that a new, larger hospital, with more services was needed in the area, why don't we all pass resolutions that we support a new hospital without specifying a location. We could lobby for the location once the funding was in place. That idea caught fire and all the municipalities in the area passed resolutions to that effect. That ended the conflict between municipalities. Fifteen years later, there has never been any provincial funding money put towards a regional hospital in the area so it would have been a lot of conflict for no reason.

AECL's original decommissioning plan for the Whiteshell Laboratories was to mothball the site and decommission in about 60 years. Our Council would have none of that and under Len Simpson's leadership and supported by the Province of Manitoba, we lobbied the Canadian Nuclear Safety

Commission that decommissioning had to take place as soon as possible while the expertise and the people knowledgeable about the site were still available to participate. This effort was successful as the decommissioning is now well underway.

I had the opportunity to lead a meeting with Premier Gary Doer in our Council Chambers. I raised a number of issues but the most important was the fact that due to the nature of funding for the School District of Whiteshell, an unfair burden was placed on the Pinawa ratepayers to pay for School capital repairs such as roof replacements. This discussion led to access to additional funding of about $600K per year from the Province for the School District of Whiteshell.

I would have been pleased to serve more terms with Mayor Len Simpson, but in 2006, Len chose to retire. It was gratifying to be elected to the position of mayor by acclamation in 2006. Two re-elections later, I still have the privilege of leading the Council of the LGD of Pinawa. Over those 10 years, I have had the pleasure to work with Councillors Lynn Patterson (Deputy Mayor), Karla Elcock, Lloyd Rattai, Clay McMurren (Deputy Mayor), Rhonda Henschell, Ron Drabyk, Dorothy Wilken, Don Daymond, Al Abraham (Deputy Mayor), Denis Sabourin, and Chuck Handford. Together, we have dealt with many important issues. Here are a few highlights:

Through the Pinawa Community Development Corporation (PCDC) Councillors Lynn and Karla tried to recruit a developer to build homes "on spec", in Pinawa but were unsuccessful due to the low risk and strong market option of building residences in Winnipeg. So upon the realization that this was not going to happen, I challenged the PCDC board to consider whether we could lead this activity. The answer was YES and in 2007 the Pinawa Housing Corporation was born, a subsidiary of PCDC. We were confident that there was a market of future residents who did not want to buy a fixer upper, or didn't want the hassle of managing the construction of a new home, but if a new home was built they would be ready to buy. Under Lynn Patterson's leadership, the Pinawa Housing Corporation built and sold 3 homes. The first one was sold before construction was completed! This success led to two local entrepreneurs taking on this challenge and I also believe was a factor in the development of the Pinawa Ironwood project. The Pinawa Housing Corporation initiative was rewarded with the Capturing Opportunities Economic Development Initiatives Award – Community in 2009. Once the private sector got involved, the Pinawa Housing Corporation operation was suspended as we did not want to be in competition with the private sector. However, the organization still exists for when we need to tackle a similar endeavor.

Discussions were led by Clay McMurren and other interested residents in developing a Seniors Housing Facility. Clay's vast network of people (he has cut almost everyone's hair in Manitoba!) led to making important connections with land owners, developers, etc. Eventually, this was taken over by the private sector and led to the construction of the Ironwood 50+ Housing and Supportive Housing complex. The project involved a partnership of the private sector investors, the developers, Manitoba Health, and the Province of Manitoba. This partnership is the first one of its kind in Manitoba and is another example of how Pinawanians have the courage to take on risk and be leaders in making a difference for our community.

Manitoba Health opened the Cancer Care Facility in the Pinawa Hospital. Anyone who was there for the opening was moved by Minister of Health, the Honourable Theresa Oswald's speech. She threw away her notes and spoke from the heart. I have spoken to patients who have shared with me how important it is to be able to get treatments without having to go to Winnipeg and also have the capability to consult with their specialist via Telehealth. This investment in Pinawa by Manitoba Health has definitely added to their quality of life during a very difficult time.

Our Councils have worked to replace infrastructure and to put a dent in the infrastructure deficit that is facing all communities. We have built a new fire hall, purchased a new fire truck, renovated the Administration Building, replaced and upgraded the Community Centre/Pinawa Secondary School gym floor, made improvements to the Vanier Centre and made it available and more accessible to people of all ages, rebuilt and improved key components of the arena and the outdoor rink, replaced the Public pool liner, supported the Friends of the Ironwood Trail to revegetate the Ironwood park and rebuild the Ironwood Trail tread to make it accessible to virtually everyone, replaced the roof, improved the HVAC system and modernized the fire alarm system at the W.B. Lewis Business Centre, built a new Public Works building for the Manager and crew, and expanded our sewage lagoon. We are also embarking on an ambitious plan for waterline renewals over the next 5+ years. Many of these projects have led to more accessible and greener (for example, eliminating the use of heating oil) facilities.

Our unbelievable volunteer groups have accomplished so much for Pinawa that it is fair to say that they are the backbone of the community. It was volunteers that won the TSN/Kraft competition for $25K for our arena and who can forget the day that they filmed Sportsdesk beside the Sundial. A group of volunteers took on the Delissio Pizza competition. The Solo Market put Delissio Pizza's on sale, cut the barcodes off at the till, the recycling workers and volunteers collected them at the depot, and the Community at large collected, as well. Then a team of volunteers wrote the required information on each and every one of those barcodes. The result was another $50K for Pinawa Minor Hockey Association, which was invested into the Arena. Pinawa Minor Hockey Association also won an additional $25K for the Hockey Goes On competition. Those volunteer efforts along with the volunteer Committee who has raised over $100K from the Celebrity/Invitational golf tournaments have resulted in the completion of over $300K of projects for the infrastructure of the Arena and the Outdoor Rink. Not bad for a community of 1,444! We are the community that will find a way to "get it done" and I am very proud to be part of that community.

There have also been some sad times while on Council. The tragic passing of Councillor Ron Drabyk touched the entire community. Ron was a hardworking volunteer, a valuable IT specialist for Pinawa, and was early in his career of being an excellent Councillor. Council was pleased to dedicate the Burrows Baseball Park in Memory of Ron Drabyk "In recognition of his distinguished volunteer services and commitment to building Pinawa as a thriving community for generations to come." When he ran for Council, Ron campaigned that Pinawa was great, but he wanted to "…make Pinawa even better." Well Ron, you succeeded.

Over the years, Pinawa Community Development Corporation lost two important board members with the passing of Doug Hall and Jane Sargent. These two people dedicated themselves to the community development and economic development of Pinawa, entirely as volunteers. In particular, Jane was involved near PCDC's inception. They are part of the reason Pinawa is such a great place to live.

Another bad day for Pinawa was the day the Pinawa Motor Inn restaurant and bar burned down. Every day, we continue to feel the loss of that part of our economy. Our residents continue to comment on the lack of restaurant options and a place to gather with friends for a beverage or to enjoy a night of the "One Man Band". This event has had a definite impact on our ability to develop a tourism industry and is a hurdle that we have yet to solve.

In 2012, we executed on a project to install water meters in Pinawa for the first time. Although, we have ample water supply, that doesn't give us the right to abuse this natural resource and the excessive use of water was also impacting our sewage lagoon capacity. We had anticipated a drop in consumption of a third. Pinawa, as usual, exceeded our expectations. Consumption actually decreased by half making us an even more eco-friendly community. The other important benefit was getting the cost of the sewer and water utility out of the mill rate on our property tax bills resulting in a much more fair distribution of the cost of the utility, particularly ensuring that the commercial sector are paying their fair share.

I was already having a good day when then Minister Bill Blaikie called me personally to inform me that the Tim Horton Children's Foundation had decided to locate their Youth Leadership Camp across the Winnipeg River from Pinawa on Sylvia Lake. The Youth Leadership Camp gives disadvantaged youths perhaps their first break in life, where they can learn they have talents they didn't know they had, where they can become one of Canada's future leaders. In sharing the news with Council and various Committees, it was Barrie Burnett who pointed out that the location was actually within the boundaries of the Local Government District of Pinawa. Until then, most people did not realize that our boundary extended to the far side of the river. I used this fact to lobby Tim Hortons to say that the location was Pinawa, Manitoba since it is within our boundaries and this was successful since it now appears on their posters as being located in Pinawa, Manitoba. We partnered with the Tim Horton Children's Foundation to extend Pinawa's water and sewer services to the Camp through lines along the river bed. This type of installation was the first of this kind and size anywhere in Manitoba and was funded entirely by the Tim Horton Children's Foundation. In June, 2015, Camp Whiteshell was officially opened in a very moving ceremony. I had the opportunity to share the stage with Premier Selinger, former Premier Gary Doer who had everything to do with the Camp being located in Manitoba, and Elders from the Sagkeeng First Nation. It was part of that special day when the now retired Bill Blaikie, who was in the crowd, came up to talk with me after the ceremony and shared that the day he had made the phone call was one of the better days in his life also. Since that day, the Camp is now fully engaged in changing young people's lives. We are fortunate to have a facility of this nature associated with Pinawa, Manitoba.

Mayor Skinner speaking at Grand Opening of Camp Whiteshell

In 2013, the Council of the LGD of Pinawa was asked if there were any concerns about the proposed amalgamation of Regional Health Authorities so we posed the question to the residents of Pinawa. A few people answered and generally it was that there were no concerns about the amalgamation but they were definitely concerned about the high turnover of doctors. This immediately became a high priority and I arranged for a meeting with the new CEO of the newly formed Interlake Eastern Regional Health Authority (IERHA), John Stinson. We had a breakfast meeting in the Pinawa Club Restaurant. We discussed the issues and ended the meeting by asking the question, "How can we help?" (A question borrowed from Chris Saunders.) This initial constructive meeting led to the formation of a Community Health Committee. Early on, it occurred to me that to be successful, we don't want to be in competition with our neighbours. So I began the process of inviting our neighbouring municipalities to join. Now the Eastern Region Community Health Committee consists of 12 municipalities in the region and a very strong partnership with IERHA all working together. As a direct result of the question I posed at our initial breakfast meeting, John Stinson called me up and asked if we would be interested in partnering with our neighbouring municipalities and the IERHA to retain an executive recruitment firm, Waterford Global, to recruit doctors for Pinawa, Whitemouth, and Lac du Bonnet. The idea was to involve the communities in recruitment. Potential candidates would get to know the job and quality of life while we would have the opportunity to get to know if the doctors would be a good fit for our community. By ensuring a good fit, the doctors would commit to the community for the long term, thus solving the high turnover/doctor shortage issue. It took our Council about 30 seconds to agree. To make a long story short, this project resulted in a significant turnaround in the future of health care for Pinawa and area. One of my favorite days of my life is August 7, 2015 when I had the privilege of driving to Winnipeg to pick up Dr. Manish Garg and his wife Karen and bring them out to Pinawa for the rest of their lives. I am looking forward to a similar great day when I go to pick up Dr. Chris Williams, who in a recent email wrote, "…my hope is to commit and contribute the balance of my professional life to serving the community of Pinawa and surrounding area, and to eventually retiring there." In the region, in a little over a year we went from days when Pinawa, Powerview/Pine Falls, and Beausejour hospital Emergency Rooms (ER) were all closed on the same to the current situation where the Powerview/Pine Falls ER is back to 24/7 and either Beausejour or Pinawa ER is open every day. Dr. Williams will bring the Pinawa Hospital ER very close to being 24/7 again. So although we have much work to do to get back to stable healthcare, we have made very good progress and I have no doubt we will succeed. The success of the Eastern Region Community Health Committee and our recruitment initiatives have shown what can be accomplished when we work together with our neighbours. Our success has led to the formation of a similar Community Health Committee in the Teulon area and one is in the process of being formed in the West Interlake. In our region, we are now collaborating with our neighbouring Municipalities on a Regional Economic Development Committee and a Regional Lobby Committee. The Lobby Committee's purpose is to lobby Provincial Ministers on common issues. These Committees are moving forward due to the success of the Eastern Region Community Health Committee.

Over the years, Pinawa Community Development Corporation (PCDC) has done a fantastic job of promoting our community. Initially, the brand "Discover the Secret" made perfect sense because very few people outside of the Pinawa area knew much about the community. In 2013, we retained a consultant to develop a 10-year Economic Plan. Their research confirmed that the promotion of Pinawa had been successful as virtually everyone they talked to in Manitoba, knew about Pinawa. Our 10-year plan required a strategic change in direction. We have hired an Economic Development Officer, Shane Li, and the new focus is on creating jobs. It is very early days, but already, we have successfully entered into a partnership agreement with North Forge to create North Forge East, a business incubator organization that is turning currently vacant space at W.B. Lewis Business Centre into business generation space. PCDC's new focus of creating jobs will result in young families making the decision to move to Pinawa.

The future of the Canadian Nuclear Laboratories (CNL) Whiteshell Laboratories site is definitely key to Pinawa's economic future. They are still the largest employer in the area with 350 employees. Over the past few years, the Government of Canada chose to privatize the management of CNL. That procurement was completed in September, 2015 and the successful consortium called Canadian National Energy Alliance (CH2M Hill, SNC-Lavalin, Energy Solutions, and Fluor) assumed management of the site. This change in model created new opportunities for new development at the site, both nuclear and non-nuclear. As opposed to the resolution we passed in 2001 where we abandoned development of the Whiteshell Laboratories, there is now hope for future economic development at the site. Again working with our neighbouring municipalities, we have formed the Whiteshell Laboratories Community Regeneration Partnership to work together with CNL and AECL to develop new opportunities for the Whiteshell Laboratories site. In recent months, we have successfully obtained funding from CNEA for the first year of the operation of the North Forge East incubator project. We have also had very promising discussions with a developer of Small Modular Reactor technology. This scenario has provided unprecedented opportunity for the future of Pinawa and area but will take a huge amount of work to realize the full potential. Fortunately, Pinawa has shown before that we can accomplish great things and I have no doubt, that along with our neighbour municipalities, we will also create a great future for the Whiteshell Laboratories site.

In the foregoing, I have listed fellow Council members. However, it would be unfair not to acknowledge the contributions of LGD of Pinawa administrative staff, Public Works crew, volunteer Board Members of PCDC, PCDC staff, and all the volunteers on so many organizations in Pinawa. The dedication of all of these people is the reason so much great work is completed and that we have such an awesome town in which to live, work, and play. I wanted to acknowledge working with Gary Hanna leading up to his retirement. He was a dedicated Municipal Administrator for more than 30 years in Manitoba and on top of the dedication required to achieve that goal, he contributed countless hours as a volunteer. The throng of people who came to his retirement party was a testimony to the respect that his colleagues in this province have for Gary and the event was a very memorable occasion.

I also have a special place in my heart for the Pinawa Lions Club and all they have done for Pinawa. Everything they work on results in a positive contribution to Pinawa. It continues to be one of my favorite tasks as mayor to carve the ham at the Seniors Supper.

To be sure, there are many more events and people who deserve to be mentioned. Over 18 years of being part of Pinawa's leadership team, there are many, many, decisions, projects, etc. that take place every day that are part of what makes this town special. In many of the things I have written about, the words "first of its kind" or "leaders" appear several times. Pinawa is the great community it is today due to the boldness of the staff and volunteers to fearlessly take on new challenges and find a way to make it work. To everyone I have had the honour to work with, I want to say thank you for what you do for Pinawa.

I want to close with the most memorable event over the last 18 years. Without a doubt, the 50th Birthday celebration was the most special event during that time period. Everything that we organized for the 10-day 2013 Birthday celebration exceeded our expectations. My fellow 50th Birthday Committee members included Jenny Petersen, Louise Daymond, Gisele Smith, Nancy Bremner, and Cheryl Ryan. These people along with a huge number of volunteers put on a celebration to remember. The usual events including the Pinawa Lions Club socials on Friday and Saturday, the parade, beach activities, fireworks, and the Sunday Town Market all went very well except there were more people than usual. But on top of those events, we also had a Winnipeg Car Club Show and Shine, a teen dance, Pinawa Secondary School Memory Lane, a Community Picnic, STARS helicopter visit, Art Extravaganza, temporary museum in the old fire hall, Whiteshell Laboratories Technical Achievement Lectures held at the Ironwood, the Community Band performances, the Pinawa Foundation Community Breakfast, the Amphicar Rides to support Parkinson's Disease research, and the special Pinawa 50th souvenir items designed, purchased, and sold by PCDC.

That list of events is exhausting already but there are 3 more events that are forever etched in my memories. We held the first ever Canadian Lund Mania Walleye Catch and Release tournament in Pinawa and it was a tremendous success. Anglers came from all over North America to compete including Bobby Hull. Who can forget the boaters standing at attention for the national anthems prior to launch? The competitors returned by 3 pm for the awards banquet that were held in the beer gardens organized by the Pinawa Lions Club. About 500 people were in attendance for the very exciting awards ceremony led by Jason Gauthier. The tributes for the tournament from the competitors were non-stop and were captured on an episode of Adventures North. The first ever winners were Dean Randell and Wayne Haner and the roar from the crowd was deafening. This has become an annual event and is an important economic development engine for Pinawa since it is the only event of its kind in Canada and continues to grow in popularity.

The second extra memorable event was the Fender Benders Reunion social. Tom Dunlop, Del Dunford, Gerry Reimer, John Hammond, and John Putnam formed Pinawa Secondary School's first band, the Fender Benders, and they decided to reunite with Gary Griffith to play for Pinawa's 50th Birthday. But here is what many will not know. They live in Seattle, Vancouver, Winnipeg, and London, Ontario. They travelled at their own expense to get together to practice at least 5 times to put on one show. For that one show, they had to travel to Pinawa and rent some of the equipment they needed, all at their own expense. The result is that the Fender Benders played to a sold out Pinawa Community Centre crowd and they brought the house down. It was magical. The performance was so good that we did not want it to end. One person remarked that they would have been happy if they had played the same set of songs a second time. I think the commitment that Tom, Del, Gerry, John, and John made to make Pinawa's 50th Birthday an event that we will always remember goes above and beyond and shows just how much Pinawa means to those who have lived here.

And finally, a very memorable event was the Founders Gala. We honoured the people and organizations that changed Pinawa and the Whiteshell Laboratories sites from bush into a town and an operating research site with an operating reactor in only a few years. I had the honour of hand delivering the invitations to the founders who came in 1963. The evening was a beautiful tribute to the founders, and I don't mind saying that I got a little emotional as we thanked the pioneers who built the town that we all fell in love with so easily. It is with great pride that I show visitors to our Council Chambers the photo of the 1963 founders who still live in Pinawa.

Every single one of the 50th Birthday Events was a tremendous success and it has to include the record of our history captured in this history book. Special thanks go to Chris Saunders for his dedication to ensuring that this project was completed. Obviously, Pinawa's journey has just begun as 50 years is just a heartbeat. Because of the people in this community, I have no doubt that we will meet the challenges that are taking place as the Whiteshell Site is being decommissioned and turn it into new chapters of success stories for a future history book.

Fire Department and Security
By Chris Saunders

The Pinawa Volunteer Fire Brigade (PVFB) was first organized in October 1963. By the spring of 1964, 25 members, grouped into 4 companies, made up the Brigade. Fire Chief T. B. Lamb was assisted by Deputy Chiefs L.A. Johnson and C. Luxton. The Brigade Officers were J.H. Allen, B. Banks, K. Dalby, D. Fitzsimmons, J.E. Guthrie, G. Hampton, P. Kingston and R. Sochaski. The LGD Fire Advisory Committee was also formed in 1964, chaired by R.B. Banham, to be a liaison between the LGD and the Fire Brigade. A few years later, the Ladies Fire Auxiliary was formed to support the Fire Brigade in a number of ways, from fund-raising, social activities, and the annual open house for residents, usually held in the fall.

Pinawa Fire Chiefs
Tom Lamb: 1963- 1980
Peter Cliche: 1980 - 1993
Orville Acres: 1993 to 2002
Shawn Elcock: 2003 to present

One of the first activities the Fire Brigade hosted was the 1963 Halloween Dance and the New Year's Dance to bring 1963 to a close. In July 1964, the PVFB hosted their first Firemen's Field Day for fire departments around eastern Manitoba. The event became an annual celebration and competition throughout the 1960s and 70s.

The first documented awards for the PVFB were in the spring of 1965; two Fire Prevention Contest Awards presented by the National Fire Protection Association. They also participated in their first canvass of Pinawa in May 1965 to support the upcoming Birthday Celebrations. This involvement with Pinawa's Birthday events has continued for the last 48 years, including their important role in the parade every year.

In 1975, the PVFB was awarded first place in the national fire prevention contest, out of 177 other entries in its class.

Over the years, the PVFB has played a key role in protecting our town and its residents. Some memories over the years include a serious forest fire in May 1984 that threatened the community, and the Pinawa Motor Inn fire in May 2010. They have also become an integral part of our Christmas Celebrations. The Fire Department

Fire Safety

escorts Santa around the community every Christmas eve, handing out small gifts to the children willing to brave the cold and snow to get a hug from Santa.

Today the group is called the Pinawa Volunteer Fire Department. Their mission statement is to save lives and protect property through prevention, preparedness, education, and response. The Fire Department currently has 13 dedicated members who train regularly. Current equipment includes a pumper truck, a wildfire response trailer and a rescue vehicle equipped with the Jaws of Life. In the spring of 2011 the town built a new fire hall to accommodate the delivery of a new pumper truck. The Pinawa Volunteer Fire

Department is a member of the North East Mutual Aid District, partnering with 13 other Fire Departments for additional resources. The Pinawa Fire Department provides fire prevention and fire extinguishing, investigates of the causes of fire, assists with emergency medical services, and provides salvage operations, hazardous material responses, ground search and rescue, fire prevention inspections, and public safety education.

To support the Fire Department, Pinawa also has a Municipal Emergency Coordinator to administer and enforce the relative provisions of the applicable by-laws; subject always to such direction as may from time to time be given by Council.

The town of Pinawa has always been policed by the Royal Canadian Mounted Police (RCMP). In the mid-1990s, Pinawa began to be policed by the RCMP detachment in Lac du Bonnet, although some officers still resided in Pinawa.

Pinawa's First Fire Chief –
Tom Lamb

Pinawa's new fire hall

An early pumper truck – mid-1960s

2013 Fire Chief – Shawn Elcock

Fire Fighter
Peter Baumgartner

Fire Fighter
Don Daymond

Pinawa's Fire Department at Fireman's Field Day
Competition – mid-1960s; Barry Banks, Unknown,
Dave Booth, Brian Finlay and Ken Faye

Royal Canadian Mounted Police Detachment

The RCMP has always played an important role in Pinawa life, as much for crime prevention programs and positive community involvement as for crime investigations. The local detachment was first formed in Pinawa in 1963. It was based out of a row house at 17 McGregor Crescent. The first constable posted to town was Nick Searle. Constable Searle was quickly followed by Torchy Torresan, who arrived in 1964, and R.M. Tramley, who came to town in 1966. Both constables were here for a 3-year posting.

The permanent RCMP office at the LGD Office was constructed in 1964. This has been the home of Pinawa's RCMP office for the past 50 years.

Pinawa has hosted over 40 RCMP staff over the years. Constables like R. Blowers (early 1970s), W.D. Epp (late 1970s), R.W. Thompson (early 1980s) and D.B. Roy (mid 1980s), along with many others, made Pinawa their home and made valuable contributions to our community, both on duty and as residents.

"Torchy" Torresan writes up a ticket to a clown for
dangerous driving.

Constable Paul Human

RCMP leading the Pinawa Parade

Constable Kevin Elliott

RCMP Musical Ride in Pinawa

Constable Pier-Luc Savaria

School District of Whiteshell – District with a Difference
By Lorne Schram, Lawrence Suchar and Helen Tomlinson

On the day after Labour Day, September 1963, Pinawa's first school opened its doors to four teachers and forty-four pupils in grades 1-8. Joyce Brown (now Joyce Tabe) had arrived the night before to take up her duties teaching a combined grade 3-4 class in the new school. To her dismay she discovered a village under construction but nowhere for her to live. The expected accommodation had not as yet been built. Joyce was able to find temporary digs in the neighbouring town of Seven Sisters. Like so many of the other new arrivals, Joyce managed to surmount the enormous inconveniences of those early days and fifty years later still calls Pinawa her home.

Pinawa, in 1963, was the spanking new town that Atomic Energy of Canada Limited (AECL) was building to house the employees of its new research station, Whiteshell Nuclear Research Establishment (WNRE). Selecting the site for both the research station and the town had depended on a great many factors but the net result was that they were built in an area of low population density. There were few existing services in place and the Company (AECL) was faced with building everything from scratch. Roger Smith was head of WNRE's Administration Division and in charge of dealing with everything that had to do with the town site. He explained that the Company faced a big problem in attracting and holding staff at WNRE. It was not easy to persuade people to come to Pinawa, an unknown place 'way out in the bush'. Keeping them was the biggest challenge. AECL could not afford a high labour turnover, so the company had to meet employees' expectations and priorities. Housing and, equally important, schools topped the list of essential services.

When asked why Pinawa has its own school district, Roger explained that arrangements for schooling in Manitoba today are quite different than they were at the beginning of the 1960s when he and Ed Lundman were negotiating with the Province. Rural Manitoba was dotted with one and two room schools. The small communities near Pinawa could not accommodate an influx of AECL employees and neither they nor the province had the money to build schools for the hundreds of children who would soon be arriving.

Andrew Davidson – Class of 1987

Andrew Davidson was born in Pinawa, Manitoba, and graduated in 1995 from the University of British Columbia with a B.A. in English literature. He has worked as a teacher in Japan, where he has lived on and off, and as a writer of English lessons for Japanese web sites. *The Gargoyle*, the product of seven years' worth of research and composition, is his first book.

Andrew is one of the bestselling novelists in the world. The manuscript was sold in more than 23 countries. Immediately after its release, the novel appeared in New York Times Book Review as the newest bestselling novel. In 2009 the novel received a nomination for the Galaxy British Book Awards.

The problem could not be resolved simply by having AECL contribute school taxes. Provincial regulations of the day required that local school boards divide funding equally among all the schools in their district. This meant that tax money paid by AECL would be diffused throughout the district but there would still be no nearby school capable of dealing with the number of children expected.

AECL would have to build the schools and also provide major funds to assist in operating them. In 1962 the Whiteshell School District #2408 was created as a 'Special Revenue District'. This arrangement, worked out between Ed Lundman representing the LGD of Pinawa, Roger Smith acting for AECL and the Province of Manitoba, became part of what is known as the 'Master Agreement'. Ed was Pinawa's first town administrator. The province also appointed him 'Official Trustee' making him the equivalent of

Superintendent of Schools and School Board all rolled into one. In November of 1963 the Province authorized the appointment of a School Advisory Board made up of Pinawa residents. This board continued to act in an advisory capacity to the Official Trustee (Ed Lundman) until 1968 when a full-time School Superintendent, Bob Dale, was hired and a School Board was elected.

When the Company undertook construction of the school buildings it was determined to build the best schools possible and would complete one project before embarking on the next. The first elementary school opened in September 1963 and was completed the following year with the addition of a kindergarten and a gymnasium. It was later named the F.W. Gilbert Elementary School to honour Fred Gilbert, who had been in charge of overseeing the planning and building of the town. Throughout 1963 Pinawa's senior students, grades 9-12, few in number at that time, were taken by bus to Lac du Bonnet High School. In 1964 with Pinawa Elementary #1 (Gilbert School) now completed there was room to add the grade 9 students. The

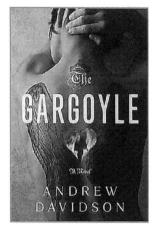

August 2008

students in grades 10-12 continued to travel by bus to Lac du Bonnet for one more year. In 1965 the first stage of the high school complex (grades 9-12) was built. This eventually would house three distinct areas: academic, vocational and a gymnasium/community centre, which included a stage and back-stage area.

The second elementary school was built as the first stage of what was planned to become a much larger complex. It was named W.B. Lewis Elementary School to honour Dr. W.B. Lewis, then vice president of AECL and a scientist of international repute. In September of 1966 when Lewis school opened its doors, a new math teacher, Wally Kukurudz, arrived to take up his duties teaching grade 8. That year the grade 7 and 8 students had been transferred from Gilbert School to join the K-6 students attending the new Lewis School. By the following year, 1967, the grade 7 and 8 students made their final move to their permanent home. The high school had been expanded to accommodate a junior high section as the District moved to a K-6, 7-8, 9-12 system. The building was initially called Pinawa Collegiate, but was subsequently named Pinawa Secondary School in 1976.

Dan Frechette – Class of 1994

Dan Frechette is a musical force. He is an award winning Canadian singer-songwriter. He's written more than 1,300 songs, was signed to a major songwriting contract at 17, and has busked on street corners and in subways all over North America and Europe. He's toured with a First Nations rock band, played solo at dozens of major folk festivals and is the man who penned hit singles "The Mists of Down Below" and "You Don't See It" among others, for The Duhks, Dervish, and other international bands and artists. Of his debut solo album "Lucky Day", Greg Quill of the Toronto Star wrote, "…an album that will surely find an exalted place in the canon," and the exalted folk music periodical Sing Out! has described Dan as, "one of the most talented singer/songwriters heard in a long time."

When Dan Frechette began writing songs in 1990, those around him were startled by the maturity of his lyrics and how his songs seemed to come from another lifetime. Dan Frechette's prolific output, iconic voice and under the radar career path have led many luminaries in the music industry to sing his songs and share their concerts, including Dar Williams, Richard Thompson, The Duhks, Blackie and The Rodeo Kings, Iain Matthews, Vance Gilbert, Ron Sexsmith, Christine Lavin, Stephen Fearing, Jackie Washington, Michael Jerome Browne, Ray Bonneville, and Kelly Jo Phelps. Today his albums earn plaudits, praise, and airplay across North America.

From the beginning Pinawa schools were never meant to be just schools. Weekdays, weekends and evenings they have been centres for the whole community. Fred Gilbert realized that AECL could not afford to duplicate buildings. Fred insisted that both the school and the community have the use of the gymnasium at the high school. Everyone in Pinawa has benefited from the many uses to which all the school buildings have been put.

In 1968 when Bob Dale, our first Superintendent, arrived on the scene, the really exciting work began. Bob is fondly remembered by his staff as someone who could listen to their ideas with respect. He supported their energy and enthusiasm encouraging them to create excellent programs.

Lawrence Suchar, who came to Gilbert School as principal in 1969, recalls that

Pinawa Collegiate

Bob Willacy, Angus Graham, Bruce Dobbin, Pat Anderson, Mike Allan, Bruce Smith

Class of 1966

families were arriving from all over the world. AECL was recruiting staff from across Canada as well as from Europe, Asia, the United States and Australia. Children were coming to school from many different backgrounds. Teachers had to use a multitude of instructional methods to meet the students' diverse educational, social and emotional needs. The District Office provided funds for staff to participate in conferences and workshops and to visit other progressive schools elsewhere. Lawrence remembers with pleasure that the schools became very interesting and exciting places to be, for both teachers and students. There was a fundamental focus on the unique and individual needs of each student. Close relationships between home and school were encouraged. Extra-curricular programs were developed to broaden the students' experiences. Pinawa gained the reputation of having schools comparable to the best in the province.

Fiona Sanipelli – Class of 2001

After receiving her Interior Design degree from the University of Manitoba, Fiona Sanipelli specialized in designing restaurants in Winnipeg. One of Fiona's Winnipeg clients had a relationship with a design firm in New York City. Next thing you know, she was hired by AvroKO.

Immediately, she began work at the Hurricane Club located on Park Avenue and 26th Street. She also received recognition for designing Beauty and Essex, located on the Lower East Side, changing an older building to a jewellery themed atmosphere. This building was the first jewellery store in New York City. Another opportunity came Fiona's way and she joined Martin Brudnizki Design Studio, a New York firm acclaimed for their expertise in hotel and restaurant design and architecture. With Brudnizki she was part of a team that worked on two major renovations: in St. Augustine, Florida she created a historical  presence to a newly constructed hotel and in Miami, the Stanton Hotel chain, Fiona converted an existing deco style restaurant/pub to a youthful vintage beach theme. In 2013, Fiona continues to work in New York.

Wally Kukurudz, who started his teaching at Lewis School with grade 8, moved with the Junior High students to Pinawa Secondary. He remembers how happy he was to be able to specialize in the math subjects that he loved. He was further challenged by helping to revise the junior high curriculum and developing curriculum at the departmental level.

In 1980 Wally became principal of Pinawa Secondary. Summing up his impressions of his years here, he confirmed that the school atmosphere generally was a happy one for both staff and students. Wally believed that students graduating from Pinawa's schools were able to take with them a real sense of confidence as they went into the workforce or on to further study.

It was a political decision in Ottawa in the late 1950s that created the town of Pinawa. Another political decision has affected the town profoundly. The Federal Government's decision to cut funding for nuclear research caused drastic downsizing of WNRE and its eventual closure. Today the student population is much smaller as young families leave to seek work elsewhere. Owing to declining enrolment the School District was forced to close Lewis School. The school building was subsequently sold to PCDC (Pinawa Community Development Corporation). It has now become the WB Lewis Business Centre.

Gerry Dougall's arrival as Whiteshell's new Superintendent in 1991 coincided with the period during which AECL began its slow withdrawal from the town. During his time with Whiteshell School District he served not only as superintendent but also shouldered the double job of high school principal and superintendent, successfully shepherding the district through some difficult times.

On his arrival Gerry was impressed by the mature attitude of the kids here, a maturity that he attributes not just to Pinawa but also to the nature of small communities generally. In a small community students are constantly interfacing with adults not just with other kids as is so often the case in large centres. Even with the changes taking place in the community Gerry could confirm that parental expectations for their children continue to be high. Although the school population has changed, the ethos of the school has been maintained. The desire for excellence remains. Pinawa teachers are enthusiastic and knowledgeable in the subjects they teach. On provincial exams our students continue to achieve scores well above the provincial average. The schools continue to receive great community support for all their activities, in sports and in the arts. Last but not least we have to applaud our school boards, past and present. Their attitude is 'education first' not 'money first'.

The most impressive accomplishment of the Pinawa school system has been the students, over 1,100 graduates from 1966 to 2013. There have been over 30 graduates that have gone on to become doctors. There are many engineers and scientists, designers and chefs, entrepreneurs, accountants and lawyers. There are also musicians and teachers, healthcare professionals, television producers and on-air personalities. The list goes on.

Sheryl Howe – Class of 1981 and Mike von Massow – Class of 1980

Dr. Sheryl Howe operates the St. David Street Dentistry in Fergus, ON. As a progressive dental office, they have focused on preventative oral health since 1991. Sheryl received her training at the University of Manitoba.

Dr. Mike von Massow joined the faculty of the School of Hospitality and Tourism Management at the University of Guelph after completing his PhD. There are two current streams of research that Mike is pursuing. The first is the development of unique food value chains. The second is on revenue management in the services industry - including hospitality. Understanding the linkages between short term pricing strategy and longer term customer expectations is very important. The role of customer feedback in value is also an area of interest.

2013 Graduating Class – Draven Galeschuk, Brett Hessian, Jessie Nelson, Lucas Jansson, Tessa Trueman, Jared Aitkenhead, Britton James-Thiessen, Avery Goodwin-Stam, Ben Dearing, Jill Lauze, Brendan Nykoluk

Dr. Sowmil Mehta – Class of 1988

Dr. Michelle Smith – Class of 1991

Dr. Robin Attas – Class of 1999

Dr. Kimberley Mulchey (nee Mills) – Class of 1994

Dr. Tamara Buchel (nee Borsa) – Class of 1986

Dr. Haris Vikis – Class of 1993

Dr. Elena Vikis – Class of 1994

Dr. John Borsa – Class of 1984

Dr. Gerald Legiehn – Class of 1984

Dr. Colin Dormuth – Class of 1988

Some of Pinawa's Teachers Over the Years – Front Row: Rosemary Sexton, George Turner, Evelyn Vandergraaf, Thelma Boase, Glenys Norman-Kukurudz, Leny Ohta, Susan Rattai; Second Row: Bob Reimer, Vivian Thomson, Helen Tomlinson, Joyce Tabe, Brenda McKenzie, Brian McKenzie, Dave McAuley; Third Row: Dixie Jung, Marg Smith, Joan Mills, Phyllis Briercliffe, Helen Hayward, Brenda Morash, Ken Sigurdson, Wally Kukurudz; Back Row: Alex Domytrak, Lorne Schram, Ann Sisler, Heather Westdal, Judy Farr, Doreen Bigelow, Michael Bigelow, Tim Fast, Doug Legall (Photograph courtesy of Stu Iverson)

Erin Selby – Class of 1986

Erin Selby spent her childhood years in Pinawa. She attended high school in Ottawa and earned a B.A. in Communications from Concordia University in Montreal. Erin began her journalism career in Montreal, first as a newspaper reporter and then as the weather anchor for Global Montreal. In 2002 Erin and her family moved back home to Manitoba. Erin was an anchor and the first Consumer watch reporter for CTV Winnipeg for four years before becoming host of Citytv's Breakfast Television. Erin was a member of the Children's Hospital Foundation Board and the foundation's broadcast committee. Erin was also a member-at-large on the Parent Advisory Council at her children's school. Through her work on television, Erin volunteered with a number of local charities. In the spring of 2007, Erin stepped down from Citytv and the board of the Children's Hospital to launch her political career.

Erin was elected in 2007 and re-elected in 2011 to represent Southdale. In 2009, Premier Greg Selinger appointed Erin the Legislative Assistant to both the Minister of Family Services and Consumer Affairs and the Minister of Culture, Heritage, and Tourism. On March 28, 2011 Erin was appointed Minister of Advanced Education and Literacy.

In 2002 the provincial government decided to amalgamate the Whiteshell School District with the Agassiz School Division and parts of the Transcona-Springfield Division to form a new larger Sunrise School Division. There was a very real threat that amalgamation could lead to the closure of small schools like those in Pinawa.

Closing schools would have a very negative impact on the community as a whole. Thanks to the enormous efforts of both the superintendent and the mayor and council, Pinawa has been able to retain its school district and its independence. Smaller they might be, but Pinawa schools continue the tradition of offering the best possible education for all students so that their years in school are not only profitable but enjoyable, providing many happy memories in later years.

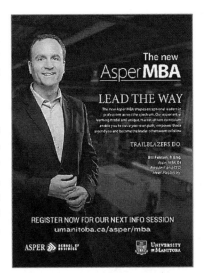

The new
Asper **MBA**

LEAD THE WAY

The new Asper MBA shapes exceptional leaders in professions across the spectrum. Our experiential learning model and unique, market-driven curriculum enable you to carve your own path, empower those around you and become the leader others want to follow.

TRAILBLAZERS DO.

Bill Fenton, P. Eng.
Asper MBA '04
President and CEO
West Plains Inc.

REGISTER NOW FOR OUR NEXT INFO SESSION
umanitoba.ca/asper/mba

ASPER ⟫ ⦂⦂⦂⦂⦂⦂   UNIVERSITY ᴼᶠ MANITOBA

Adam Donnelly – Class of 2001

A graduate from the culinary arts program at Winnipeg's Red River College, Adam Donnelly has worked for Michelin star chef Tom Aikens and at the award-winning Dehesa Charcuterie & Tapas Bar in London, England. Most recently, Adam completed a short stage position at St. John Bread and Wine under Chef Fergus Henderson.

Before opening the award-winning Segovia Tapas in Winnipeg, Adam spent six weeks travelling throughout Spain, learning everything he could about the Spanish way of life and the food and wine found within the country. For Segovia's menu, Adam gracefully melds Spanish recipes and techniques with fresh ingredients and modern ideas. The end result is an inspiring menu of delicious small dishes designed for sharing with good friends and family.

Robin Ledoux – Class of 1988

Robin Ledoux (Stage name Robin Black), is the lead of a Canadian glam rock band originally known as Robin Black and the Intergalactic Rock Stars, formed in 1998. He moved to Toronto in 1998 to form the band. Robin also made an appearance on Showcase's TV series KinK and was a judge on the 2006 Much Music VJ Search. He holds a second degree black belt in Tae Kwon Do. Robin won the 2008 Naga World Championships. In 2006, Robin all but walked away from a successful music and television career to pursue his real passion: Mixed Martial Arts.

A true MMA obsessive, Black is an Analyst and On Air personality for The Fight Network and The Score, a color commentator for English broadcasts of Sengoku and DEEP as well as Ringside, CFC, AFC, MFL, The Score Fighting Series and other shows. He has also ring announced and done post-fight interviews for WRECK, CFC and other shows, and is a writer for The National Post and Maxim Canada. In addition, Black manages a stable of 18 athletes (and growing) as managing partner of Black and Associates Fighter management.

THE BLACK EYE
with Robin Black

School Advisory Boards, School Boards, 1963-2013

Ed Lundman was appointed School Trustee in 1963 by the province of Manitoba, in addition to his duties as Resident Administrator. The election of a School Advisory Board merited the distinction of Pinawa's first elected body.

Advisory Board 1964-65: Mrs. Kirkham, Mrs. Green, Mr. Stromberg, Mr. Hillier, Dr. J. Weeks, Mr. A. Mayman, and Mrs. G. Unsworth

Whiteshell School District – Did You Know?

The school budget for 1963 was $24,060; the actual expenditures were $23,675.

The Advisory Board recommended in 1964 that three elementary schools be built to accommodate the predicted growth of the LGD.

The high school opened August 31, 1965.

1965, Mr. D. Graham was hired as Acting Secretary-Treasurer.

In August 1965, questions arising from a letter regarding Rules and Regulations for students attending the Collegiate:

Question – whether it would be advisable to lay down rules on hairstyles for both girls and boys, due to the many unconventional styles seen these days? Upon discussion with the Board, it was suggested that this would be hard to enforce as "new fads" are continually changing and it would be best left to parental discipline.

Question – As girls would not be allowed to wear slacks or shorts in High School, would there be any restriction on boys wearing jeans? Board felt that this was not the same, as there was not the element of distraction and that as long as jeans were clean and presentable they could not find any objections to them.

Question – Would students be liable for breakages or damage caused by them?

1965 December, Mr. P. Thiessen submitted his letter of resignation.

November 1965 attendance: Elementary school 317 students, including 52 in kindergarten; High school – 65 students; average attendance 96%; December move-ins – 11.

The first agreement for shared costs between the LGD and School District was developed in 1965: 55%/45% respectively.

Advisory Board 1966: Mr. W. Litvinsky, Mr. C. Hillier, Mrs. G. Unsworth, Mrs. R. Kirkham, and Mrs. J. Putnam.

Feb 1966: Mr. Rowan was offered position of supervising principal for the Elementary School.

F.W. Gilbert School has a Citizenship Award every year, in honour of Mrs. Chris Gilbert.

Board Chair
Edward Olchowy (1968-70)
Alex Mayman (1971-72)
John Boulton (1972-74)
Bernice Putnam (1974-75)
Donald Amundrud (1975-76)
Harold Peterson (1976-78)
Alma McCormac (1978-83)
Alice Chambers (1983-88)
Zona Dmytriw (1988-90)
Alice Chambers (1990-92)
Neil Miller (1992-93)
Barbara Sanipelli (1993-95)
Terrance Andres (1995-97)
Ed Bueckert (1997-99)
Barbara Sabanski (1999-2001)
Rhea Galeschuk (2001-05)
Neil Miller (2006-07)
Rob Murray (2008-10)
Brian Wilcox (2010-present)

Superintendent
Robert Dale (1968-80)
Roland Ledoux (1980-86; 1987-89)
Walter Kukurudz (1986-87)
Malcolm McMurray (1990-91)
Gerald Dougall (1991-2006)
Michael Borgfjord (2006-08)
Bob Derousie (2008-13)
Tim Stefanishyn (2013-present)

Pinawa Co-operative Nursery
By Pat Amundrud

The Nursery School offers three and four year aids an interesting, stimulating and caring environment where they learn to work and play with other children. The Pinawa Co-operative Nursery School is licensed under the Manitoba Government Day Care Act and is required to abide by the regulations set out in this legislation. The Pinawa Cooperative Nursery School has been located at various sites around town, including room 34 at the Community Centre (the kitchen), in the basement of Kelsey House (previously the Women's Centre), room 8 at the Lewis Center, and twice located at room 9 in F. W. Gilbert Elementary School where it is currently located.

The teachers over the years included Wendy Allison, Merna Wolstenholme, Barbara Barnett, Gloria McAuley, Alice Jones, Doris Summach, Carol Dyck, Sue Wallace, Marg Haugen, Leny Ohta, and Jackie Sturton.

The teacher-aids and special needs assistants have included Ingrid Betteridge, Jan Molinski, Chris Crosthwaite, Kelly Murray, Tammie Powaschuk, Wendy Gibson, Elise Shewchuk, Tamara Tinant, Clint Chaboyer.

The first attempt to start a nursery school ran into difficulty when they couldn't find a teacher. In the spring of 1973, a group of twelve including the families of Allison, Barnett, Barker, Derkson, Dutton, Faile Fisher, Mehta, Penner, Nuttall and Wright, went looking for a teacher. The group spent many evenings discussing aims and goals of a cooperative nursery school venture and establishing a common understanding. The Pinawa Cooperative Nursery School was officially incorporated on October 2, 1973.

The teacher that first year, Wendy Allison, had primary teaching experience and held a kindergarten certificate. The Pinawa Cooperative Nursery School held memberships in Parent Cooperative Preschool International, Early Childhood Education Council, and West End Cooperatives. During the spring of 1974, the Nursery School Board investigated the amalgamation with Rosemary Minn's private nursery school. No decisions were ever made. It was then discovered that Rosemary was leaving Pinawa. At that time the following people were elected to the Board: Barbara Barnett, Chairperson, Liz Barker, Treasurer, Glenys Dutton, Secretary; Ilona Komzak, Equipment Committee Chairman; Marjorie Campbell, and Rota Chairman (Rota resigned at the end of the summer and was replaced by Fiona Wright).

In the summer of 1974 the Board, led by Chair Barbara Barnett, established a policy regarding the assessment of a fee for working mothers not serving rota duty. In September, 1974, Merna Wolstenholme was the new teacher. Merna was a pediatric nurse. She taught 18 children for one term. That fall was a busy time for the Nursery School with several fund raising activities.

With Merna's resignation effective after Christmas, Barbara resigned as Chair to apply for a teaching position. She had a background in nursery school training and taught the older class of youngsters. Gloria McAuley was a primary teacher and taught the younger children. Fiona Wright assumed the Chair position.

June 1, 1975 marks the day that Pinawa Cooperative Nursery School became a registered charitable organization, with Marg McDowall elected Chair.

At the May 1977 Annual General Meeting, many were shocked to hear the announcement that Barbara and Gloria had both resigned. Carol Dyck became the senior staff member. She and Sue Ennis formed a hiring committee and advertised for two teachers. Doris Summach and Alice Jones were hired. Activities in 1978 included the Children's Shop whereby Don Nisbet Toys, Child's Place and Growing Minds set up at the Pinawa Club. In the spring, the children all boarded a bus for a trip to "Where Daddy Works". The summer of 1978 was highlighted with two activities. The Nursery School sponsored a summer playground for three and four year olds. During the Birthday Party weekend, Actors' Showcase, Winnipeg, presented the children's theatre production of Snow White. The only problem that seemed to occur in the operation of the Nursery School resulted when Alice Jones closed her nursery school. With no other choice, parents wanting to send their children to nursery school were forced to send them to the Cooperative.

At the Annual General Meeting in 1979, the following people were elected: Carol Moyer, Chairperson, Shirley Kozier, Vice Chairperson, Pat Amundrud, Secretary, Marie Stobbs, Treasurer, and Louise Mellin, Equipment Chairperson. In 1978 and 1979 the incoming children were taken on a "tour" of the Nursery School in small groups during the month of August. During the year both Marie Stobbs and Pat Amundrud left Pinawa. They were replaced by Elizabeth Ross and Barbara Sabanski respectively.

Melissa Simmons – Class of 1992

After receiving her Masters of Organizational Psychology at Columbia University, Melissa Simmons started Melissa Simmons Coaching, a professional service company that provides career, life, and leadership/business assistance for executive and senior management clients throughout the USA. After receiving her Industrial Engineering degree from the University of Manitoba she was hired by Nygaard International as the Manager of Merchandising and Product Development. She was promoted by Nygaard to work in New York; she was responsible for recruiting, hiring, training and evaluating new associates joining the company. She was noted for increasing efficiency of communications with overseas mills and factories. After her Nygaard experiences she worked as a Senior Manager for the world famous designer Coach. She coordinated design and merchandising with international suppliers in the highly competitive fashion industry. At Melissa Simmons Coaching, Melissa has a passion for helping people uncover true potential and passion, as well as helping them pursue more fulfilling lives and careers. She helps clients achieve change and goals.

Pinawa Secondary School Athletics
By Lorne Schram

Pinawa Secondary School's (PSS) athletic accomplishments over the past 50 years have been part of the school's well-rounded reputation it carved for itself early into its history. Academic excellence, especially in the sciences, as well as a strong arts and music program were already at the fore when the school keenly encouraged the development of an equally impressive physical education program. Fun and fitness were the flagship qualities the new Phys Ed. program hoped to instill in all students. By having all students physically active, and encouraging them to become involved in as many different sports as possible, regardless of their ability, PSS achieved their goal throughout the seventies of maximum participation. The mantra was, "Athleticism is not important-involvement is important!"

The gym, as the hub of physical activity, was the place to build confidence and comfort in the physical realm of students' lives. It was seen as a safe haven for all, and not just a place for jocks. Winter carnivals and track and field meets became one-day fun events, featuring a variety of activities, in which teams were made including students from Grade 7 to 12. House Leagues were founded, enabling everyone an opportunity to play in all the sports throughout the school year. This acted as a "feeder" system for the extra-curricular sports program, where teams would be formed to compete against schools in the Agassiz School Division (the northern part of what is currently known as the Sunrise School Division). Schools that did well in local competition were invited to face off against the top performing Eastman schools in the Zone 13 championships. Winning the zones meant not only a banner for the school, but a trip to the provincial championships.

Just a few of Pinawa's high school athletes

In the mid-1970s, PSS teams met with moderate success against established teams from the nearby communities of Lac du Bonnet, Pine Falls and Beausejour. A few short years later, PSS had established itself as a contender in athletic competitions, winning divisional, zone and provincial tournaments in boys and girls events. Cross country running and soccer were our school's early consistent winning teams. PSS then became a powerhouse in basketball and volleyball. Later on, golf, curling and track and field teams added to our winning tradition.

In 1982, PSS was chosen, along with two other schools throughout Manitoba, to present their physical education programs at a provincial conference. PSS was noted for offering the maximum daily amount of physical education, having a house league program for both boys and girls that included everyone from Grade 7 to 12, and participating in the standard Manitoba schools fitness program each year.

To build such a provincially renowned program took a true team effort. A large percentage of the teaching staff was involved with coaching and supervising teams and house leagues. Many community members also volunteered as coaches for the Panthers teams that took to the courts and pitches of competitor schools. High school students helped coach junior high teams, and were trained as scorekeepers and officials for Panthers home games.

An outdoor education program was added as well, enabling students to go on excursions of one to several days, including wilderness camping, canoeing and bike trips into the nearby Whiteshell and Nopiming Provincial Parks. Winter camping trips provided an especially unique challenge. Trips often combined students from different grade levels, creating bonds among new friends, while strengthening old ones. These trips were well received by students--both those who had not been involved in such trips in any setting, and by those who appreciated the chance to do so with a large group. Trips were planned to appeal to all age levels and abilities. As with school sports, high school students were also given leadership opportunities to accompany junior high trips.

Taking a look at the walls of the PSS gym today, it's evident that the school's physical education program has been a boon to school spirit, and led to the success of Pinawa high school sports teams over the past 5 decades. Visitors to the gym are greeted by a large mural of a fierce black panther, a symbol of PSS pride, painted by PSS students. Over 150 championship pennants and banners surrounded the home of the Pinawa Panthers at the start of the 2012/2013 school year. Seventy-one of these banners celebrate provincial and zone championships, while 87 pennants represent division title victories. Seven other banners the school has won, all in the past 7 school years, show that the emphasis on fun and fitness that were rooted in establishing an active community of PSS Panthers has not been forgotten. These are the Quality Physical Education Program banners, awarded to schools that meet or exceed the provincial Department of Education physical education curriculum guidelines. These banners, the school's current offerings of competitive and house league teams, as well as outdoor education trips and student leadership opportunities, are all indicators that the "maximum participation" mantra started nearly 50 years ago, is still alive and well today. Go Panthers!

Pinawa Secondary Provincial Championship Banners
Provincial AA Senior Girls Track and Field Champions, 1983/84
Provincial Junior Boys Cross Country Running, Runners Up, 1983/84
Provincial Boys Soccer Champions, 1983/84
Provincial A Boys Basketball Finalists, 1992/93
Provincial A Boys Basketball Champions, 2003/04
Provincial A Boys Basketball Finalists, 2005/06
Provincial Junior Varsity Boys Basketball Finalists, 2011/12
Quality Physical Education Program Banners
Eight consecutive banners won from 2005/06 to 2012/13

Reach for the Top
By Brian McKenzie

In 1961, the CBC affiliate in Vancouver began televising "Reach for the Top," an academic competition for secondary schools. As schools from other provinces joined the series, a national final was organized in 1965 with Manitoba an early member. Schools established their own Reach teams and applied to the CBC to join the provincial competitions that selected representatives for the Nationals. In participating provinces, the CBC arranged the schools into a series of four-team flights, each flight using "knock-out" rounds (elimination on the first loss). Flight winners were formed into new flights with new competition until a final victor could be decided.

1984 RFT Team – John Truss, Rob Thomson, Gerald Legiehn and John Borsa

Under Principal Ken Sigurdson, PSS applied for entry but was put on a waiting list as so many other schools were seeking the same. Our opportunity came in late 1975 when one school dropped out just two weeks before its competition was to be taped for television. The CBC began phoning hopefuls on the waiting list, but all the early contacts refused because of the limited time for preparation. Principal Sigurdson and teacher Brian McKenzie offered to enter a team, realizing this was an opportunity to get Pinawa into one of the limited number of regular positions. McKenzie approached a number of Grade 12 students with the offer of a chance "to humiliate themselves on TV" for the good of the school. Four were willing to make the sacrifice: Jill Boulton, Cheryl Payne, Tim Olchowy, and Ed Oravec. With no equipment and only a set of rules and two old scripts supplied by the CBC, the team held a few brief practices before heading to Winnipeg. In their first game of the "knock-out," they fell behind early as they adjusted to the buzzers and pace of competition. Learning quickly, they narrowed the gap steadily before time ran out. After the game, the rival coach complimented the team and admitted their resiliency had him very worried. Thanks to the "first four," Pinawa lost the game but won a regular spot on the "Reach" flight-board.

1988 RFT Team – Back Row: Coach Brian McKenzie, Team Member Karen Heinrichs, Two CBC Producers and Coach Alex Domytrak

In succeeding years, Pinawa students vied for a place on the team and built a provincial reputation for the school's academic prowess. For the first six years, the team usually won the initial game in its flight and then lost the second to one of the large Winnipeg high schools. In 1982, however, Pinawa got to the finals of its flight and 1983 won its first flight on three straight victories, losing the CBWT Championship 310-305. Next year's team built on that accomplishment by winning the CBWT Championship and the Great West Life scholarship, while placing third in the Provincials. PSS was now seen as a formidable competitor and not just "another rural school."

Unfortunately, just when our momentum was building, the CBC in 1985 stopped broadcasting "Reach for the Top," claiming that, despite good audiences, the program was not reaching enough of the "desired demographic."

The rights to the program were purchased by a Toronto group "Reach for the Top, Inc." which soon revived the competitions under the name of "School Reach." Subscribing schools organized tournaments on a regional basis. For example, Manitoba was organized into five or six regions, depending upon the number of schools paying to join each year. Regional winners competed for the provincial title. In 1988, the "Reach for the Top" National finals were revived with Pinawa almost attending, winning all its games until the last one of the provincial finals. Locally, the Agassiz School Division organized a league that included the Agassiz high schools and Pinawa, the latter winning the first two tournaments (1986 and 1987).

1996 Team – Provincial Champions:
Barrett Miller, Coach Brian McKenzie,
Scott McCamis, Riley Kearns and
Jennifer Vandergraaf

In 1987, an Intermediate level was added for students up to Grade 10. Pinawa's Intermediate team won a bronze, silver, and gold in its first four years of competition in this league. In the School Reach Provincials, Pinawa continued to do well, finishing fourth in 1992 and 1993, third in 1994, and then in 1996 first in the province with the right to represent Manitoba in the Nationals. Many individuals and organizations from Pinawa rallied behind the team with financial support, enabling it to attend the competition in Toronto. Riley Kearns, Jennifer Vandergraaf, Scott McCamis, and Barrett Miller finished seventh in Canada. Unfortunately, in the next year, Pinawa was eliminated from the Provincials, losing by 10 points on a disputed decision by the judge.

In 1998, Pinawa returned to winning form as Barrett and Scott were joined by Robin Attas and Joey Baumgartner to win the regional tournaments and the Provincials. With renewed community financial support, the team finished third in Canada at the Nationals held in Halifax. By invitation, the team also appeared at the 1998 convention of the Manitoba Association of School Trustees to compete with a select panel of trustees and a CBC representative.

In 1999, Pinawa repeated as Provincial Champions and went to the Nationals in Toronto where Barrett, Robin, and Joey were joined by alternate Jesse Attas as regular team member; Craig McDougall was unable to attend. The team got to the semi-finals before being defeated, tying for third in Canada. Also in 1999, the first Intermediate Reach Provincial Championship was held in Manitoba and was won by the PSS team of Jesse Attas, Maria Baumgartner, Ryan Bilinsky, and Cole Drew. In each of the next three years, the Pinawa Intermediates placed second in the Manitoba Provincials.

A succession of teachers, individually or in pairs, has coached the Senior and Intermediate teams. In 1975, Principal Ken Sigurdson and teacher Brian McKenzie worked to prepare the team for its first competition. From 1976 to 1981, McKenzie was joined by Dennis Holmlund, from 1981 to 1997 by Alex Domytrak, and from 1997 to 2001 was occasionally assisted by other teachers, in the last couple of years especially by Scott Smith. Since 2001, now-Principal Scott Smith has been responsible for the teams.

More than thirty-five years after its introduction, the "Reach" program continues to be a popular extra-curricular activity at PSS with both Senior and Intermediate teams competing in regional tournaments. The program provides an academic equivalent to sports teams, allowing participants to test their general knowledge and reasoning skills while interacting with other students from a variety of schools.

Pinawa Piano Teachers Association
By Joan Lidfors, Bev Dougall and Jane Petkau

Names of some of the piano teachers in the early years of Pinawa included Caroline Penner, Gwen Greenstock, Beryl Briercliffe. Jane Petkau, Don Thompson, Diane Kelly, Delores Velie, Joan Lidfors, Priscilla Thibault, Cheryl Ellila, and Jackie Snider.

There were no music programs in the schools and several interested people filled this void by teaching piano. Every other music program grew from this lack with two examples being Caroline Penner's Choral group and Peter Hayward's "Baby Band". The band consisted of interested adults at that time.

The piano teachers also started music mornings in the schools biweekly giving students a chance to play and experience recital performances. Sometime in the 80s a beautiful grand piano was purchased for the community centre, thanks to the E.M.C.A. board. The Piano Teachers Association was fortunate to have access to this wonderful instrument and regular recitals started at the community centre.

Making music in Pinawa

By 1990 only Jane Petkau, Joan Lidfors, Priscilla Thibault and Cheryl Ellila were still teaching piano. They were joined in 1991 by Bev Dougall and Deborah Semchuk. Bev had been a coordinator for The Royal Conservatory of Music for several years. In 1992 Bev applied to become an exam centre. A week later R.C.M., Centre 448 Pinawa was born. Since then students have been able to write theory exams and perform practical exams and vocal exams here in Pinawa.

Heather Westdal and Bev put on several musicals and show choirs in the high school from 1992 to 2004 featuring students from grades 7 to 12. These were always very popular and extremely well attended. During these years some students started performing in the Honour Choir in Winnipeg and participating in the Steinbach Youth Choir. Our town is still an exam centre, but numbers are dwindling.

Presently Bev Dougall is the only active teacher in Pinawa, but Clara Thurmier and Audrey Lehman both send students to the centre to take exams in June. These students come from communities north of Pinawa. The music examiners belong to the College of Examiners and mostly come from Toronto.

Pinawa Hospital – The Early Years
By Dr. John Weeks

In January, 1965, the first patients were admitted to the present Pinawa Hospital, but it was not the first hospital in town. I joined the then Whiteshell Division as Plant Physician at Chalk River in early 1962 and was asked to take on the additional responsibility of planning, organising and operating the medical services for Pinawa. Dr. Gordon Stewart, Medical Director at Chalk River, had already obtained AECL agreement to the building in Pinawa of a hospital that would provide services comparable with that of any small town. A site for the hospital had been chosen and when I first saw it in the spring of 1962, the town was an uninspiring collection of mud clogged cuts through the bush. But even then, one could see that Pinawa was going to be a good place in which to live.

The plan was for a town that would eventually have a population of some five thousand and which would provide hospital services for people living in the nearby communities as well as for the large summer population of the Whiteshell Provincial Park. The "five thousand" figure had an important bearing on the planning and layout of the hospital, for although the number of adult beds was initially to be 17, the services of the hospital were built so that the number of beds could be doubled without need for the expense of adding more service capacity. The government of Manitoba at that time proposed to extend Highway 211 I at least as far as Pointe du Bois and to develop the north shore of the Winnipeg River as a major tourist area. Where there are busy roads there are accidents and to deal with this pessimistic thought, an extra operating room, to be used only for the surgery of trauma, was added to the O.R. suite of the hospital. The extension of Highway 211 has never materialised.

Throughout the rest of 1962 and into 1963 planning continued; the layout of the hospital was firmed up, budget cuts were accommodated (even in the golden years there were budget cuts), suppliers were sought for everything from "Q-tips" to x-ray and operating room equipment - it is amazing the number of things needed even in a small hospital. Importantly at this time we set up our relationship with Manitoba Hospital Services Commission (MHSC). There was some pretty hardnosed negotiation, but we managed to convince the Commission staff that we were not a bunch of "wild-eyed scientists" and that we knew a bit about managing both a hospital and a budget. Thereafter we worked very well with MHSC. At this time too, Dr. Henry Beaumont, the first family doctor in Pinawa, provided a great deal of help in organising the medical and surgical supplies needed in the hospital.

By early 1963, it was apparent that although construction contracts were being let, the hospital would not be ready when the first residents of Pinawa were due to arrive that summer. What we needed was a temporary hospital and plans were quickly made to convert a house for that purpose. There is a house in Pinawa with floors that have been sufficiently stressed to take the weight of operating room equipment and which may still have explosion proof electrical fittings. This then was the second Pinawa Hospital and a nice little hospital it was, too. With three beds and a well-equipped O.R. suite it provided a base for Dr. Beaumont during the next fourteen months, a time in which he was helped by Dr. Petkau who was also planning his research program at the plant. The first "Pinawa" baby, Tracy McAllister, was born in this temporary hospital. But the first Pinawa hospital was in one of the row-houses. Little more than a first-aid post, it had to be set up because even the "temporary" hospital was not going to be ready by the summer of 1963. Fortunately during that high summer there were no serious medical or surgical problems.

John Weeks (1926-2006)

Dr. John Weeks was born in Bath, England. In 1943, he joined the British Army. In 1947, after service in India and the Far East, John left the military with the rank of Captain and entered the St. Thomas's Hospital Medical School where he graduated in 1953. John joined the London Transport Executive in 1955 and served the rest of his life in occupational medicine, with the exception of a two-year stint as a family physician in Newfoundland.

In 1958, Dr. Weeks and his family immigrated to Canada where he worked in the forestry, mining, and nuclear industries, until his retirement in 1992. John devoted a great deal of effort to the development of occupational medicine as a field of study in Canada. He was an examiner for the Royal College of Physicians (Canada); and from 1989 to 1991, president of the Canadian Board of Occupational Medicine. Dr. Weeks was awarded the 'Canadian Forces Decoration" in 1984, the 'Meritorious Service Award of the Occupational and Environmental Medical Association of Canada' in 1993, and the 'Health and Safety Award of the Manitoba Medical Association' in 1995.

For more than 40 years, John and his family made Pinawa his home, where he enjoyed its scenic beauty and wide-open spaces. He was widely read in history, especially in the fields of art and aviation history; and most importantly, he was devoted to his wife and family.

Then in early winter the "real" temporary hospital was on line and patients could receive care in adequate surroundings. People are the most important part of running a hospital and here we were very fortunate. I was able to hire from across Canada a group of first class nurses and laboratory technicians. They were delightful people and with the first Nursing Supervisor, Marion Hutchinson, they soldiered on through mud (there was no thought of importing mud to Pinawa in those days!) and primitive conditions, providing nursing care and basic laboratory services as well as baby care and lifeguarding at the beach. It was a beautiful staff and I rather think that all hands enjoyed themselves quite a lot. During the summer of 1963 the Health and Safety Branch WNRE was formed, with Pinawa Hospital as part of its responsibility.

Come 1964 and I did need someone to look after the non-medical aspects of the hospital. One day Roger Smith rang me to say that he was talking to John Minton from Bissett, who had some hospital experience and would I be interested? It seemed like no time at all before John Minton was on board and I had gained a fine colleague. For a period of thirteen years John Minton, as Hospital Administrator, ensured that the hospital worked smoothly, that our relationship with MHSC continued to be good and that there was no friction between the nursing and administrative components of the hospital staff. Those who have worked in a hospital setting will appreciate the extent of this tribute to an able administrator and to a number of dedicated nursing supervisors. John Minton continued as Administrator until his retirement in 1977, when he was followed by the equally competent and friendly Peter Cliche who, on his own initiative, had earned a diploma in Hospital Administration from the University of Saskatoon.

Pinawa Hospital - 1964

Henry Beaumont (1929-2009)

Dr. Henry Beaumont was born near Barnsley, North Yorkshire England. His early childhood years were spent growing up at Kirkburton, Yorkshire. At age 11 he attended Huddersfield College Boys Grammar School until graduation, where he excelled at academia, was captain of swimming for three years as well as enjoyed soccer, cricket, rugby and bridge. He did one year at University of Sheffield, before joining the army shortly before the end of the war and was posted in Egypt. On his return he enrolled in Medicine at the Royal College of Surgeons, Dublin, Ireland, graduating in 1955. He held a rotating internship at St. Charles Hospital, Toledo Ohio, and then returned to the U.K. He then did general practice in Romford and Conception Bay before moving his family to Lac du Bonnet in 1960. Henry then remained there and was the first doctor at the new Pinawa Hospital in 1965. He built his home in Pinawa and raised his family.

Henry's greatest times were held at his offices in Lac du Bonnet and Pinawa where he always said he was privileged to have so many wonderful patients and friends. He was the consummate country doctor and looked after two and three generations of families. He did it all: he made the house calls, worked the long hours, and was on call many long hours at the Pinawa Hospital. Henry had a great sense of humour, loved to tell a good joke and loved to hear one. Henry also liked to swap his gardening stories but somehow the garden always had too many weeds.

Henry retired from medicine in 1995. He loved to travel and he made many trips to Mexico, England, Hawaii, Madeira, Australia, all parts of Canada and the U.S. Henry was a great father and even took his children with him when he took a job in Saudi Arabia. They all remember it as a high time in their life.

In the late 1970s, F.A. (Sis) Smith was the Director of Nursing, responsible for all aspects of patient care, until her retirement. Judy Coleman became Director of Nursing when Sis retired. Some of the doctors who were part of the Pinawa Medical Clinic and who attended patients in the hospital were: Dr. Opie, Dr. Beaumont, Dr. Johnson, Dr. LaRue, Dr. Corn, Dr. Petkau, Dr. Younger-Lewis and Dr. Reich. Office staff included Mary Peterson, Iowna Meek, Donna Raleigh, Dorothy Wilken, Laurel Johnston, Fran Schultz and Judy Platford.

Pinawa Hospital staff kept a statistical record of where patients who presented at Pinawa Hospital resided (remember that the average age of people living in Pinawa was quite low). The out-patients presenting from Pinawa made up about 20% of the total, with the R.M and the village of Lac du Bonnet representing the largest percentage. The outpatient visits on the weekend during the summer indicated a high volume from Winnipeg.

The in-patient statistics were about the same except that the majority of children born at Pinawa Hospital were from Pinawa. Pinawa Hospital at that time had a well-equipped operating room where minor surgical procedures were performed. The Pinawa Hospital served people from the U.S.A., Mexico, China, Korea, Japan, the United Kingdom and many European Counties.

Bud Opie (1925-2014)

Dr. Bud Opie quietly retired after 39 years of serving Pinawa and the surrounding communities in 2004. Born in Albany, New York in 1925, Dr. Opie moved with his family to England in 1932 where he later went into medicine and qualified as a doctor in 1952. For a time, he practiced in London, England, before spending nine years in North Wales and then coming to Pinawa in 1965.

Bud and his wife Dawn were among the earliest folks to arrive in Pinawa at a time when the community was in the early stages of development. The prospects of practicing in a fully equipped hospital and good educational opportunities for their children played a big part in the move to Pinawa. During his tenure at the Pinawa Hospital, Dr. Opie was awarded the 'Doctor of the Year' distinction by the Manitoba Medical Association; and over the years has taken care of our aches and pains, delivered our babies, mended our broken bones, sewed up our wounds, and counselled us about our concerns.

Raymond Hawkins (1931-2014)

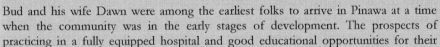

Dr. Ray Hawkins was born and educated in the United Kingdom. He obtained his Bachelor of Surgery and Bachelor of Medicine degrees and a Diploma from the Royal College of Obstetricians and Gynecologists in 1954 from London University. On graduating, he was appointed the Resident Obstetrics Officer at Charing Cross Hospital, London, after which he served as an army surgeon at the British Military Hospital, Rinteln, Germany for five years. On his return to Britain he was admitted as a member of the Royal College of Physicians (Faculty of Occupational Medicine), London, and delved into the world of occupational medicine, toxicology and environmental medicine with Imperial Chemicals Ltd, U.K.

In 1968, Ray immigrated to Canada and became a certificant of the Canadian Board of Occupational and Environmental Medicine and joined AECL in Pinawa. He was also appointed as a Medical Advisor to the Atomic Energy Control Board of Canada. He eventually became the Chief Medical Officer and Head of the Medical Services for A.E.C.L. By Order in Council, Ray also became a Provincial Medical Examiner in the mid-1970s. Ray retired in 1992 devoted much of his time as a divisional coordinator with the Winnipeg Police Service thoroughly enjoying the camaraderie he shared with the police staff. Ray also proudly served with the Royal Canadian Legion in many positions culminating in Branch President.

In the late 1980s and early 1990s the move toward healthcare reform in Manitoba caused all Healthcare Administers and Directors of Nursing in the North Eastman area to establish a series of planning meetings. This was fundamental in bringing the Lac du Bonnet and District Health Centre and Pinawa Hospital together to form the Winnipeg River Health District (later to become part of the North Eastman Health Association). Pinawa Hospital up to that time was operated by AECL under an operating agreement with the Province of Manitoba.

On the date that the Winnipeg River Health District became an entity, Ms. Beth Dyck, the CEO of the Lac du Bonnet and District Health Centre, was appointed as the new CEO.

Abe Petkau (1930 – 2011)

Dr. Abram Petkau was born in Lowe Farm, Manitoba where he attended a one room school for grades 1-9. He graduated from Hiebert School and went on to obtain a teaching certificate. He taught for two years in country schools to save enough money to attend the University of Manitoba where he completed a Bachelor of Science and Master of Science (Physics) in 1956. While attending medical school, he met Jane who was a student nurse and they were married in 1959. Abe graduated from medical school in 1960. After completing his internship at the Winnipeg General Hospital, he was awarded a post-doctoral fellowship at Yale University in New Haven, Connecticut. Abe accepted a research position with Atomic Energy of Canada Limited (AECL) in 1962 and worked at the Chalk River Laboratories before moving to Pinawa where he became Head of the Medical Biophysics Branch. Abe, his wife and young children were among the earliest residents of Pinawa. Dr. Petkau returned to medical practice at the Pinawa Medical Clinic in 1990 where he worked until 2010. He was dedicated to his research, his patients and his family. He loved intellectual challenges and derived great pleasure from learning. He was passionate about medicine and committed to his work. His faith was foundational to who he was. He saw God's hand even in the smallest particles, remarking that the world at the molecular level was sheer beauty.

Pinawa Ambulance Services
By Chris Saunders and Don Daymond

In early 1985, Peter Cliche, Pinawa Hospital administrator, put out a call for volunteers to staff a new ambulance service in Pinawa. Up until then, AECL Protective Services staff was responsible for ambulance service out of Pinawa. Every evening AECL staff brought the AECL ambulance into town and left it at the hospital ambulance garage until morning when it was taken back to the plant site. As AECL owned the hospital, ambulance, and employed both protective services and nursing staff, the system seemed logical. But the decision had been made to create a separate EMS entity.

The initial meeting had an overwhelming response. Over 25 people showed interest in donating their time to a community-based volunteer ambulance service. Training began shortly after, with first aid and CPR courses, acquisition of Class IV driver's licenses, and the beginning of a First Responder (FR) training program. It was truly a volunteer service then with countless unpaid hours devoted to 24/7 emergency coverage for Pinawa. Staff members also provided first aid service for community events such as triathlons and ski loppets. By 1988, training had increased to the EMA (Emergency Medical Attendant) level. Defibrillation and IV maintenance had become standard for EMRs (Emergency Medical Responders – formerly FRs) and EMAs.

Serving Pinawa – Primary Care Paramedics
Tony Wiewel and Marilyn McNeill

Eventually, Pinawa joined with Lac du Bonnet Ambulance to become the Winnipeg River Ambulance Service operating under one administrative board with one coordinator. Two new ambulances were purchased to replace the three outdated units in service in Pinawa and Lac du Bonnet. The Pinawa

Ambulance garage was modified to allow storage of the bigger ambulance. EMAs had become EMTs (Emergency Medical Technicians) and, at the discretion of a medical director, EMTs were given a number of transfers of function, including starting IVs and giving certain medications on the ambulance. The medical service provided was more than just splinting and giving oxygen.

The next logical step, regionalization, saw the formation of the North Eastman Health Association (NEHA) encompassing Bissett, Pine Falls, Lac du Bonnet, Pinawa, Whitemouth, and Beausejour, and the RMs of Springfield, and Reynolds. Pinawa EMTs were now trained to the Paramedic level with more responsibilities and further transfers of function (including cardiac drugs). The old "volunteer" service now had one full-time and two part-time employees as well as a group of dedicated casual employees. The quality of care available to the residents of Pinawa has come a long way from the "scoop and go" philosophy of 1985.

March 1, 2013 marked the 28th anniversary of our ambulance service. Time has seen many changes and many committed individuals have come and gone. Some stayed for a short time, others for years. Familiar names that have been with the ambulance service over the years include Allan Campbell, Tanya Cutting, Don Daymond, Kent Truss, Myles Drynan, Barb Payne, Barb Zerbin, Joan Lidfors, Alice Chambers, Daryl Woodbeck, Karen Ross, Arlene Boivin, Marilyn McNeill, Tony Wiewel, Bonnie Lortie, Bill Gallinger, Tina Christianson, Paul Flynn, Diane Hannah and Glen Podaima. No longer are they "ambulance drivers" but qualified medical personnel committed to treating the sick and injured in our community whenever the need arises.

Pinawa Dental Clinic
By Dr. Ken Young

The Dental Clinic in Pinawa has been providing care to patients since 1966. The original location was in the hospital and the dentist hired was Dr. Howard Cross. He recalled to me that he needed more space to work from; the building used today for the clinic was designed to be double in length as part of the expected future growth of the community. Dr. Cross was completely booked for in excess of one year. He moved back to Winnipeg after two years to pursue a career in Pediatric Dentistry as a specialist. He was a teacher of mine at dental school. He left Pinawa in 1968 and he is still working today at the Health Sciences in the Pediatric Dentistry department.

Ken Young

Dr. Gary Derksen came next and was well liked in the community for the four years he worked here. He was followed by Dr. Ron Rice who worked at the clinic four years and then moved out west. These doctors settled in the community and became part of its fabric.

There were over 100 active clubs when I moved to Pinawa and everyone needed to be on the executive of several clubs for these to operate. In 1976 Dr. Cliff Swanlund arrived. He sold the practice to me and I worked at the clinic from 1980 until this time. I had been looking at other rural locations in my last year but Pinawa was a great attraction to me as it is on the Canadian Shield.

I spent 35 plus years at the clinic and the great memories of staff and patients are numerous. There was a very low turnover on staff and this led to many long-term relationships that developed between staff and patients. Paulette Schram, Janice Schellenberg, Dorothy Meyer, Christine Donnelly, Barb Zerbin, Sharon Howe, Rena Corbett, Debbie Mayoh, Cari Hamilton, Angela Hayes, Nancy Gregoire, Michelle Shier and Shelly McLean were some of the members of the dental team who provided great service for many years. As the population aged there was a need for more periodontal care and hygienists joined the team. Maria Findlay, Glenda Genoway and Donna Davidiuk excelled in this department. There was many other fantastic staff that worked to assure fine dental care was received by all that entered the building.

Emergency service was provided 24/7; although the calls were infrequent, they were usually from someone in great need. Living in the community made it easy to provide this service. Although there was remodeling done on several occasions, the format of the building was set out well and usually required maintenance only. There was also large community garden installed on the Vanier Drive side of the lot that was in full view to all driving into town.

Experiencing great appreciation from your patients for providing them a service that brings you a livelihood is very satisfying. Health care in a rural

Pinawa Dental Clinic

town is so important to its development and success and I was very happy to play a part.

Business Community
By Chris Saunders

In October 1965, Premier Duff Roblin addressed the Pinawa Association. His talk included a discussion on regional development and the economy. He knew that AECL was planning for the key services to be provided to residents: the Hudson Bay Company, the Bank of Montreal, Texaco, the Pinawa Pharmacy, the Pinawa Motor Inn, the Pinawa Hospital and the Pinawa Dental Clinic. The question was how the other services would be provided to the region. Pinawa had limited commercial and retail space available, so it became famous for its small home-based businesses. The first record of such businesses were in late 1965 with Tom Morecraft and Cy Luxton as sub-dealers for Melnick Garage, Morgan Insurance Agencies, operated by Barrie Banks, and Pinawa Moving and General Cartage, operated by Gerry Hampton.

Over the next two years, a significant number of local businesses were established, as illustrated by the growth in local print advertising. Some new home-based businesses that made their first public appearance by 1967 included Faymous Driving College, Avon by Mrs. Walters, Pinawa Barbers and Texaco Bulk Oil Sales by J.P. Cronin.

By the early 1980s, Pinawa had over 50 home-based businesses registered with the LGD. Companies like Rashmi's, Argosy Travel, R&L Boat Sales, Jardy of Pinawa (framing and art), Children's Place Daycare, Pinawa Florist, Lorna's Place and Jarvis Carpets advertised in the local paper, produced by another local business, the Pinawa Press. Other businesses included Hampton's Moving and Storage, The Pop Shoppe, Mont St. Benoit Cheese, Pinawa Print, Pinawa Plumbing and Heating, Don A. Thompson Piano School, Bailey's Bush Gear, Whiteshell Electronics, Shoreline Realty, J.D.'s Accounting & Income Tax Services, the Craft Basket, Jackson Custom Cabinets, Garry Robertson Music Services, Cramer Jewellers, Lorne Swanson Enterprises (Whirlbird Turbine Ventilators), Lloyd's Sporting Goods, Bailey's Sportswear, Pinawa Hardware, and Tufford Enterprises.

The late 1980s saw some businesses close and new ones emerge. Companies like South Interlake Credit Union, Pinawa Furniture, D&D Enterprises, Winnie's Oriental, Sharon's Perm & Cuts, French's Lot Maintenance, and Home Computer Consulting by Alex Thomas began to advertise in the local papers. Other companies that were trying to get established included Styles Jewellers, Shirley's School of Music, Roto-Tilling by Wayne Early, Oliver Agencies, Interlocking Paving Stones by Gary Plunkett, Phil's Exercise Equipment & Sportswear and Coralie's Whicker Where? Local advertising continued and tradeshows were held to find customers.

Christmas Gift Ideas from

BAILEY'S SPORTSWEAR

- Cords & Denims (Basic to Fashion Styles)
- Blouses by Arrow & Sweet Baby Jane
- Sweaters   -- Curling Sweaters
- Apple Bee Shirts   -- Vests
- Penman Track Suits   -- Hand Bags
- Penman Turtlenecks   -- X-Ski Packs
- Pioneer Parkas   -- Sleeping Bags
- Bomber Jackets   -- Sheepskin Mitts
- Windshells   -- Sheepskin Slippers
- Lifa Underwear   -- Sheepskin Dust Wands

**OPEN AFTERNOON & EVENINGS (6:30-8:30)
SATURDAY 10:00 - 4:30**

18 Prescott   Phone 2233

The 1990s saw many of the long-term businesses continue to thrive. Companies like Whiteshell Electronics, Lorna's Place, Sharon's Perms and Cuts, Jarvis Carpets and Shoreline Realty continued to advertise and generate sales. New companies also began to advertise and promote their products and services; Movies and Munchies, Aloette Beauty Consultant with Joan Mills, Cassidy and Company, Pinawa Painting and Decorating, Nancy's Place Hairstyles, Watkins Products, Pinawa Hair Centre, L.D. Rattai Holdings, deWitt Massage Clinic, Eastman Community Computing, Granite Internet Services, Mike's Cycletech, G. Clark Plumbing, Eastman Woodcrafts, ECOMatters, Acsion Industries, Northern Environmental Consulting, and Channel Systems.

The past 15 years saw a growth of realty companies as RRR Realty, RE/MAX and Century21 began to operate in Pinawa. New companies continued to be formed to provide services to Pinawa residents: Home Interiors and Gifts, M. Berry Locksmithing, Kelly's Music, Whiteshell Physiotherapy, Pinawa Marine and Industrial Sewing, Brian's Appliance Repair, PinePro Automotive, Software Solutions, Pinawa Recycling, Rustic Charms, Baking by Dawn, Simply Ethnic Interiors, The Paper, J.D. Wellness, The Burger Boat, Nancy's Place, GeoGems, Book Break, Purity Personal Day Spa, Whiteshell Agencies, Uniquely Pinawa, Horizon Insurance, Core Action Fitness and Rehab Centre, Solo Market, Tupperware by Barbara Sanipelli, Sheppard Environmental, Pinawa Automotive Services, Aquatic Life, Sunova, Karen's Market and Quilt Stop, Dynamic Wind Technologies, and Shaun Thompson Design, Whiteshell Computers and Channel Systems.

Simcha Stroes-Gascoyne – GeoGems
at Pinawa Trade Fair

The past 50 years have seen over 150 small businesses call Pinawa home, including only those companies that registered or were included in advertising or articles in the local papers. Many more home-based businesses provided for everything from cross country ski equipment to childcare services; lawn care to snow plowing; accommodations and vacation rental; electricians, plumbers, handymen, carpenters and general contractors; plus many more. As the community moves forward, we expect the local business environment to evolve; new companies will be formed to meet our needs and older companies will continue to grow, move on, or wind down. Pinawa's business community has been unique over 50 years; thriving and adapting with limited commercial space and a small customer base.

Pinawa Business Women's Association
By Brenda McKenzie

When the town of Pinawa was developed in 1963, the planners established both a residential and commercial area for the future population. However, there was no provision made for small businesses run by entrepreneurs and the "business sector'" consisted only of the Mall on Burrows Avenue. Within a few years local entrepreneurs had begun to open small businesses in their homes. The term "basement business" was used to describe this local commerce.

Advertising was done via word-of-mouth, door-to-door flyers, or posters on the bulletin board in the mall. Eventually, Grant Bailey put together a directory of the businesses. The flyer became known as The Purple Pages because it its colour. However, many of the businesses were seen only as "after hours" initiatives or a way for some people to earn a few extra dollars. Sales were not as great as expected.

Business owners came together to form a "business community within our community" to sponsor the first Pinawa Trade Fair. The Community Centre became a bazaar of banners, booths, door prize displays, and a showcase for all the services and merchandise available locally. The theme was always "shop locally". The mix of businesses was "ad hoc'" for the event until the women business owners/operators decided a better method was needed to make their businesses more visible. Through a series of informal meetings the Pinawa Business Women's Association (PBWA) was born on February 04. 1984.

Name of Member	Name of Business
Bea Jarvis	Jarvis Carpeting
Bonnie Bailey	Bailey's Sportswear
Bonnie Lortie	Calm Water Inn
Brenda McKenzie	Argosy/Marlin Travel
	Brenda's ArtWorks
Brenda Popple	Amway
Carol Moyer	Carol's Bed and Breakfast
Chris Spinney	Kids Only Clothing
Deb Smith	I Have a Notion
Dianne Boczek	Rustic Charms
Dolores Bird	Whiteshell Electronics
Donna Warenko	Granite Internet
Elaine Greenfield	Shoreline Realty
Jane Cramer	Cramer's Pharmacy and Jewellery
Janet Dugle	Jardy of Pinawa
	Custom Picture Framing
Joan Mills	Aloette Cosmetics
Judy Platford	Avon Cosmetics
Lisa Brooks	Best West Pet Foods
Karen Mauthe	Lorraine's Travel
Karen McDougall	Whiteshell Sewing Centre
Karen Strobel	Indulgence Expressed
Leslie White	In Stitches/Indisposables
Lori Evenden	Parkland Properties
	Pinawa Beer & Winemaking Supplies
Lorna Truss	Lorna's Place
Rae Gurela	Pinawa Florist
Louise Daymond and Cathy Beauchamp	Software Solutions
	Beauday Publishing
Rashmi Mehta	Rashmi's
Ria Moreau	Pinawa Hair Centre
Rita Brown	Pinawa Channel Newspaper
Shirley Staerk	H&S Creations
Wendy Berry	Pinawa Furniture

The first members were Rashmi Mehta (Rashmi's Giftware), Lorna Truss (Loma's; all things for knitters, crochetters and craft people), Ria Moreau (Ria's Hair Centre), Brenda McKenzie (Argosy Travel), Sharon Beaumont (Pinawa Florist), Dolores Bird (Whiteshell Electronics), Bonnie Bailey (Bailey's Sportswear), Maureen Lyon (Lorraine's Travel), and Elaine Greenfield (Shoreline Realty). The meetings were held monthly at the Pinawa Motor Inn. Members often brought their children to the meeting as the members recognized the dual nature of the lives of women as both family and business people.

The first project was to raise funds for a Business Women's Association bulletin board for the Pinawa Mall. Here were displayed the business cards and promotions for the various members' businesses. To add to their promotional capabilities outside of Pinawa, the PBWA hired Barrie Burnett, a local cartographer, to draw a map of the town site. The PBWA kept the copyright to this item and then had it reproduced as a map for distribution by the members of PBWA, the gas station, the Pinawa Club and the Pinawa Motor Inn. Later this map was incorporated into a placemat form for use in the restaurants.

Shopping in Pinawa

The PBWA next began a "Welcome Basket" promotion. Using the "Welcome Wagon" idea, new people to Pinawa received a basket of promotional materials, coupons and the map as a way of learning about their new town. The envelope would be delivered by a member of the PBWA who would add the personal welcoming touch to the promotion. "The Binder" was another promotional item first developed by the PBWA. In the pre-internet days, it represented a "one stop look" at Pinawa by newcomers.

The idea of the Trade Fair was re-organized and opened up to other business women in the S.E. Manitoba region. It was held in mid-October when the school participated in the annual Manitoba Teachers' Conference in Winnipeg. For Christmas the PBWA booked the main conference room in Kelsey House for the annual "Holly and the Ivy" Trade and Craft show. These two events ran on alternate years. The fees charged for the booths to these events would eventually pay for the "Pinawa Famous for Home Shopping"' sign now on Highway 211.

Pinawa Community Development Corporation
By Blair Skinner

The Pinawa Community Development Corporation (CDC) was formed in 1996. The role of the Pinawa CDC was to implement the town's economic and community development strategy. The Board of Directors included 5 people elected from the Pinawa CDC membership, a representative appointed by the Pinawa Chamber of Commerce, and the Council of the LGD of Pinawa. The Pinawa CDC employs a Community Development Officer and support staff. The staff also partners on many activities with the LGD of Pinawa Resident Administrator who has economic development responsibilities. The Pinawa CDC is funded mainly by the LGD of Pinawa through an operating grant.

The Pinawa CDC Vision statement is "…for Pinawa to be a growing, prosperous, vibrant, and sustainable community". The Pinawa CDC Mission Statement is "…to promote the LGD of Pinawa, and lead the growth of business, community development, and enhancement of quality of life. We work through cooperative efforts with other groups".

The primary function of the Pinawa CDC is to market our community with a goal to attracting new residents to live, work, and play in Pinawa. Residential growth will naturally lead to commercial growth as the demand for goods and services will increase accordingly. Marketing activities are planned by the Pinawa CDC Marketing Committee. Some of the marketing activities over the years have included:

- Advertising in numerous publications, on Pinawa Club restaurant placemats, signs in the arena and curling club, highway signs, advertisements for local events, various tourism magazines, Pinawa Discovery Guide, etc.
- The Visitor Information Centre located in the Sunova Mall. There are many information guides, bulletins, brochures, etc.
- The Pinawa CDC staff has operated a booth at one or two trade shows per year such as the RV Show and the Cottage Country Show. This is an opportunity to meet many potential new residents to Pinawa and provide them with information about our community.
- The Pinawa CDC operated the Uniquely Pinawa Gift Shop for many years located in the Sunova Mall. Staff developed Pinawa-themed souvenirs for sale. Promotional items were also developed to be given away such as pens, balloons, tattoos, etc.
- Pinawa CDC provided information for articles in various papers or magazines. Typically, Pinawa gets mentioned about 50 times a year and this was doubled during 2013, Pinawa's 50th Birthday year.

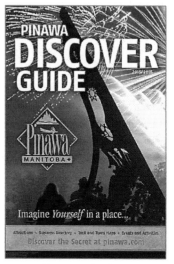

Discover the Secret

- Additional marketing is arranged as opportunities arise. For example, in 2013, Pinawa CDC initiated radio advertisements for the first time.
- Pinawa's website www.pinawa.com is operated by the Pinawa CDC. This is a valuable tool for promoting the Pinawa brand.
- Pinawa CDC also has a presence on Facebook, Twitter, and Flickr.

Pinawa CDC also supports businesses in a number of ways:

- Funding the Business Incubator program at W.B. Lewis Business Centre.
- Operating the Vanier Kiosk for local businesses to advertise.
- Writing letters of support for grants or license applications for local businesses or organizations.
- Promoting local real estate developments in various ways including at Trade Shows.
- Providing administrative support to the Pinawa Chamber of Commerce.
- Maintaining a current Jobs Bulletin Board on the Pinawa website.
- Assisting new businesses by providing information and referrals to Community Futures Winnipeg River for loans or assistance for preparation of Business Plans.
- Partnering with the Pinawa Chamber of Commerce to maintain a current list of businesses in Pinawa.

Pinawa CDC also is the sole owner of two subsidiary corporations:

The **W.B. Lewis Business Centre Incorporated** was formed to purchase the W.B. Lewis Elementary School from the School District of Whiteshell and convert it into office space. The purchase was mainly funded by a grant from the Whiteshell Community Adjustment Fund, a fund that was set up to help the communities in the region adjust to the downsizing of Atomic Energy of Canada Limited. This office space has facilitated many new businesses and was the home of the North Eastman Health Association Corporate Head Office until 2013. W.B. Lewis operates a Business Incubator program funded by the Pinawa CDC to help new businesses to get started.

The **Pinawa Housing Corporation** was formed to stimulate housing development in Pinawa. The Pinawa CDC tried to recruit developers to build "on spec" housing based on the assumption that there were potential new residents who would buy a new house in town if they were available. The Pinawa CDC was unsuccessful in recruiting a developer since they were all able to make more money in Winnipeg with less risk. So the Pinawa CDC took the bold step of doing it ourselves with some support from the

Whiteshell Community Adjustment Fund. Three homes on Cameron Road were built and sold. At that point, local entrepreneurs took up the cause and began constructing homes "on spec". The Pinawa Housing Corporation has since been idle; it was not the intent to be in competition with the private sector. Pinawa Housing Corporation has some resources remaining from this work and is waiting for the next opportunity to stimulate the housing market.

Called Together: 50 Years of the Christian Fellowship
By Bob McCamis

The Pinawa Christian Fellowship all began in January, 1963. A group of future Pinawa residents, living in Deep River, Ontario, took upon themselves the privilege of making arrangements to hold Sabbath worship and Church School in Pinawa as soon as possible after "the settlers" began to arrive. The first meeting of the "Pinawa Church Group" was held on Sunday, Jan 20, 1963, in Deep River, to discuss and plan the organization of a combined church in Pinawa. At this meeting, Mr. F.W. Gilbert read a letter from Atomic

Rob and Kelly Murray

Energy of Canada stating that they were setting aside three serviced lots in the new town for the building of churches. Mr. Gilbert also noted that AECL buildings in Pinawa would be available for worship services; the first building to be ready for use, in 1963, would be the public school. The new church would spend the next 50 years worshipping in the elementary school.

The first meeting of the Pinawa Christian Fellowship was held in Pinawa in early October, 1963. On November 3rd, 1963, the first Sunday morning worship service of the newly formed Pinawa Christian Fellowship. The service was conducted by Rev. A. Friebert from the United Church in Dugald, Manitoba. At this service Kerri, the daughter of Mr. and Mrs. G. Bailey, and Robert, the son of Mr. and Mrs. D. Graham, were baptized. On August 11th, 1965, an induction service was held for Donald R. Ross, of the United Church of Canada, the first full-time minister of the Pinawa Christian Fellowship. The PCF originally represented Anglican, Baptist, Lutheran, Mennonite, Presbyterian and United Church denominations. The Lutherans withdrew from the PCF congregation in the late 1960s.

One of the prime focusses for the 1970s was to assist First Nations communities, led in large part by the Senior Youth Group. One major effort, which was in fact started in the late 1960s, was the "Fort Hope Project". A similar project involved Little Grand Rapids, Manitoba. The Youth Group also spent some considerable amount of time in Winnipeg, repairing inner-city mission facilities. The youth also formed a Rock Band and ran a Youth Church service in the early 1970s. Brian Gilbertson and Harvie Barker were the PCF ministers in the 70s.

The early 1980s were a vibrant time in the PCF. AECL was expanding its Pinawa staff, and this led to an influx of young families with children. Richard Corman was the minister throughout the decade. In the mid-1980s, a thriving Junior Choir was established under the leadership of Janet Melnyk. A highly successful and well-attended Family Retreat to Camp Arnes, near Gimli, was held in the spring of 1986.

The 1990s saw Robert Ewing and Robert Murray split the decade as PCF ministers. Rev. Murray was called to the PCF in 1996, and he has remained with the PCF to this day. One initiative of Rev. Ewing was to establish ties with the National Shared Ministries organization. This resulted in the "PCF Story" getting significant, national exposure as a model for shared ministries. Another highlight, in 1998, was the sponsoring the immigration of a Bosnian family to Pinawa. The family still lives in Pinawa.

The mid to late 1990s saw the town numbers shrink and many long-standing and faithful PCF families were transferred east. The result was a much smaller and older congregation. Now, the dominant demographic in the PCF congregation was snowbirds and retirees. The PCF began holding worship services at the Milner

Ridge Correctional Institute, and the Lac du Bonnet and Whitemouth Personal Care Homes. With the construction of the Ironwood Apartments in Pinawa, outreach to the Ironwood also began.

One constant with the PCF (led by the Senior Choir) for almost all of its existence, is the custom of hosting, with the Pinawa Players drama group, a Christmas Carol and apple cider event in the Pinawa Shopping Centre in December each year.

Currently the PCF is relatively stable in numbers, and in its financial status. The PCF has survived for 50 years as a financially self-supporting, single point, multidenominational congregation in a small, rural town in eastern Manitoba. This remarkable and unique fact would

Called Together: 50 Years of the Christian Fellowship
(Photograph courtesy of Stu Iverson)

certainly have surprised that initial group of future Pinawa residents that held the first meeting 50 long years ago. One can only wait to see what the next 50 years brings to the Pinawa Christian Fellowship!!

Pinawa Lutheran Church
By Peter Cliche

October 9, 1966 –Forty five "Lutherans" met for worship with Pastor Bob Jacob from Winnipeg leading the service. The following Sunday we held our first Sunday school. Thirty two children were enrolled. Sunday school was every week at W.B. Lewis while church services were every second week. Rev. W.K. Raths from Lutheran Church of the Cross arranged for Pastors to come and preach in Pinawa. June 24, 1968 we officially became a Lutheran Church. A retired Pastor, Mathias Aalen moved to Pinawa. He immediately visited all the homes and drew up a membership list of 112 people. Our church directory for 1970 lists the following:

Church council: Norm Roy, Chair; Ad Zerbin; Peter Cliche; Delores Velie; Jake Frederick; Henry Schnellert and Roy Slettede.

Church Women: Sharon Howe, Pres.; June Roy; Norma Johnson; Clara Cooper; Marlene Fanning and Val Frederick.

Sunday School: Supt. Jim Saltvold; Marg Haugen; Karen Schnellert; June Roy; Arlene Schnellert; Shirley Cliche and Jake Frederick.

We still have nine family names on our records from Pastor Aalen's original membership list as of November 2012.

Pinawa's Lutheran Church

PASTORS that served us full time through the years: *Mathias Aalen; Elwyn Josephson; Rudolf Zwingel; Jim Peterson; Barry Bence; Kolleen Karlowsky and Jake Frederick.*

Over the years many men and women served as Pastors, some of them only came once or twice while others came regularly for months. We give thanks for all of them.

December 20, 1992 we had our first services in our new church building.

Our relationship with the Pinawa Christian Fellowship has meant we have joint worship through the summer months and key times during Advent and Lent. We see our corporate worship, community service and fund raising events as opportunities to make a difference in our community and the world through prayer and dedication of resources.

Pinawa Roman Catholic Parish
By Marvin Ryz

During 1963, the first permanent residents of Pinawa began to arrive to begin work at the new Whiteshell Nuclear Research Establishment as it was called in those days. The majority of these residents were AECL employees transferring from Chalk River Laboratories in Ontario, however, some were new employees from other parts of Canada and around the world. The Catholic residents of Pinawa first became members of the Notre Dame du Lac Parish in Lac du Bonnet. With the opening of the F.W. Gilbert Elementary school in the fall of 1963, the Roman Catholic Parish of Pinawa was established with Sunday Mass being held in one of the classrooms of the school. Father Albert Frechette (resident Parish Priest in Lac du Bonnet) was also our first Priest. Upon completion of the Pinawa Community Centre (which also doubles as the PSS Gymnasium) in the fall of 1966, Sunday Mass was moved to that location and was held at the Community Centre until the fall of 2007.

St. Francis of Assisi Roman Catholic Church

The Parish registry shows: Anne Jennings was the first child baptized on January 26, 1964; there were eight first communicants on July 4, 1965; and 24 children confirmed by Bishop Antoine Hacault on May 27, 1967.

During the fall of 1968, Father Gideon Trudeau accepted a teaching position at the PSS and became Pinawa's first and only resident Priest. During Father Trudeau's term in Pinawa, a constitution for a Parish Council was established. The Parish Council consisted of the Parish Priest and four council members (administration, liturgy, catechetical and social action). This Parish structure remains to this day.

The desire by the parishioners for a church goes back to the mid-sixties. The formation of the first committee, for the purpose of investigating the possibility of building our own church, occurred in the early 1970s. The building proposal at that time was to acquire two or more trailer units from the Lac du Bonnet Secondary School. These had been used as temporary classrooms while the new Secondary School was under construction. The plan was to develop a small chapel with a residence for the Priest, an office and a meeting room. The chapel would be too small for Sunday Mass but would adequately serve the needs of the Roman Catholic congregation during the remainder of the week. However, at that time we simply did not have the financial resources to be able to undertake such a building project.

Since that early attempt, throughout the 1970s and 1980s, there was a succession of building committees and church construction concepts, all supported by a majority of the parishioners. However, these all succumbed to the same fate. Our congregation was simply too small to be able to undertake a project of this magnitude single-handedly.

During the 1990s, an attempt was made to jointly share the cost associated with the construction and operation of a church with one or more of the other Pinawa congregations. The Roman Catholic and Pinawa Christian Fellowship congregations even went so far as to each purchase adjacent lots on which to build a church. While this church building option appeared to be within the financial means of the two congregations, this attempt failed due in part to the varying requirements of the participating congregations and the uncertainties surrounding the viability of the Pinawa town-site at that time due to downsizing by AECL, Pinawa's principle employer. This period also witnessed a significant change in the demographics of the Roman Catholic congregation. The congregation had gradually transformed from one with many

Time for Mass

young families with children, requiring several classrooms for religious instructions, to the present day where the community is more retirement-based. In recent times though, the community is again attracting young families, as well as retirees, and our congregation is benefitting from this.

In November 2003, interest in building a church was renewed with the formation of a Foundation Committee with the mandate to see our church building dreams fulfilled. The success of this initiative was immediate and a letter was sent to Emilius Goulet, Archbishop of the St. Boniface Diocese in December 2003, advising him of our intentions. The church building plan continued to progress to the stage that in October 2004 another letter was sent to the Diocese to seek approval to continue with our church building efforts. This was followed by a meeting with the Diocesan Financial Secretary and Diocesan Building Committee. At this meeting members of the Foundation Committee made presentations to support our request for building approval. In September 2005 we received a letter of support from the Diocese with authorization to advance our project to the "design stage". This meant that we were able to have preliminary plans drawn for the purpose of obtaining cost estimates for the church. In September of 2006, with the design and cost estimates in place, another letter was sent to the Diocese requesting authorization from the Archbishop to proceed with construction. In October 2006 we received that final authorization. Now the work of building a church could begin in earnest! MMP Architects were contracted to prepare the architectural drawings and the construction contract

Priests who have served the Roman Catholic Parish of Pinawa include:

Parish Priest	From	To
Fr. Albert Frechette	July 1963	July 1966
Fr. Paul-Emile Boisjoli (assistant)	July 1963	June 1964
Fr. Maurice Jeanneau (assistant)	July 1964	Dec. 1966
Fr. Allen Soucy	July 1966	July 1968
Fr. Gideon Trudeau (Pinawa only)	Aug. 1968	May 1972
Fr. Allen Soucy	Jun. 1972	July 1973
Fr. Edward Bonin	Aug. 1973	July 1977
Fr. Olivier Valcourt	Aug. 1977	July 1978
Fr. Paul-Emile Boisjoli	Aug. 1978	July 1980
Fr. Gerard Oblonczek	Aug. 1980	Apr. 1984
Fr. Patrick Murray	May 1984	July 1984
Fr. Reginald Prescott	Aug. 1984	Jul. 1987
Fr. Gerald Michaud	Aug. 1987	Jul. 1992
Fr. Martin Houston	Aug. 1992	Apr. 1996
Fr. Real Gingras	May 1996	Jul. 1996
Fr. Richard Machura	Aug. 1996	Jul. 2003
Fr. Miroslaw Szynal	Aug. 2003	Present

was awarded to Clearline Construction with the signing of the contract on January 31, 2007. First work on the foundation pilings began in March 2007 and Church construction was completed in October 2007. The first Mass was held in November 2007 and the grand opening and blessing by the Archbishop was held in December 2007. The name chosen for the Church was St. Francis of Assisi Roman Catholic Church.

Pinawa Alliance Church – A Look Back
By Brad Nelson

Pinawa Alliance Church began as Pinawa Baptist Church in 1970 as an off-shoot or church plant of the Whiteshell Baptist Church in Seven Sisters Falls. A number of families from Pinawa had been attending Whiteshell Baptist Church for worship services. Soon there seemed to be enough people to establish a congregation in Pinawa. With the encouragement of the Seven Sisters Church and the mentoring and preaching of Rev. Bruno Voss, pastor of the Seven Sisters Church, meetings were held on Sunday evenings in Lewis School gym. Eventually, with financial and spiritual support from the North American Baptist Conference, Pinawa Baptist Church was founded. Our first pastor Rev. Siegfried Schuster and his wife Grace joined us shortly after.

Pastor Brad Nelson

Following Pastor Schuster's installation, the Pinawa Baptist Church (PBG) moved to the home economics room in the high school. This was a great opportunity since the school board and the school administration at the time allowed the PBC to use classrooms for Sunday School. There were enough children in the congregation to have 5 or 6 classes as well as an adult class. These were in the early days of Pinawa when there were many young families with correspondingly many children of various ages. There were some Monday mornings when the regular classroom teachers found things not quite as they were left on Friday! However, all survived.

The home economics room was soon outgrown as the congregation increased in size and was allowed to move to the high school gym, which space was shared with the Roman Catholic congregation. This arrangement worked fine with seasonal changes in service times ... Baptist service first and Roman Catholic service later, and vice versa for the next half year.

When Pastor Schuster went on to other assignments in the North American Baptist Conference, Andrew Wolstenholme, a young, recent seminary graduate became the pastor. Andrew, the son of a pastor in England, was young, recently married and full of ideas and ambitions. With the anticipation of the arrival of

Pinawa Alliance Church

the new pastor, the PBC purchased the house at 2 Stanley Ave. While regular morning services continued in the high school, he and his wife, Myrna, opened their home to Sunday evening song and devotional meetings. These were good times, too. In 1979, because of the varying church backgrounds of its membership, the PBC became an independent Baptist church.

After Pastor Wolstenholme moved to Alberta, Brian Heaney accepted the role as pastor of PBC. Brian, a recent seminary graduate, and his wife, Sharon, grew in faith along with the congregation as they served and worshiped together. During Brian's years in Pinawa, discussion from time to time turned to erecting our own church building.

When an opportunity came up for Pastor Heaney to enter the field of social work in his home province of Saskatchewan, he made the move there. For a time, the PBC was without a regular pastor and several capable men served to continue the ministry.

Now the PBC's search for a pastor was solved with the arrival of Pastor Al Gordon and his wife Sue who served as pastor until he moved to a larger congregation in Winnipeg in 1989. Being an independent church has several drawbacks. One of these is the lack of contacts or resources when calling a pastor. Established church conferences have seminaries and Bible schools from which to recruit workers like pastors and missionaries. There is support for member churches, financial, personnel, training, etc. The independent church is not generally limited in its choice of pastors and leaders, but it is also hampered by its independence.

Another drawback is that the independent church does not usually have a network of pastors with which its pastor can find fellowship and support. Established conferences and denominations also generally have benefits for their pastors such as pension programs, health plans, and other benefits that other professions have. After Al Gordon moved to Winnipeg, the PBC inquired about affiliating with the Christian and Missionary Alliance denomination of Canada. After a number of meetings, PBC became Pinawa Alliance Church, and was able to welcome a new pastor in the person of Pastor Ken Dittman with his wife Ethel. Pastor Ken was also a new pastor fresh from seminary. Ken, having been a manager in business was a great organizer and mover which the church seemed to need after the years of independence. One of the most notable events in Pastor Ken's leadership was the planning and building of the present church building at Burrows Road and Bessborough. The new church was dedicated on February 5, 1995. Now there is a permanent place of worship and a church home! The premises provided by the local school board have been so much appreciated, but a permanent place of worship is great! Pastor Ken moved on to Alberta and was followed by Pastor Ken Cooke and Louise who served here for about three years, and under his leadership, Pinawa Alliance Church (PAC) settled in to its new affiliation with Christian and Missionary Alliance of Canada (C&MA).

After Pastor Cooke retired, the PAC was blessed that Pastor Henry Hiebert and Lorraine came out of retirement to take the leadership of the PAC. His pastorship was to be temporary, but was temporary for three years. Here again the PAC had sincere leadership and teaching. But, time marches on, and Pastor Hiebert decided it was time to really retire.

In 2003, Pastor Brad Nelson was invited to become the PAC pastor in Pinawa. He and his wife, Lorraine, and family have given us and continue to give us great pastorship, encouragement, and leadership. Over the years the PBCIPAC has experienced many memorable events:

Baptism services in the Whiteshell Baptist Church facility, in the Pinawa swimming pool, in the Winnipeg River, and in the Pinawa beach, as well as in the PAC baptism facility.
There have been Sunday School picnics in Whitemouth Falls Park, Lake Nutimik Baptist camp, Pinawa Dam Provincial Park.
Vacation Bible schools have occupied Pinawa children in summer times.
Baptist camp has been the scene of family camps and retreats for times of worship, fellowship, and fun for all ages. Recently, Otter Falls and Lake Nutimik camp grounds, and Blue Lake campground in Ontario have been the scenes of August summer weekend camping trips. Again great times of worship, singing, swimming, boating, etc. were had by all.

On a sadder note, over the years, PBC/PAC have lost members and loved ones as age and illness have claimed members and friends. Now they are fondly and sadly remembered and missed greatly. As PAC goes ahead serving God in our community, whatever is in store in the future, He will see us through.

Pinawa Interdenominational Bible Study
By Pat Ramsay

In 1963, Jane Petkau started a Bible Study in her home. It was open to women interested in studying the Bible in an informal home setting. It grew over the years to include women from all the churches in Pinawa (the Baptist, Catholic, Lutheran and Pinawa Christian Fellowship). We would meet in each other's homes on Wednesday mornings and took turns leading the studies. We would end our study time with refreshments and some good visiting. It was a wonderful way to meet other women in Pinawa and to learn more about the Bible. This continued on until the late 1980s and the number of women taking part would average 15 to 20; in fact, when we met in the latter years, we would divide up into 3 groups to do the study. In the 1980s, we added a Wednesday evening group for those women who were working or who preferred an evening study time. Each year the ladies would plan a Christmas party, and always in the spring, we held a windup which was, quite often, a big affair with delicious food dishes, special musical numbers, etc. We had great times together. It was a unique experience and strong bonds were formed between all these women from different backgrounds and churches which are still evident today.

Pinawa Library
By Helen Tomlinson

"Just change that 'they' to 'I' or 'we' and you'll have the answer," said my husband. We had just returned home from an information meeting and get-together with other families who would soon be moving from Deep River to Pinawa, the Company's brand new town …way out in Manitoba!

I wasn't thinking too much about the initial drawbacks involved in the move. Limited access to services like banking, shopping and recreation hadn't really engaged my attention… yet. What did clutch at my heart, though, was how would I survive without something to read? With no stores and no library, how could 'they' (the Company? Somebody? Anybody?) expect us to survive a long, cold winter in isolation without books?

Helen Tomlinson

"What are THEY going to do about it?" I demanded.

Mike repeated "Just change 'they' to 'I' or 'we'." The next day I went to talk to Dorothy Robertson. She in turn telephoned Bunny Putnam, who spoke to Gladys Guthrie, who contacted Marg Smith who called Mari-Ann Weeks, and so on. We decided to advertise in the local paper and ask for donations of books. "Just give us a call and we will be happy to pick up any of your old paperbacks or old books of any kind," went the ad.

The response from the community was amazing. Boxes and boxes of books made their way into the homes of those of us who would soon be heading west to Pinawa. Deep River librarian, Joy Herringa, greeted our request for material with enthusiasm. Her library was crammed to overflowing and she was ready for a big clean up in order to make way for new items. Dr. Lewis, long-time supporter of the Deep River library, treasured its collection and was reluctant to part with anything. He was, however, seduced by the idea that the Deep River Library could help found a new library in Pinawa and so he gave his blessing to the librarian's projected clean-up.

AECL would pay expenses for families moving from Deep River to Pinawa, but how would we cover the cost of sending all these books? The problem was quietly resolved. We were told to distribute the boxes of books among those of us making the move during that summer of 1963. These boxes would simply be treated as family household items. And so Pinawa's infant library was delivered to the new town in the form of many, many cardboard boxes full of dusty books travelling side by side with beds, lamps and teddy bears.

Ed Lundman greeted the arrival of our strange library with enthusiasm. He was immediately helpful and continued to support the growing library in every way he could. Ed was the administrator of the Local Government District of Pinawa. This meant that he wore many administrative 'hats'. He was Mayor and Council and School Superintendent and supervisor of just about everything else all rolled into one. As soon as space was available in the new elementary school, our boxes of books were given a home in an empty room (no shelves). There were few permanent residents in town as yet, so Phase 1 of Library Services was casual to say the least. If you fancied something to read, you'd sashay round to the school and rummage around in one of the many boxes looking for anything that might catch your attention. It was a lucky dip.

In addition to having no shelves and no money, we didn't have a real 'librarian' among us. Still, the early arrivals to Pinawa seemed to feel an attachment to this chaotic 'library', partly because there were few, if any, other organizations or clubs operating in town to fill their time. Hence many volunteers appeared who were prepared to invest considerable time and effort into organizing this mess.

In order to address the lack of funding in those first few months we resorted to basic money raisers such as bake sales and selling Christmas trees. Standing outside on the Christmas tree lot one evening, with the temperature marking what felt like at least 1,000 degrees below zero, the revelation struck that these kinds of efforts would raise barely enough money to buy a good book or two and certainly not enough to support a library. At that time there were no libraries in the nearby towns, although a Manitoba Public Library Bookmobile came around. The selection of books here was limited. We were invited to request any item that might be of interest but the waiting time

Donna Wuschke, Lyn Ewing, Ann Quinn, Michael Luke, Marg Stokes (head librarian), Michelle Long

was long and this arrangement precluded browsing for something that might take your fancy.

Ed Lundman stepped in to suggest that we apply to the province for library funding. If our request was approved, the funding would meet our needs for the establishment of a real library. In order to ensure provincial approval, he counselled that we first circulate a petition approving an increase in the mill rate. The petition asking residents to support a tax increase for the purpose of funding a library met with overwhelming town support.

Armed with our petition results Ed and I went to Winnipeg for an appointment with the Provincial Librarian. The Provincial Librarian was understandably curious about this hitherto unknown town and perhaps even a tad suspicious of a place which had barely begun to exist. In the course of our chat with her she was impressed with the efforts we had made to start our library and very gratified with the results of our petition. Our town administrator (Ed) was able to confirm that the new Public Library would be housed permanently in the new High School / Community Centre, currently being completed, and that it would serve both the High School as well as the community of Pinawa; there would be more than enough volunteers to staff the library throughout the week and public access to the books would pose no problem.

The Librarian's response, to our great delight, was to confirm the necessary funding. She was quick to reassure us that Library Services would make the book selection on our behalf and that the books would be sent to us catalogued and ready to lend. New selections would be made as and when we'd exhausted the first lot and so on. Of course we could submit special requests and they would try to accommodate us.

For a moment we were speechless. Knowing we had the funding was wonderful. The second part came as a shock. It hadn't occurred to us that we wouldn't be making our own selection of materials. Pinawa had eager readers and volunteers planning on making their own selection of books for the town. As gently as possible we explained that we would prefer to undertake our own book selection. Our readership represented a very wide range of tastes. There was a big requirement also for non-fiction material unlikely to be addressed by Library Services.

It was the Librarian's turn to be speechless. If Pinawa was set on being independent, doing all its own ordering as and when it felt like it, then it would have to look after cataloguing its own accessions. This Pinawa didn't even have one qualified librarian to its name. It would be an impossible situation! We demurred. We could learn how. Please let us try. A truce was called. It was with reluctance that the Librarian agreed both to our funding and to permitting us to go it alone. She was sure in her heart that within the year, possibly even in a few months, we would be back with a big mess for them to sort out and begging for their help.

And so began the next phase of the library's development. To the relief of the messengers (Ed and me), all the Pinawa volunteers agreed that the independent route was absolutely the way to go. They pulled together and faced the challenge of learning how to catalogue the collection we already had. For a short time we had

the advice of Eva Sutherland, a qualified librarian but she did not remain long in Pinawa. In addition to those first on the scene, I remember others who gave hours of their time: Sheila Dyne (we'd have been lost without her), Sheila Hilborn, Rowe Lundman, Bea Mathers, Alice Mooradian. The first Library Board (made up of Ed Lundman, John Minton, Helen Tomlinson, Dick Tuxworth (chair), Eyfe Walterson and Mari-Ann Weeks) was appointed to direct the operation of the library. Many more volunteers came out on a regular basis to give out books, replenish the shelves, repair damaged books, shelf read, select new materials and serve on the

Barrie Burnett's 3D Puzzles at the Library

Library Board. Finally it became apparent that the library needed to employ someone regularly who would provide continuity and take on the business of ordering and accessioning new material.

Enter Edna Graham. Edna was the sole daytime Library employee for many years. She brought love and dedication to the job and, together with Barb Sabanski and Linda Swiddle who supervised evening hours, kept our library running smoothly. This sums up the early period during which the library was established. The Pinawa Public Library has, without a doubt, the finest volunteers one could wish for. Without them the library would never have come into existence. It would not have continued to exist without regular employees like Edna (retired), Brenda Johnson (now living in Switzerland) and Marg Stokes who have provided the glue to make it all hang together.

Over the years, under the direction of the Board, volunteers all, the Pinawa Public Library has grown and changed with the times. It continues to come up with improvements and refreshing new ideas. For example, next time you're in, look at the hand-painted signs and artwork on the walls, courtesy of the high school art class, and keep your eyes open for special contributions from the younger school children. The Library continues to exert its independence. Our collection of books, videos and audio books is growing, thanks to the efforts of our book selection committees. Extra funding generated through raffles and other activities, allow us to have special presentations over the cold winter months - like author readings, selections by the school choir and information on new and unusual hobbies. The Library provides employment for librarians and summer students and an outlet for our many volunteers. Over the years, our volunteer base has been solid, stable and enthusiastic and is the envy of town libraries across the province. "We" and our Library are an ongoing success story.

Pinawa Authors

Author	Title
Ates, Murat	Life. Fire. Prose
	Life. Fire. Prose: Volume 2
Attas, Amy	Navigating Customs: new travel stories by twelve writers
Banerjee, Anjali	Enchanting Lily
	Imaginary Men
	Invisible Lives
	Looking for Bapu
	Maya Running
	Seaglass Summer
	The Good Neighbor
	The Twilight Wife
Beirne, Gerard	Digging My Own Grave
	The Eskimo in the Net
Bellamy, Irene	Welcome to Pinawa, a town for all seasons!
Bernardin, Lois et al	Stories and Poems by Winnipeg River Writers
Campbell, Nicola	Friends at last
Dale, Gordon	Fool's Republic
Davidson, Andrew	The Gargoyle
Finlay-Young, Jane	From Bruised Fell
French, Alice	My Name is Masak
	The Restless Nomad
Gibson, Shannon	Made to be Broken
	The Iron Horse: A Collection of Short Stories Written by Young Canadians
	The Memory Machine: A Collection of Short Stories Written by Young Canadians
	Inkspots: A Collection of New Canadian Short Stories
	Formation: A Collection of New Canadian Short Stories
Gillespie, Colin	Time One: Discover How the Universe Began
Gould, Deidre	
(writing as Elle Rush)	Drama Queen
	It Girl
	Leading Man
	Screen Idol
Grayson, Gloria	In Those We Trust: Only They Can Betray Us
Heimann, Robert B.	Ancient and Historical Ceramics: Materials, Technology, Art and Culinary Traditions
Henschell, Alex	Memoirs of a Whiteshell Trapper
Horn, Leonard N.	A Log Cabin in the Manitoba Wilderness
King, Alexandra	Diary of a Powerful Addiction
Lodha, Manju	125 Poems for Preservation - Peace - Pleasure
	Stories of Feelings of You and Me
	Stories of Prejudice, Pain and Peace
Lopata, Vince	'C' Force: Decorations, Medals, Awards and Honours
Luke, Michael O.	The Perfect Candidate
	The Morning Light Conspiracy
	Great Science Fiction Stories You've Never Read
	Some Great Enterprise
McKenzie, Brenda	Loving You
Minton, R.J.	Golden Memories of Bissett
Montgomery, John H.	To the Edge and Back
Munn, Karen	Forget Salt, Cook with Herbs
	Treat Your Heart - Eat Smart
Palmer, Wayne	Across the Grain: The Inside Stories 1986-2011

Author	Title
Pinawa Centennial Committee	Pinawa
Pinawa Christian Fellowship	Called Together: 50 years of the Pinawa Christian Fellowship
Roy, Pat & Daymond, Louise	Pinawa - 20 years
Saunders, Chris	Whiteshell Laboratories – A Legacy to Nuclear Science and Engineering in Canada
Saunders, Chris and Daymond, Louise	Pinawa: 50 years of Families, Friends and Memories
Stermscheg, Robert	POW #74324: triumph over adversity: the Life of John Stermscheg
Taylor, Peter	Wings Along the Winnipeg
	The Birds of Manitoba
Tomlinson, Michael	A Yorkshire Inventor: Tales of Harry Brammer
Valgardson, W.D.	Vikings on a Prairie Ocean: The Saga of a Lake, a People, a Family and a Man
	Gentle Sinners
	The Girl with the Botticelli Face
	God is not a Fish Inspector
	In the Gutting Shed: Poems
	Sarah and the People of Sand River
	Thor
	Frances

Pinawa Teen Centre
By Louise Daymond

Pinawa teens in the mid-60s lobbied the town for a place to get together, separate from the church and children's groups, and under their own supervision. In 1965, at the urging and support of the Recreation Director Jim Spencer, they were granted permission to use the basement of the recently vacated hospital in the bi-level on McDiarmid Road. Here they played records, ran a small canteen (on the honour system), and generally hung out. Don Plunkett was the first president of their newly-elected council, which established rules and membership fees. They held a talent raffle (babysitting services and odd jobs) to raise money for furniture, and spent Saturday mornings cleaning, waxing floors and keeping things tidy.

The teens were forced to move in 1966, and during that summer the kitchen (room 34) in the community centre was transformed into the Psychedelic Pearl - a canteen and drop-in centre, run by women volunteers. That fall, three ATCO trailers were affixed to the south side entrance of the community centre, with room for an office, TV room, pinball area, ping-pong table, jukebox and card-playing area.

Jim Dunford

The centre was initially supervised by the older teens, then for a time by the high school student council. The Recreation Department hired two women to monitor the building, halls and washrooms every evening, up until 1970 when Jim Dunford and Gary Griffith were hired. In 1971 Jim took over the operation himself, and re-organized the centre and incorporated programming to keep the teens active, rather than just 'hanging around'. Under Jim's direction, the entire centre was redecorated, with all of the labour courtesy of the teens themselves. Committees were set up for various activities, including community fundraisers, and the teens challenged themselves to come up with novel ways to raise money, kept to a schedule of weekly cleaning, and adhered to rules they themselves helped create. Failure to adhere to the rules meant expulsion for a week or two, depending on the severity of the infraction.

Eventually the trailers were demolished, and the teen centre moved to 19 Alexander Avenue. It was now called the Youth Activity Centre, and many of the activities that started in the 70s continued for over fifteen years under Jim Dunford's guidance. Santa's Workshop and refereeing the annual Jam Can Curling every year were fixtures on the teens' calendar. They also raised money for many years for charitable organizations such as Muscular Dystrophy and Manitoba Heart and Stroke. In addition to Santa's Workshop (where typically 400 visitors would come for the chance to sit on Santa's knee, receive a treat and enjoy special activities during the 10-day event), the teens gathered food and toys for a Christmas hamper each year, which they delivered themselves to those in need in northern Manitoba. Safe to say, the teens of Pinawa were highly engaged in the community for many, many years.

The teens started fundraising and planning for a new building of their own while they were in the trailers; plans moved forward and a committee was formed to make it a reality during the time on Alexander. Funding was augmented from the LGD, the Lions Club and other service groups.

The Vanier Community Centre was built in 1979, and with the exception of the excavation and pouring of the basement and foundation, the entire structure was built from volunteer labour; Don Daymond was the project manager. The teens moved into the building December 1, 1981. Right from the outset, the teen council hoped that the community would use the rest of the building, too. A new committee with representatives from the LGD, Parent Advisory Council, a high school student representative and the Recreation Department and the teens was formed.

While the number of teens using the teen centre has dropped significantly since the mid-90s, the Vanier Centre continues to be a gathering place, not only the teens, but the rest of the community, as well. Jim Dunford would be very proud.

Pinawa and Age-Friendly Communities in Manitoba
By Marsha Sheppard

The Seniors and Healthy Aging Secretariat has chosen Pinawa as one of its pilot communities for the Age-Friendly Communities in Manitoba Initiative. As a member of the Pinawa Committee, I would like to tell you a little more about how we are involved and some of the events that have taken place as well as the challenges ahead.

Marsha Sheppard

Age-Friendly means making day to day things easier for all ages, not just seniors. Think about it, if you don't have the strength to open the post office door, and then neither does a child. Sometimes it's not strength but just the angle the force needs to be applied. Issues like font size in printed materials such as our phone books has been raised and we'll see how MTS will respond.

The University of Manitoba's Centre on Aging and the Secretariat came to Pinawa in November and carried out a survey with an invited focus group to give us some ideas of how we could make Pinawa more age-friendly. Here are the results of questions that were asked about housing, transportation, infrastructure, safety, social participation and recreation, work force participation, information/advocacy, respect and social inclusion and health and community services.

Our First *Pinawa* Age-Friendly Questionnaire

Score of >70% - what we do well

Seniors feel safe walking alone, day or night
Seniors are generally treated with respect
Seniors have enough volunteer opportunities
Local parks and walking trails are accessible to seniors

Karen Munn teaching students to cook

Information about community events, services and programs by various organizations is readily accessible
Snow clearing is done in a timely manner

Score of < 20% - what we could improve

Health care services not provided in Pinawa are not convenient to access – i.e. services too far away, appointment times not convenient.
Housing for seniors is not plentiful or affordable.
Subsidized housing for low-income seniors is not sufficient.
Waiting times to get into senior housing, such as assisted living, are not reasonable and not available in Pinawa.
Public transportation to and from medical appointments is not sufficient.
Public transportation to and from medical appointments for those individuals with disabilities is not sufficient.
Public transportation to shopping, senior centres, church, cultural events is not available.
There are not enough seniors' advocacy services available.
There are not enough paid job opportunities for seniors.
There is no congregate meal program or Meals on Wheels program available.
Public telephone answering services are not adapted to the needs of seniors – i.e. instructions are not given slowly or clearly enough.

Don't know >30% - the focus group wasn't certain of these

Whether planning processes specifically consider needs of seniors.
Whether the home care services for seniors are sufficient.
Whether services that help seniors (lawn care, garbage help, snow clearing, etc.) are sufficient.

Priorities areas were then identified by the participants as:

- Building accessibility
- Recreation/social activities
- Civic participation/social inclusion
- Sidewalks
- Transportation
- Building maintenance and
- Housing

Mike Tomlinson and Will McKay
(Photograph courtesy of Darcia Light)

Grants are available to fix some of the infrastructure issues, such as heavy access doors, sidewalks, and modification of curbs for strollers and scooters. Other things require programs to be set up, such as congregate meals, grocery and pharmacy delivery and Meals on Wheels.

We have a very dedicated Age-Friendly Committee set up to initiate some improvements in Pinawa. The Chair is Clay McMurren, and the members are Marsha Sheppard, Lloyd Rattai, Alf Wikjord, and Bill Early. The Committee has the full support of Council and already several things have been put on the Public Works list of "to dos" for the coming summer. In addition, the Pinawa Chamber of Commerce will be working with businesses to help make them more accessible and age-friendly.

Stay tuned for more age-friendly initiatives and speak to one of the Committee if you have some suggestions as to what could make Pinawa more Age-Friendly.

Chapter 4
Clubs and Organizations

Like most communities, Pinawa is home to a long and diverse list of clubs and organizations. All of these groups can point to the original Pinawa Community Group, established in early 1963, for their beginning. The group, initially formed in Deep River, Ontario by the families planning to make Pinawa their home, focussed on establishing church congregations, youth activities, sports clubs and arts groups. Meetings were held, plans were made, funding was secured and the first clubs and organizations were formed almost immediately as families moved to Pinawa in the summer of 1963. By January 1964, there was:

- Beginners Square Dancing, led by Cy Crawford.
- Minor Hockey: The town already had three rinks and three teams, including one all-female team. New sweaters had been purchased and the Rink Committee was hard at work. The Committee was led by Orville Acres as Chairman, with Len Horn (Maintenance Committee Chairman), Ken Murphy (Program Committee Chairman), Ray Sochaski (Curling Committee Chairman) and Don Green (Hockey Convener) taking leadership roles.
- A Public Library
- A Roman Catholic Mass
- A School Advisory Board, including John Weeks, Bruce Stewart, Tom Stromberg, Don Green, Ray Kirkham, Ray Sochaski, and Ed Lundman.
- A Recreation Advisory Committee, including Dr. R. Robertson, Mrs. C. Cameron, Mrs. F. Gilbert, Jane Petkau, John Rankin, Barbara Hart, Mr. I. Striemer, Mr. J. Guthrie and Mr. D. Fitzsimmons
- A Women's Club, focussed on "meeting your neighbor"
- An Oxfam Committee was tasked with raising funds for famine relief around the world. The group chairman was Peter Thiessen, with Jane Petkau and Cecile Schmidt as secretaries, Jean Murphy as treasurer, and Bud Bjornson as the Public Relations Officer.

Pinawa is a story of cooperation and constructive action. What needed to be done was done and what appears to be needed for the future was being planned for. There has never been any indication of hesitancy on the part of residents to promote or take part in endeavours that interest them. We sometimes joke at our "over organization" - about the many clubs and activities which have been formalized. But what was the alternative - to sit around complaining about nothing interesting to do?

Since 1963, hundreds of organizations have called Pinawa home. Volunteers have been and continue to be at the heart of all of these activities. This chapter describes many of these clubs and groups. Some lasted for only a few years; many have had their 50th anniversaries. As you read about each organization, we hope you remember the faces and how each club helped make Pinawa our home.

Lions Club
By Chris Saunders and Judy Farr

Lions Clubs International is a non-political service organization founded in 1917. It currently has over 46,000 local clubs and more than 1.4 million members in over 200 countries around the world. The organization aims to meet the needs of communities on a local and global scale. The Lions motto is "We Serve." Local Lions Club programs include sight conservation, hearing and speech conservation, diabetes awareness, youth outreach, international relations, and environmental issues. The discussion of politics and religion is forbidden. The Lions acronym stands for *Liberty, Intelligence, and Our Nations' Safety.*

Pinawa Lions Club started in 1964 with 40 members. The meetings were held on the first and third Wednesdays of the month, in Kelsey House (now known as Wilderness Edge Retreat and Conference Centre) in the VIP lounge, meals from the staff house cafeteria and drinks from the Lions own bar. A key theme of the club has always been "Lions pay their way"; all money raised from the public goes back to the community. The Lions pay all their administration costs by means of annual membership fees.

The local Lions Club has been an integral part of Pinawa for 50+ years. The first major event was the 1964 New Year's Eve Dance, with proceeds to hockey sweaters for kid's hockey.

The first Pinawa Birthday Celebrations in 1965 saw the Lions Club begin their relationship with this important annual event. In 1965, Everett Dobbin started the fishing derby at 5 am. A very full day ended with the traditional fireworks. Sometime in the late 1960s the Pinawa Birthday Dance began being held in Kelsey House with two bands; one for the younger folks and one for the older folks! The bar was in the in the courtyard, rain or shine. The dance has moved over the years and is now housed in a large tent near the sundial. For decades, the Lions Club was also the organizer of both the beach activities and the parade during the Pinawa Birthday weekend.

Old Fundraisers
Rubber Ducky Races in the Pinawa Channel
Wood Tick Races
Circus and Fertilizer Sales
NYE Dances
Broomball and Millionaire's Night
Dunk Tank
Birthday Dances at Kelsey House and then PMI
Giant Garage Sale
Bike raffles, Barbeque and Solo gift coupons
Ladies only Fashion Extravaganza

Current Fundraisers
50/50 draws
Fireworks Canvas
Springtime Social
Pinawa Dance in Big tent at the Sundial
CNIB Canvas
Bingo Tuesday night in the winter

The Lions Club has contributed to many major initiatives over the years, including:

- A substantial contribution to the purchase of an ice plant for arena in 1972.
- Championing the building of the Vanier Centre in 1976. In 1980, it became a reality, a place for teens and other community groups to use.
- Supporting the Canadian National Institute for the Blind annually since the 1970s.
- Helping to form the first Lioness Club in Pinawa in 1983. The first big projects for the Lioness Club were funding the

Acute Care nurses Laurie Pilon, Derek Edwards, Heather Mueller and Meredith Kinghorn were on hand for the donation from Lion Peter Sargent

Cemetery Gates and a massive blood clinic at WNRE. As a result of a Lions International initiative, the Lionesses joined the Lions in 1992. The first woman President of the Pinawa Lions was Sandy Campbell (1993/94).

Pinawa Lions supporting Kidsport

- Numerous donations of equipment to the hospital.
- Discreet assistance for families in need, particularly medical treatments of children outside Manitoba.
- A large donation to the arena for renovations in 2010.
- Sponsoring Pinawa Little League Ball
- Donations to Kidsport
- Contribution to the Pinawa swimming pool renovations in 2014
- In 1986, the first Seniors' Christmas Supper was sponsored by the Lions Club. The event was a potluck and 30 seniors attended. In 2015, over 300 seniors attended the event, which has become an important part of the local holiday season.

As with many service clubs, the Pinawa Lions Club has seen their membership decline over the years. A dedicated core has been sustained by recruitment of new members; however, to continue their many activities around Pinawa, the Lions have come to depend on volunteers and partnering. For example, the Birthday parade and beach activities while sponsored by the Lions are organized and run by others. Thank you to all those that have been part of the Lions Club for the past 50+ years. Keep us strong - new members are always welcome.

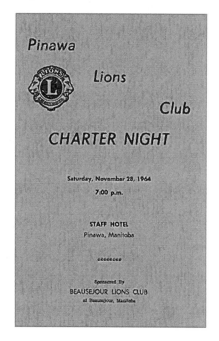

Pinawa Lions Club Charter Night – November 28, 1964

Past Presidents

1964	Torchy Torresan
1965	Barrie Banks
1966	Jack Macleod
1967	George Takeshima
1968	Dennis Fitzsimmons
1969	Bill Dunford
1970	Bill Chelack
1971	Bob Dale
1972	Howard Gilmour
1973	Alex Mayman
1974	Metro Dmytriw
1975	Len Molinski
1976	Ted Copps
1977	Wally Stober
1978	George Turner
1979	Peter Cliche
1980	Harry Johnson
1981	Frank Theriault
1982	Hal Peterson
1983	Peter Sargent
1984	Doug Blais
1985	Chris Saunders
1986	Harold Bender
1987	Jeff Knight
1988	Dale Lidfors
1989	Ranjit Singh
1990	Bud Biddiscombe
1991	Jerry Farr
1992	Alex Domytrak
1993	Sandy Campbell
1994	Ron Bratty
1995	Dean Murray
1996	Marty Jacob
1997	Wally Kukurudz
1998	Dorothy Wilken
1999	Brian Corbett
2000	Judy Farr
2001	Rena Corbett
2002	Karla Elcock
2003	Dorothy Wilken
2004	Dean Popple
2005	Gerry Tretiak
2006	Marty Jacob
2007	Alex Domytrak
2008	Sandy Campbell
2009	Barb Sabanski
2010	Barb Sabanski
2011	Barb Sabanski
2012	Gisele Smith
2013	Gisele Smith

Pinawa's Birthday Dance – Alex Domytrak and Barb Sabanski

Pinawa's Birthday Dance – Barb Sabanski, Alex Domytrak and Gisele Smith

CancerCare Program staff Connie Randall, Michelle Rosentreter, Susan Barnett and Dr. Edwin Spence accept a new iPod and iPod Dock from Lion Peter Sargent

Pinawa Health Auxiliary
By Sandy Campbell

Sandy Campbell

One could say that Pinawa Health Auxiliary (formerly Pinawa Hospital Auxiliary) owes its beginning to decisions made during a meeting of the church ladies. It was in the fall of 1965, with lady members of the church having increased sufficiently in number to enable them to consider forming and participating in the usual church type groups, one of which would be to work for the hospital. A meeting was called with the then current Hospital Administrator, Mr. John Minton, to discuss the possibilities of such a group. Six of the members committed themselves to form a hospital guild. This group carried on informally, without executive or organization, and needless to say with no success in recruiting new members. For the March 15th, 1966 meeting each member of the group was asked to bring a friend. A letter was sent to the Seven Sisters Guild requesting their help. Seven Pinawa ladies and five guests from Seven Sisters were in attendance. Together they decided to form an executive. The president was selected by proclamation with the balance of the executive being drawn from a bowl. During the course of the meeting it was agreed to invite the Ladies of Lac du Bonnet to join. This constituted the first official recorded meeting. The Lac du Bonnet Ladies decided to form their own auxiliary sometime in 1973. Membership has varied over the years, but even during the lean years (1980s) we had approximately 12 members.

Pinawa Health Auxiliary – Front Row: Jackie Snider, Mary Frances Spiers, Alma Alexander, Mary Beth Spitz, Christine Nuttall, Glenys Norman-Kukurudz; Back Row: Irene Verrier, Vivian Thomson, Shirley Mustard, Shirley Pellow, Carol Sulkers, Carolyn Kirk, Joan Ticknor; Missing: Sandy Campbell (member for 44 years), Carol Breton, Karen Guse, Mariann Hiebert, Irene Sedge, Bev Stanley, Joyce Tabe

The Auxiliary have held numerous fundraisers over the years, our Annual Pie Sale, our BBQ at the Beach every Birthday weekend, Christmas Bake Sale, community soup lunches, several fall suppers, tomato plant sale, Carnation sale, Christmas Basket Raffle, and until it reorganized we held twice a year Regal Sales, catered to EMCA concerts, the Act Festival held in Pinawa, chartered bus to Winnipeg for Christmas Shopping, our snack machine and pop machine in the hospital (for interest purposes our biggest fundraiser has been our pop machine).

The gift cupboard was built by Harry Staerk. It is in the front hall of the hospital. It sells one of a kind items, like lap blankets, slippers, and knitted items. Twice a year, it goes to the town market sale. The gift cupboard contributes well to auxiliary funds.

With these fundraisers, we have been able to supply the daily paper to the hospital and supply favours on the patients' trays once a month. We have renovated several special rooms in the hospital (i.e. Children's Ward, Cancer care ward, Palliative Care Rooms, Lounges, Waiting Rooms and Outdoor Patio area). We also supply plants for the Court Yard and maintain the plants.

The monies raised over the years have allowed us to purchase over $300,000 worth of equipment - whirlpool bath, bed, furniture, railings, TVs, as well as donate to local requests (e.g. equipment for the ambulance, training of first responders, and the original rescue truck for Fire Department). We donate a bursary to 1 or 2 local graduates entering the field of medicine each year. And we cannot forget our "friends" who have taken the cart around to the patients with items to sell and spread a little friendliness to the patients. We now have approximately 21 members, one who has been a member for 44 years and three have been presented with their 25 year pins.

Health Auxiliary donates rescue vehicle to the Fire Department. Fire Chief Tom Lamb and Deputy Chief Peter Cliche

Pinawa Foundation
By Chris Saunders and Carol Findlay

Most people believe their community is special; usually because of the people, the setting, the clubs and special events that make their town a home. Pinawa is no exception.

The Pinawa Foundation was established in 2010. The original board of the foundation included Chris Saunders as Chairman, with Lynn Patterson, Connie Plunkett, Carol Findlay, Pat Sullivan, Chuck Vandergraaf, and Jane Sargent as the first directors. The foundation is a non-profit group focused on financially supporting the many groups and clubs in Pinawa.

As one of Pinawa's newest organizations, the foundation raises funds from corporations, the estates of local individuals and numerous activities throughout the year. These funds are invested and the investment revenue is given back to the community.

The Pinawa Foundation distributes funds to local charities that work in the areas of Health and Recreation, Social Services, Education, and Arts and Culture. The foundation offers a variety of giving tools to help people and organizations achieve their charitable goals, offering a simple, powerful, and highly personal approach to giving.

Over the first three years of operation, the foundation has grown from an idea to an important part of the community, giving all of us a way to leave a permanent legacy to the community. Since 2010, the foundation has supported a number of important initiatives, including an active scholarship program, the Pinawa Club Capital Renewal Program, the Sign-Up for Life Organ Donation Program, Survivor's Hope Crisis Centre and numerous programs directed towards the local seniors, health care and schools. They also presented every student and staff member at the local elementary school a pair of Olympic mittens to celebrate the Vancouver games.

Foundation Board Member Carol Findlay presents scholarships to Anna McDonald and Amelia James-Thiessen in 2012

Over the next 50 years, the Pinawa Foundation plans to continue to grow the endowment fund to support the local charities and groups that are so integral to making Pinawa our home.

Pinawa 50+ Club
By Glenys Norman-Kukurudz, Barb Jones and Bernice Hawton

As Pinawa matured from a fresh new community with a mostly younger demographic in 1963 so did its citizens. By 1989, our community had many retirees looking for recreational outlets to augment those already offered in our town; thus the formation of the Pinawa 50+ Club. Spearheaded by Barb Jones, Shirley Harding, Elna Grant and Bob and Dorothy Willacy with the assistance of then Recreation Director Heather Sagert Ayres, the Club came together unofficially in the fall of 1989 and by February 1990 had a constitution in place. Pinawa 50+ Club was officially incorporated on February 13, 1990. The first Executive Committee was President Marg Haugen, Vice President, Dan Fundytus, Secretary, Ron Wiggins, Treasurer, Barb Jones, Membership, Robert Willacy and Program and Special Events Co-ordinator, Sheila Martino. Initial membership was approximately 20 people.

In the beginning the Club met at the Vanier Centre moving to the Lewis Centre in October 1994. In 1999 the Club was on the move again to The Pinawa Club where we still meet monthly from September to June. The objective of the Club from the beginning and continuing today as stated in the constitution is to "provide opportunities for Club members to engage in recreational and educational activities (e.g. Health clinics, legal, tax etc.), be entertained and to socialize." The Club shall address issues that are of concern to Club members by taking collective action on issues that affect the local and regional communities."*

As mandated in the Club's constitution there has been member representation on several committees studying issues such as the potential closing of our pharmacy, the need for senior's housing and the medical needs of our community in regard to the hospital itself and recruitment and retention of physicians in Pinawa.

Social activities abound in the 50+ Club. Our meetings have morphed into lunches and sometimes dinner with speakers or cards and games at every meeting as well as numerous extra activities such as golf tournaments and nature walks. Club members have participated in bowling parties and taken numerous "road trips" to Winnipeg Goldeyes games, Royal Manitoba Theatre Centre, the Winnipeg Symphony Orchestra, the Manitoba Legislature and Assiniboine Down racetrack. Attendance at one or more dinner theatre productions in Beausejour, Oakbank and Stonewall are usually an annual event. A highlight for some members was a trip to Churchill in

> ### Pinawa Support Group
> ### By Marg Haugen
>
> Our group was started in 1991 by Isabel Acres and Marg Haugen. We wanted to help folks who had lost a loved one.
>
> As widows and widowers, we meet twice a week for coffee, lunch and companionship. Our group also began to travel the world, attend special events and, above all, support each other through the grieving process.
>
> Today we all enjoy each other's company and have made life-long friends, celebrating birthdays and special events in our lives.

50+ Club in the 1994 Pinawa Birthday Parade: Ruth Dobbin, Doreen Dick, Eileen Loudon, Sylvia Bjornson, Marg Haugen, Beth Kenny, Dorothy Willacy, Sheila Martino, and Shirley Harding

October 2005. The group, led by Gail Schatzlein, flew from Winnipeg to Thompson and took the train to

Churchill. The group spent four days visiting the town of Churchill and Cape Merry as well as touring the tundra to see the polar bears, dog sled rides at the Northern Studies centre and beachcombing along Hudson's Bay. True to their 50+ spirit the group sampled the restaurants and shops for unique meals and keepsakes and then retraced their route with enough memories and photos to last a lifetime. Membership continues to grow as the Club celebrated its 25th anniversary in November 2014 with the 2011-2012 membership at approximately 120.

*Pinawa 50+ Club Constitution amended October 2011.

Pinawa Players
By Les Crosthwaite

The formation of the Pinawa Players had its roots in the already established tradition of amateur-theatre presentation in Deep River, Ontario. In the early 1960s, when AECL decided to expand its operations by creating a new research laboratory in Eastern Manitoba many of the new employees were active in the Deep River amateur theatre group, called the "Deep River Players". These amateur thespians were determined to continue their love of participation in live theatre and so, in 1964, formed the fledgling Pinawa Players.

1964's "The Alley Cats" - Lynette Olsen, Pat McWilliams, Don and Doreen Thompson, Maureen Dobbin and Linda Thompson

The first Pinawa Players production was presented in the spring of 1964, at the gymnasium of the Pinawa Elementary School. Entitled "Variety - The Spice of Life", the production featured a one-act play entitled "Mother's Day", several dance numbers by various groups, an all-male barbershop quartet, an all-female "beauty-shop quartet", and several solo and dance acts.

The production entitled "The Bachelor's Baby", directed by Helen Tomlinson and Jo Kingston was presented in the spring of 1965, featuring 15 actors. This was the last production presented in the Pinawa Elementary School. By the autumn of that year, the new Community Centre Auditorium, complete with stage, was ready. In the fall of 1965, the new auditorium was home to "Welcome to Pinawa" dance with music by a group called "Jo Banana and His Bunch", in conjunction with a "musical melodrama" entitled "No, No, A Million Times No".

Keith Chambers and Friends

Over its 39-year history, the Pinawa Players have presented almost every type of play including comedies, dramas, musicals and performances for children. On special occasions, a play has been held in conjunction with a dinner and dance to celebrate, for example, the group's 25th and 30th anniversaries.

Since its inception, the Players have presented (including productions that included several one-act pieces) almost 100 plays for the entertainment of Pinawa and surrounding-area audiences. The Pinawa Players is a member of the Association of Community Theatres of Manitoba (A.C.T. Manitoba), an organization of similar groups from across the province devoted to the promotion and development of amateur theatre in Manitoba.

Jane Sargent

Jane was born in Saskatoon, Saskatchewan in May of 1944. She grew up in Fort Qu'appelle, Saskatchewan. During her high school years, she met and was greatly influenced by Florence James who inspired her lifelong interest in amateur theatre.

After graduating from high school, she studied Education and completed a BA at the University of Saskatchewan. During this time, she met and married her husband of 48 years, Peter. In the summer of 1967, daughter Karen was born and, shortly afterwards, they all moved to the UK to live in Yorkshire for 2 years where her son, Kurt, was born. Returning to Canada in the fall of 1969, she and her family settled in Pinawa, Manitoba.

Jane was an active volunteer in Pinawa (Brownies, Guides, Figure Skating, Teen Centre, PCDC, Pinawa Foundation, Manitoba Science Academy; many others). Jane's commitment to community was also demonstrated by her long term involvement in the Pinawa Players. Although her specialties were makeup and costumes, she also pitched in where needed, painting sets, mopping floors, organizing the Pinawa Players cupboards, and serving as Treasurer for many years.

Each year, A.C.T. sponsors a drama festival hosted by one of its member groups. Of the 25 A.C.T. Festivals held since 1979, the Players have participated in 20 and hosted the event twice.

The Players also play an active role in community activities such as participating in the annual Pinawa Birthday Weekend Parade, sponsoring an annual Carol Sing at the Pinawa Shopping Mall at Christmas and, on occasion, helping with Pinawa Secondary School stage productions.

The Pinawa Players welcomes anyone with an interest in amateur stage productions, whether it is acting onstage or helping backstage such as in makeup, lighting, sound, set construction, set decoration, props, stage managing, costumes, publicity, etc. Just to show up to a casting meeting. And no previous experience is required!

Pinawa Players' Frank Hughes

Eastern Manitoba Concert Association
By Shirley Cann

The Eastern Manitoba Concert Association (EMCA) is a community presenter of professional musical entertainment in the Eastman Region. An incorporated non-profit, volunteer organization, EMCA has maintained a professional venue for artists, provided educational opportunities for students and enriched the cultural life of Eastern Manitobans for 40 years.

The concept of EMCA began about 1971 in the basement laundry room of a Pinawa apartment block. Two young mothers, Yvonne Oldaker (ballet tutor and examiner) and Joyce Hart (formerly with the Winnipeg Art Gallery) met each other while folding diapers. They discussed their previous artsy lifestyles and discovered they were both feeling culturally deprived. Ideas were shared and the concept of bringing entertainment to the community was born. Neither partner had any money, but they decided to take a chance on selling enough tickets to cover their costs. The first concert was held in Kelsey House and featured a quartet. It was a financial success and proved that the community would support such an endeavor. A second concert was held at the F.W. Gilbert School and featured a Winnipeg contemporary dance group. A third event featured George Swinton (artist and historian) and is believed to have been held in the Pinawa Public Library.

Starting in the fall of 1973, Pinawa became a host for Overture Concerts run by world-class bassoonist, George Zukerman of Vancouver. For six years, three or four performances were held annually in the Upper Lounge of Kelsey House, and, later the Pinawa Community Centre. In 1979, local volunteers took over the series and the independent Eastern Manitoba Concert Association was launched. The incorporation document was signed by Brian Turner, David Torgerson, Stuart McIntyre, Martha Owen, Barbara Zerbin and Fenella Lane.

The EMCA formula is simple: quality concerts and a rewarding community volunteer experience. In its beginning, the concert organization introduced primarily classical music but over the years, performances have become considerably more varied to include jazz, folk, Celtic, country, big band, comedy and some indefinable categories. EMCA has presented over 235 professional performances of Manitoban, Canadian and International artists. More than 25 Juno Award Winners, numerous Prairie and East Coast Music Award winners and even Grammy and Oscar

EMCA Board of Directors, March 2013 - Back Row (left to right): Elly Hudson, Bonnie Popowich, Derrek Owen, Colin McConnell, Robert Munn, Karen Munn, Bob Wakeman, Gail Shillinglaw, Barrie Burnett, Terry Hayward; Front Row (left to right): Joye Platford, Cathy Harding, Shirley Cann, Connie Hill, Carol Randall; Missing: Judy Platford, Bill Hicks, Sean Roberts, Wendy Rachuk, Manuela Nalichofsky, Steve Sheppard

Winners have performed on the EMCA Stage. Examples are Buffy Ste. Marie, Leona Boyd, Ian Tyson, The Borodin String Quartet, Finjan, Stan Rogers, Lois Marshall, Winnipeg Symphony Orchestra and Natalie McMaster. With volunteer production and local business sponsors, almost every dollar of ticket revenues goes to artist fees. EMCA gives Eastern Manitobans A-list performances at affordable prices.

EMCA subscribers come from a large area, encompassing much of Eastern Manitoba. EMCA is also a customer for equipment (more than $100,000 has been invested in sound, lights and stage hardware), services (advertising, publishing, agencies, equipment rentals) and hospitality (hotels, restaurants, events), contributing to the Eastern Manitoba economy.

EMCA enjoys the lovely baby grand piano we have today due to some blunt words from Leonard Isaacs (pianist, conductor, arranger and Director of the University of Manitoba School of Music). Isaacs performed in Pinawa during the 1978-79 Season and was reportedly offended by the piano he was given to play. He told the Pinawa committee that if they expected to have professional musicians come to Pinawa they needed to purchase a decent piano. Thus began the drive to raise the funds to purchase the baby grand piano that EMCA and other community members use today.

EMCA provides many services to the community. These include technical support with lighting and sound to other community groups such as theatre and band, a music scholarship, and music education support to area schools. EMCA also provides fundraising opportunities for non-profit community groups to raise funds for their activities by supplying refreshments during intermissions.

A volunteer Board of Directors runs EMCA, responsible for Administration, Publicity, Advertising, Membership, Staging, Lighting, Sound and Artist Liaison.

EMCA has grown deep roots in the community. In its 40-year history, more than 200 citizens of the region have been a volunteer director.

Fun, achievement, community enrichment, a quality venue, an audience for artists, and of course, enjoyment of the concerts defines the substance and value of EMCA to cultural life in Eastern Manitoba. After 40 years of hard work and careful spending - attracting a faithful audience and paying its bills, EMCA is a favorite destination for performing artists across the country.

Eastman Community Band (Formerly the Pinawa Community Band)
By Peter Hayward

The origin of the Eastman Community band probably lies in the pick-up band that was formed by Heiki Tamm to provide the music for "Annie Get Your Gun," an all-consuming musical production that was put on by the Pinawa Players during 1977. After the musical was over, a few of the players, including Heiki, Sandy McDowall, Alec Robertson, Harold Smith and Grant Koroll, formed a basement band dedicated to playing music and/or consuming beer, not necessarily in that order.

Eastman Band – 2009; Peter Hayward Conducting
(Photograph Courtesy of Stu Iverson)

While the musicians' range of instruments (four trombones and an alto sax) was not ideal, their enthusiasm was infectious, and they were soon joined by other musicians new to town, including Peter Hayward (trumpet), Karen Hoffman (alto sax), Dave Watson (guitar), Ken Young (electric bass), Rich Hamon (drums), Robyn Johnston (flute), Lawrence Dickson (trombone) and his wife Anne (clarinet), who was the town's first Secondary School music teacher. Two school students, Scott Hamon (trumpet) and Dave Westdal (alto sax) also played with the band.

The basement band survived for many years, playing at numerous dances and other local functions. Eventually, it morphed into the Pinawa Stage Band, originally directed by Heiki and currently led by Sandy McDowall.

In 1985, Anne Dickson came up with the idea of forming a community band. As the only person with any conducting experience, she was the obvious choice for leader. She directed the band until 1987, when she moved to Chalk River with Lawrence and their family. The baton was then passed to Glenys Norman-Kukurudz, an experienced choir director. Glenys directed the band for the 1987/8 season. Mike Pohorily, the school music teacher at that time, took over the band in September 1988, but stepped down in December. Finally, Peter Hayward was coaxed into taking over the director's role in January 1989 – a position that he has held ever since.

During its lifetime, the band has developed into an integral part of the Manitoba community band scene. One reason for our success is that we have always welcomed students into our ranks; in fact, it would be difficult to keep the band going without them. They are encouraged to join by Donna Wyryha, the Pinawa schools' music teacher and a community band member since 1990. In the mid-1990s, Donna, together with Gerry Dougall (then school superintendent) and the Whiteshell School Board, started to allow students to use band membership as part of their music credit. The Board remains an enthusiastic supporter of the band, allowing us to use the school band room, percussion instruments, music stands and other school equipment.

More recently, Dave Westdal, a Sunrise School Division music teacher and former community band member, recruited band members from his Lac du Bonnet and Whitemouth students, three of whom have gone on to study music at Brandon University and the University of Manitoba. Other recruits include a music teacher and assistant teacher from the Edward Schreyer School in Beausejour. To reflect the increase in membership from surrounding communities, the band changed its name in 2008 to the Eastman Community Band.

Right from the early days, the band has had to adjust constantly to the ever-changing Pinawa population, partly from the numerous transfers of AECL staff and families and also from the loss of many students after graduation. For this reason, Peter Hayward offered to form a beginners' band in 1991, to teach more adults to play wind instruments and (ultimately) to fill some of the gaps in the band's ranks. Approximately 50 adults – many with no prior experience – took up the offer, borrowed or rented an instrument of their choice, and started to learn by playing together in what soon became known as "Baby Band." For two years, this band rehearsed weekly from September to May, although not everyone stayed for the duration. Finally, in 1993, the Baby Band survivors were absorbed into the community band, and many of them have remained to the present day.

From its inception, the community band has been a member of the Manitoba Band Association, and has participated in every one of the MBA's "Community Band Festival" concerts. These concerts typically involve individual performances by four or five community bands, after which the bands combine to perform a massed-band selection involving around 150 musicians.

Massed Band – 2011 (Photograph courtesy of Stu Iverson)

During 1987-2002, these annual concerts were invariably held in Winnipeg because all the bands (apart from the Pinawa band) were Winnipeg-based. However, the audience for these events was never very large, probably because Winnipegers have such a wide variety of concerts to choose from. As a result, the band leaders and MBA executives decided to make the event biennial and, in 2003, moved it to Pinawa.

The response of the local community has exceeded the expectations of all the Winnipeg bands, with typical audiences of 200+ filling the Community Centre. At the time of writing (July 2012), the event has been held five times in Pinawa. The next Community Band Festival concert is scheduled for April 21, 2013.

Apart from the MBA concerts, the Eastman Community Band regularly performs with the Secondary School bands and choirs in a Community Christmas Concert. We end the band season with the Community Spring Concert in May, sharing the program with the Pinawa Stage Band and Pinawa Community Choir.

Many band members also play in other groups, including the Pinawa Stage Band, the Satin Dolls, the Manitoba Millenium Band, the JABaH saxophone quartet, the Pinawa Birthday Parade Dixieland band, and a German-style "Oompah" band. Several of our members regularly attend the annual International Music Camp at the International Peace Gardens on the US/Canada border, and also the annual Roland Community Band Workshop.

J A B a H
By Helen Tomlinson

Judith, Alice, Betty and Helen had recently graduated from Peter Hayward's Baby Band. This "Baby Band" was his brain child, an idea he dreamed up to address a big problem. Atomic Energy of Canada Limited had begun to transfer many employees and their families to Chalk River in anticipation of shutting down the Whiteshell Nuclear Research Establishment. Peter, the director of the Pinawa Community Band, feared it would soon be forced to fold because so many band members would be moving away to Ontario.

Peter put an ad in the local newspaper inviting anybody wishing to learn to play a musical instrument to come out to a meeting. The part of the ad that really grabbed the reader's attention read something like this:

Prior knowledge of how to play an instrument is not required.

Ability to read music, while useful, is not necessary.

A willingness to learn . . .

. . . would be your passport to participate in the practice sessions held on winter Sunday afternoons. On completing your two year apprenticeship you would be eligible to join the Community Band.

Well, how could a musically challenged person resist such a come-on?! Peter later confessed he hoped a half dozen people would come out to his proposed meeting. To his surprise (and horror??) about 45 musically naïve people showed up. Most people had no idea of what band instrument they wanted to play. (What does a trombone sound like? What is a euphonium? etc.). We selected our instruments and joined the Baby Band.

JABaH at the Bookbreak in December 2000: Judith Simpson, Betty McCamis, Alice Iverson and Helen Tomlinson
(Photograph courtesy of Stu Iverson)

As already mentioned, Judith, Alice, Betty and Helen (you can guess how the name of our quartet, JABaH, came to be) responded to Peter's ad, did their apprenticeship and then moved on to the Pinawa (now Eastman) Community Band in September 1992. We were so captivated by our new-found musical passion that we took every opportunity to develop our skills. For a few years we participated in the International Music Camp sessions for adults held each summer in the Peace Gardens.

Six or seven years elapsed from the time when we four saxophones made our first (terrified?) appearance in the Baby Band. Finally the Eureka moment struck. We decided to form a saxophone quartet. It was a big commitment. After many sessions with two alto saxes and two tenor saxes, both Alice and Judith decided to purchase new instruments – Alice, a splendid baritone sax and Judith, a lovely soprano sax. Our group now had four voices, Soprano, Alto, Tenor and Baritone.

During the early days of JABaH we encountered many hurdles. The biggest was finding music for us. We could purchase music but it was very costly and our skill level wasn't up to many of the arrangements. We had access to a gold mine of good songs in four parts (SATB) – written for piano or voice … but here's the rub. Each part (soprano, alto, etc.) had to be transposed for the instrument playing that part. If you don't play a band instrument then this probably sounds like Greek to you … so just take it from us that transposing the music and writing it out by hand took hours to do and was depressing to say the least.

Thanks to advice from Donna Wyryha, the local school music teacher, we purchased a computer program that enabled us to transpose and print readable sheet music. It still took a long time but it was a big improvement.

Feeling more confident, even sassy, we knew it was time to perform in front of a live audience. JABaH's first appearance came in 2000 when we played outdoors at the Town Market. In December we had an invitation to play at Book Break. 2001 was soon upon us and there were more invitations to play – first for the 50+ Club on Valentine's Day, next at the Hadashville Seniors' Centre and then for the Pinawa Health Auxiliary. Over the next four years we played for the Lions' Christmas dinner in Lac du Bonnet. The Whitemouth Personal Care Home invited us to come several times over the next few years. By 2002 we played for one wedding and another one again in 2005. A dear friend asked us to play at a funeral – we were very touched to have been asked.

David Westdal transposed a number of well-known and several lovely, but lesser-known Christmas carols for us from the Oxford Book of Christmas Carols. We played these carols several times in the Pinawa Mall or elsewhere when the season was upon us. For a few years we provided background music at the Pinawa Club for tired skiers and their families who had come for the loppet.

The Pinawa Christian Fellowship was a great support to us as they issued many invitations to play for them. We would play for the complete service, replacing the organ. That meant playing as people were arriving (the Prelude). Then we would accompany the choir and congregation, playing all the hymns and such portions of the service where sung responses were required. We would also select an anthem to perform and finally would play after the service (the Postlude) as people were leaving. This required transposing of hymns etc. but was always very satisfying to do.

The United Church invited us to a few functions. We played for the United Church Women's conference at Wilderness Edge and for another at the Dr. Jessie Saulteaux Centre near Beausejour. We have happy memories of travelling to Deloraine MB to play for Betty's mother in the Personal Care Home there. Another great memory is playing for Dorothy Willacy's 90th birthday party which she had catered at the Lutheran Church in Pinawa.

When we were asked what we charged for an afternoon or evening of music we always replied that we did not charge. Some people who asked us to play were uncomfortable with this response and asked if we would accept an honorarium. In that case, if they insisted, we would accept. This gave us the opportunity to buy new music. The more we played, the more we improved and so the chance to purchase more challenging music was a boon. Often groups who booked our services would offer us a meal or tea and cookies … whatever seemed appropriate at the time. We were always happy to accept invitations to play. This was our main reward as we never wished to charge for our services.

JABaH played our last gig at the official opening of the newly completed Ironwood Seniors' Residence in July of 2010. Sometime after that, as the saying goes, "all good things must come to an end". It was time for JABaH to retire. Over the ten years we were together we played for many different events in Pinawa, Lac du Bonnet, Whitemouth, Beausejour, and beyond. We tootled our horns for school kids, seniors and those in between. It was a privilege to have been invited to play. As they say - It was a blast!

Acappella Choral Singers
By Pat Ramsay

In 1969 or 1970, an acappella singing group was formed in Pinawa. There were so many accomplished musicians at that time and thus different ones wanted to direct the group. The first year Roy Lampard directed followed by Nancy Murphy and Carolyn Penner each taking a year. By this time, many of the choral group had moved from Pinawa and Keith Chambers continued on directing the singers for a number of years. Occasionally, piano accompanists were required for some pieces, and Beryl Briercliffe would come and ably accompany the group. During those years, the Acappella Choral Singers put on a number of concerts at Christmas and in the Spring. They also went into Winnipeg and performed at the Centennial Concert Hall in a Festival. The ladies sewed up beautiful long gowns of the same design but different colors to wear when they performed and the men looked sharp in their attire. The repertoire consisted of madrigals, classics, and contemporary pieces. Those were memorable years for those participating, and hopefully, as well, for those listening.

Pinawa Art 211 and the Gallery
By Vivian Thomson

Pinawa has had an active art community for more than four decades. Under the leadership of the local art specialist, Vivian Thomson, of the Whiteshell School district, the formal organization of the art group Pinawa Art 211 began in the late 1970s. The artists held regular exhibitions and sales. They fundraised by producing a calendar featuring the works of twelve artists annually.

The Gallery

Pinawa Art 211 annually combined with the Eastern Manitoba Artists Co-op (later, Collective) for a larger exhibition each July as part of the Pinawa birthday events. The artists also held workshops to teach their skills to others while developing their own talents as teachers and mentors.

In 2013 members of Pinawa Art 211 decided to open an art gallery in the W.B. Lewis Business Centre. From here the work of all the gallery members could be seen by the viewing public three days a week. The Gallery is run by the artists on a volunteer basis. The mediums displayed range from oil paintings to water colours, pen and ink, glass work, fabric art using silks and felted wear, copper and silver jewelry, and photography .

Following its tradition of reaching to the community, several artists now provide lessons in oil painting, flower arrangement, and basic drawing skills in the gallery's workshop room.

Vivian Thomson, founder of Pinawa Art 211, and Janice Charko at an exhibition/sale in 2012 at F.W. Gilbert School

Currently members exhibit in The Gallery and are part of the Pinawa Birthday weekend and Christmas sales events under the title Artisan Square. Members also attend the Eastman Judged Art Exhibition where all the entries are professional adjudicated. More information about Pinawa Art 211 and the Pinawa Art Gallery may be accessed through Facebook (Pinawa Art Gallery) or www.pinawaart211.

Pinawa Association for Photographic Art (PAPA)
By Anita Schewe Drabyk

The Pinawa photography group aka Pinawa Camera Club has been ongoing for years. The group has had meetings, field trips, contests, and learning activities. The Camera Club has usually held meetings once to twice a month from September to May or June. Field Trips were often help in the spring, summer and fall. Destinations have included old buildings and farm landscapes in the Brokenhead area; Allegra, Lowlands and environs; Patricia Beach and crocuses of Agassiz Forest; graveyard for old cars and trucks; Pine Point Rapids; Old Pinawa; Narcisse area and Whitemouth Falls. Travelogues from around the world were presented at meetings. In our meetings, we had local critiques and learning sessions by our own photographers. In early years of the club, slide photo instruction sets from the National Association for Photographic Art (NAPA) and travel sets were ordered and viewed by members. A yearly event was the "Shoot-out", which was started by Hans Tammemagi. Slides, and now electronic photos, are divided into two groups. Two projectors show two photos. Members vote for their favourite photo. Then the photos are re-grouped and members vote again until one slide or photo is left, the winner of the year.

The group also participated in interclub competitions and events with other camera clubs in Manitoba. In one contest, three of our photographers had photos in the top 25 slides (Manitoba Camera Club, Brandon Camera Club and Winnipeg South Camera Club as well as PAPA). In 1989, PAPA entered the Prairie Zone Challenge. Our slides were pitted against the finest of those from other clubs in the prairie is (mostly large city groups). We rated 10th, which was a great feat from a small group of photographers from a small area. Club members have attended seminars or presentations by Freeman Patterson, Courtney Milne, and Mike Grandmaison.

Club members for 1982 to 83 (one of the first complete set of records) were Barb Sanipelli, Hans Miller, Peter Taylor, Bill Murray, Jan Dugle, Maureen Miller, Peter Chow, Sam Hosein, Steve Mihok, Phil Davis, Pat Lamaga, Jack Turner, Ben Richter, Karen Hoffman, Martha Laverock, Jean Kruchak, Greg Pool, Colin Chung, Len LaRue, Ed Sexton, Sham Sunder, Andrea Meyer, Eleanor Brown, Erwin Schatzlein, Gail Schatzlein, Carol Boase, Eric Cowdrey, Christina Cowdrey, Hans Miller, Keith Greenfield, Nick Ostash, Barrie Burnett, Ed Wuschke, and Ted Melnyk. Over the years other members have also included David Head, Brian Turner, Jim Bridges, John Dean, Dennis Graham, Peter Sargent, Frank Walton, Darrell Hartrick, Calvin Chan, Guy

Pinawa Camera Club
(Photograph courtesy of Anita Schewe Drabyk)

Strobel, Barb Sabanski, Doreen Bigelow, Harry Johnson, Jack Jackson, Cathy Younger-Lewis, M. Cooper, Dale Hiscock, Mike Einspenner, Alden Bushman, Anita Schewe Drabyk, Edith Olson, Thea Anderstedt, Ann Duncan, Ann Deschamps, Cathy Stewart, Wayne Stewart, Shirley Kurian, Stu Iverson, Nathalie Slavik, Gayle Rutherford, Helen Olchowy, Thecla Melnick, Isabel Acres, Kim Simpson, Shaun Thompson, Sandra Ramsden, Linda Huisman, Karen Munn, Keith Reid, Ken Duncan, Lori Robb, Robert Tiede, Don Heinrichs and Jen Heinrichs.

Over the years, Frank Walton, Bill Murray, Harry Johnson, Barb Sanipelli, Maureen Miller, Jen Heinrichs, and Anita Schewe Drabyk have managed the club. Other very active members over the years have been Derrek Owen, Sam Hosein, Janet Dugle, Hans Miller, Peter Taylor and Erwin Schatzlein. Derrek has spent much time in doing teaching sessions on portraits and slide duplication.

PAPA had been invited to participate in many events and projects. Our members participated in advertising for Atomic Energy of Canada Limited and for the Local Government District of Pinawa. Local photos of people, places, birds, plants and animals have appeared in local advertisements and brochures to promote the town and the area. As a group, many of our photographers took photos of the 1988 Manitoba Summer Games events taken place in Pinawa.

Pinawa Club
By Ken Meek

Sports and socializing have always been the focus for the Pinawa Club. It was created by AECL in 1963 as a non-profit corporation to hold the assets of the newly constructed Curling Club/Clubhouse, the Golf Course, and whatever other Sections evolved in the future. Initially the Curling Club consisted of two sheets of ice, a small viewing area and a kitchen. Volunteers staffed the kitchen and primarily provided snacks but also provided meals for special functions.

Ken Meek

They did a remarkable job considering the limited facilities. As Pinawa grew two additional sheets of ice were added and the Clubhouse doubled in size. The golf course opened in 1967 and soon became a popular venue for people from Winnipeg and the surrounding area. After the official opening Ed Dearden, a reporter for Winnipeg Tribune, described the ninth hole as, "the best finishing hole in the province". Thousands of volunteer hours cleared brush, widened fairways and continued to groom the course until it was not only challenging but picturesque. Later a Tennis Section with four courts was added to the Pinawa Club. The initial surface was special red shale but was changed in later years to a hard surface as the popularity and demand grew. The fourth section to join The Club was Duplicate Bridge.

Pinawa continued to grow and the clubhouse facilities were expanded to meet the need. Bonspiels, golf and tennis tournaments kept the place very busy and the expanded clubhouse facilities greatly increased the social functions to included dances, New Year's Eve parties and many other social gatherings. It was truly the center of Pinawa activities. The golf course became so popular with members, green fee players, tourists and regulars from as far away as Winnipeg it was expanded to eighteen holes in 1982. A liquor licence had been added and operating the Clubhouse, which was now serving full course meals, soon became too much for volunteers.

Executives over the site for the new Pinawa Club – D. Morgan, R. Sochaski, M. Allan, W. McKeown and F. Jones

The Pinawa Club constitution ensures that the organization remains non-profit for the benefit of the members and guests. There are probably as many stories to tell about the history and growth of the Club as the number of volunteers involved. There is no doubt the Pinawa Club was responsible for enticing people to come to work at Pinawa and more recently to retire here. AECL foresaw the need for such an organization and the volunteers can be very proud of making it such a vital and successful part of Pinawa.

Golf Section

Legend has it that AECL management involved in the planning stages of the town felt that we needed some "firebreaks". J.L. Gray, an ardent golfer, agreed that it would be prudent to have 9 such breaks. This may or not be true but it is more likely that he realized that our town needed to have good recreational facilities to attract and retain people to Pinawa.

The first Annual General Meeting of the Golf Club in 1964 saw Bob Jones become Chairman. Clearing for the golf course began in the spring of 1964. Within six months, the clearing was done, low lying areas were filled in and the drainage system was completed. In 1965, Bob was joined on the Board by E.V. Graham, A. Sawatzky, J. Martino, and R.E. Hollies. The spring of 1965 saw the tender for construction of the tees, greens and fairways awarded. The irrigation system was also being designed. Work progressed into the fall of 1965.

Before we had the course in town the golf members played out of the Pine Falls course. One memorable story was in the fall of 1965 when the members decided to travel to the Falcon Beach course to hold our wind-up tournament. They experienced an early snow and there was some trepidation amongst some of our members to playing in the cold. Sterner wills prevailed, Edna Graham to be honest, and off 24 members trekked to play a cold round with some snow on the ground. Maybe Englishmen go out in the midday sun, but Pinawa golfers go out in an overcast

Official Opening of the Pinawa Golf Course – August 26, 1967: J. M. Putman, W. A. Kovacs, J.L. Gray, R.G. Hart and J.A. Martino

and freezing morning to golf.

Although play began in Pinawa in the spring of 1967, the official opening of the course took place on August 26, 1967 when J.L. Gray was here on a business trip from Ottawa. Needless to say we wanted him to be here for the opening. Without his backing there wouldn't have been a golf course in Pinawa. Ken Meek was Chairman of the Golf Section at the time, Bill Kovacs was Club Captain, Bob Jones was Greens Chair, and Bob Hart was Pinawa Club President.

At the opening there were a lot of lost golf balls. Bob Hart commented that he lost more balls on one hole than he had lost playing the entire 9 holes at the Deep River Golf Course. The rough was pretty dense in those early years. The brush came right to the edge of the fairway as the "deer" hadn't started to eat away the brush in town and on the course.

William Dunford

The first Pro Shop was the building now situated at the tennis courts. It and the bridge between holes 2 and 3 were donated by AECL. They were the first Public Relations Building and raised viewing platform at WNRE. They were situated along the north boundary fence of the parking lot so that visitors could see the excavation and construction of the WR-1 reactor. Once construction of the reactor building was completed they were surplus so the Club got them. The first Golf Pro was Jack Castelane and he inhabited the pro shop for several years. Nick Kalupar was our first Greens Superintendent.

Throughout the 70s and 80s, the Pinawa Golf Course matures and membership grew as the facility became a key recreational facility and an important course in Manitoba. In the late 1980s, members began planning the expansion of the course. Course designs were produced, approvals were secured and financing was put in place. With pristine and undisturbed boreal forest available to the west of the existing course, the second nine was added in 1992. The official opening of the expanded course was on July 19, 1992.

William Dunford of Pinawa served 17 years with the Manitoba Golf Association, beginning in the late 1960s. For 10 years, he was chairman of rural activities for the MGA and helped the Manitoba rural amateur championship held each year at Hecla Island. He was vice-president of the association for many years and was in line for the presidency before ill health forced him to step down. Bill Dunford was a valued leader in Manitoba golf.

The forest and wilderness are inspiring and the granite outcroppings are evident throughout all 6,589 yards of the par-72 layout. Many will see that maximum yardage and reach for the driver to bring Pinawa to its knees, but a dash of a conservative approach serves most players well. The course can be a bear (and likely is home to a few nearby) and has been a regular host of Golf Manitoba's provincial men's amateur championship, three times since 2000.

Early days of Pinawa Golf Club

HOLE	1	2	3	4	5	6	7	8	9	OUT	I N I T I A L	10	11	12	13	14	15	16	17	18	IN	TOT	HCP	NET
BLUE (0-8 HCPS)	432	384	363	200	472	215	474	343	332	3215		168	415	411	225	403	535	338	525	354	3374	6589		✓
WHITE	426	379	358	165	462	210	470	338	327	3135		162	375	377	182	371	509	309	510	340	3135	6270		
HANDICAP	3	1	13	17	11	15	5	7	9			18	4	2	16	10	8	14	6	12				
Tavis Donnelly	3	3	3	5	4	4	5			32		3	3	6	3	4	4	5	6	8	35	67	3	64
PAR	4	4	4	3	5	4	3	5	4	36		3	4	4	3	4	5	4	5	4	36	72		
Bob B	5	5	4	3	8	5	7	7	7	51		3	7	6	5	5	6	4	6	4	46	97		
RED	403	350	295	134	351	182	410	303	279	2742		137	267	334	143	390	409	245	472	311	2625	5337		
HANDICAP	3	9	13	17	11	15	5	7	11			18	14	6	16	10	2	12	4	18				
MARKER:															PLAYER:								DATE: Aug 17/08	

Tavis Donnelly shot a course record of 67 on August 17, 2008.

Early Years of Curling: 1963 to 1983

Curling started very early in the Pinawa area with a one sheet rink being constructed on AECL's property while the reactor was being built. Gerry Hampton and some of the building crew that stayed in the onsite bunk houses enjoyed a few games outdoors. What a sight that must have been!

In the fall of 1963 Ray Sochaski relates the story of moving 16 rocks in the trunk of his 63 Chevy Biscayne from the plant site to a one sheet outdoor curling rink that was constructed behind 13 Burrows. The car sat so low to the ground that the local RCMP stopped Ray because the officer thought he had a load of illegal sturgeon in the trunk. The rocks are thought to have come from Pointe du Bois and were later stored under the old fire hall. The interesting thing about these rocks is that they had a standard 5" running surface on one side but a 4" surface on the other for wet conditions attesting to their use outdoors. Sometime in the 1980s they were sold to LDB curling club.

The rink on Burrows only lasted one season as a new two sheet rink was being constructed at 1 Willis Drive. This building was a flat roof type that was not normally used in Manitoba but it did fit into the general décor of the town. Curling commenced in the 1964-65 season with Grant Unsworth being the first Curling President. Gerry Smith remembers making ice with Ray Andrews, who was an A.C tech. at AECL. White ice colour back then was Keen's white cement sort of flooded on to the ice. The game was so popular that ice time still had to be rented in Seven Sisters so two more sheets were added in 1966 with state of the art clubrooms upstairs and locker rooms downstairs. The four sheets were open for the 1966-67 season and all the leagues were full with all the week nights being used except Friday because this was when bonspiels usually started.

Because the ice area ceiling was lower than traditional western rinks the ice area was borne to a lot of condensation problems which caused many a headache for the ice makers. Over the

M. Allan throws the first rock at the new Pinawa Curling Club

years ice makers struggled with a brownish water condition from the town supply and heaving ground conditions and yet delivered good quality playing ice. Hats off to Nick Kalupar (1966/76), Ron McDowall (1977/78), Al Abraham (1978/81), Duane Keenan (1982/88), and Darryl Mistelbocker (1989). The rink was also very noisy due to the tin lined walls and the rink rat brooms being used at that time. In the early 1970s the walls were lined with blown on cellulose which added to the heat in the building and reduced the noise level. Two large propane heaters were also installed by Harry Haugen and Jack Longmore which helped the cold problem on the ice. All in all a very nice looking rink.

From 1964 to 1984 the curling rink enjoyed prosperous times with men's, ladies and mixed leagues fully subscribed. Bonspiels were the best of many rural rinks with good prizes and lots of parties far into the night. One of the social highlights of the year was at the end of the season when the awards presentations were done at a sit down dinner and dance held at the high school gym with around 250 curlers attending. Dinners were catered by Bill and Jo Chelack and were not to be missed! All the aggregate winners and square winners garnered trophies and bragging rights for the year! All these spots were hotly contested through the year and made for exciting curling.

The competitive side of curling was not forgotten as many highly skilled teams played off for zone spots and the on to zones and then to provincials. Some names that come to mind at the Provincial level are Men's team skipped by Grant Bailey, Ian Kirk, and George Duncan. Mixed teams skipped by Ian Kirk, Dennis Smith and Dave Litke, Ladies teams skipped by Marg Smith, Cindy Litke and Farrel Rice.

The junior curlers were not forgotten as after school leagues were organized, curling schools were set up and a developmental program was started that was the blueprint for many curling clubs in the province. Many volunteers spent countless hours at the rink teaching and coaching these young people the finer points of the game. Names that come to mind are the Benders, Smiths, Shermans, Litkes and many parents who took their turn being fourth man on the team. Teams skipped by Michelle Smith and Katherine Boivin won the under 14 division in the Ladies Winnipeg bonspiel while teams skipped by Lesle Cafferty and Michelle Smith captured Zone spots. The junior teams also won or placed highly in several Manitoba Winter Games.

The financial part of the club was always handled by AECL. They put up the facility, paid for the maintenance and the operation of the curling club through a yearly grant that was paid to the Pinawa Club which was the umbrella organization. It was left to the curling club to pick up any difference in funding but all the surplus went into the coffers of the Pinawa Club leaving the curling club at a yearly operating profit of zero.

In 1975 Ron Rice was elected curling president and he instated a reserve and replacement fund for the curling club. This was a fund to cover future ice plant repairs or major building repairs as AECL was not leaning towards funding large replacement costs. Over the years profits from the curling operations were put into this fund and when it was decided to add the restaurant in 1983 about 70K was available from this fund. Well done Ron!

In 1976 the club elected Bev Ayres as the first Female President and in 1977 a ladies team skipped by Marg Smith played in the Provincial Ladies final at the Elmwood CC. but lost to D. McKenzie. That particular Monday there was not too many people at work including the AECL president! Marg repeated this feat in 1980 but lost in the semi-final. In 1983, Marg's team again played in the final of the provincial Scott Tournament of Hearts, but lost to the Patti Vande rink from Winnipeg.

In 1983 the restaurant was added to the Pinawa Club and certainly changed the dynamics for the curling club. Volunteers were no longer needed to run the bar and kitchen which were a major source of extra revenue. In fact one year it was noted that over twenty thousand drinks had been sold through the volunteer bar! But the offset was that the curling club lost the revenue streams from these operations.

Middle Years: 1984-1994

During this period curling continued to prosper but an aging population made keeping the leagues full become more of a challenge for the executives. Howard Gilmour after his retirement started an afternoon drop in league which was very popular and even drew curlers from the surrounding district. This league is still active today. Basic maintenance was carried out to the plant and building with AECL still picking up some of the costs. Around 1990 ice making duties where taken over by a group of volunteers and over the years to present that position has been chaired by Dennis Smith, Harry Noel, Bob Payne and Mike Smith with countless hours donated by the curlers.

Later Years: 1995 to Present

The 1994/95 season was an exciting year for the club. The ageing building and plant finally demanded attention. Under the guidance of Sharon Turner the old tar roof was stripped from the rink and a new tin roof was installed in November 1994. April 1995 saw insulation and vinyl siding installed by D. McTaggert and volunteers on the inside of the rink. New score boards were installed, painting was done, and Cimco overhauled the top end of the compressor. Total cost for these renovations was 66K with about 34K of this covered by grants. About 700 volunteer man hours were used on these projects. The curling club then embarked on a series of fundraising schemes which included a successful car raffle chaired by Blair Skinner for two years. In 1996 a used wide blade ice scraper was purchased from the Heather Club which led to much better ice conditions and was paid for by running an annual book sale for four years. This scraper was later replaced with a state of the art Ice King scraper around 2005 utilizing a grant that was available

In 1998 AECL shutdown with large layoffs affecting all memberships in the Pinawa Club sections curling included. In a couple of years the curling club lost the ladies and junior sections and suffered severely reduced membership in the men's and mixed sections. The club continues to operate to this day with volunteers putting in the time to maintain the club.

The main plant was completely overhauled in 2010 and the condenser was replaced in 2011. Also in 2011 material became available due to the closing of the Grain Exchange C.C. in Winnipeg. Forty new lockers, 1280 sheets of 1.5" Styrofoam, a large ice dehumidifier and 20 chairs, plus miscellaneous curling supplies were salvaged from this rink. Again many volunteers stepped up with donations of time, vehicles and trailers. During the summer of 2012 under the direction of Dennis Smith and Mike Smith material was removed from sheets three and four, weeping tile was installed on the north side of the rink and three inches of Styrofoam was installed on these sheets. To date the notorious hill on sheet four is gone! New heaters, new side boards and puck board was also installed. Part of this cost was covered by grants and at least 1000 volunteer hours have been used on this project. It is planned in 2013 to do sheets one and two to the same standard.

Going into the next fifty years the curling club will continue to make improvements to their facility so the roaring game can be enjoyed by future generations.

Pinawa Tennis Section
By Dennis Chen, contributors Christine Nuttall and Kelly Deveau

The tennis section of the Pinawa Club was founded in 1965 under the presidency of John Boulton. A number of founding tennis members were the Allan, Hilborn, and Hemmings families.

Three clay courts were constructed at the present site of the tennis courts in 1965. The courts were designed to include a top red coloured clay playing surface (a special red clay was trucked in from Alberta), a thin layer of Manitoba clay to maintain moisture levels and a gravel base containing drainage tiles to remove excess rain water. The clay courts required a watering system to keep the courts from drying out. At the beginning of the day, the courts had to be dragged to smooth out the surface and then watered to produce a good playing surface. At the start of each tennis season the courts were cleared of all vegetation and leaves by a member work party and PVC tape was laid down to

Tennis courts in Pinawa

outline the three courts. The old golf pro shop was moved behind the tennis courts to serve as a club house.

The membership grew from about 25 to over 100 members during the first five years of operation. The tennis section hosted a yearly Manitoba Tennis Association mixed doubles tournament which was well attended by tennis players from Winnipeg and rural tennis clubs. The club held a number of weekend tournaments during the year with a windup BBQ after the tournaments.

The constant level of maintenance of the clay courts became a burden to the tennis club and it was decided to convert to hard courts to minimize the maintenance effort. To finance the construction of the hard courts the Pinawa Club floated a debenture to residents and Pinawa Club members. The construction of the hard courts was successfully completed in 1974. This time period saw the zenith in tennis popularity and the membership grew to over 150 adult tennis players. The popularity of the sport resulted in the installation of lights in 1986 to extend playing time in the evenings.

The junior tennis program for children from 8 to 18 years also boomed during this period with up to 80 registered juniors. The program ran from May to June after school and the summer program ran from July to August. We were fortunate to have Anne Green for a few years provide instruction and run the junior program with junior coaches. The junior tennis coaches were skilled tennis players who had to take and pass the Manitoba Tennis Association coaching clinics. During this period, two junior members Paul Nuttall and Sandra Wright made the Manitoba provincial tennis team. They competed in junior tournaments in Manitoba and Saskatchewan. Paul Nuttall won both the singles and doubles tournament in Saskatchewan in 1984.

Tennis memberships declined in the late 1990s. This was in part due to the decline in popularity of the sport, some movement of AECL staff to Ontario, and Pinawa's aging population. However, there continues to be a small but enthusiastic group of tennis members. Kelly Deveau, a certified tennis instructor, along with husband Claude has given tennis sessions to students in Pinawa's two schools. In 2012, Kelly became certified to instruct the exciting new Cardio Tennis program. Plans are in the works to repave the three hardcourts in the foreseeable future. The Pinawa tennis club looks forward to welcoming new members of all ages in the coming years.

Pinawa Duplicate Bridge Section
By Jerry Smee and Lorne Swanson

The initial staffing of AECL at Pinawa took place in the early summer of 1963 when the majority of the Whiteshell Branch, as it was known then, moved from Deep River. Several of us had played duplicate bridge at the Deep River Duplicate Bridge Club but for the next few years the only bridge in Pinawa was "Marathon" and social bridge played at one another's homes in the evenings and weekends and lunch hour games at the plant.

The first duplicate bridge games were actually played using bridge hands paper clipped to bristol board cards and home-made movement cards. The very first games were played at the W. B. Lewis School gymnasium. The date of the first game is uncertain but Lorne can recall leaving his "frozen-up" car there overnight after a game and he sold that car in summer of 1968! In 1969 Jerry was temporarily assigned back to Chalk River for a 2-year project. Of course he immediately rejoined the DRDBC and began thinking about starting such a sanctioned club in Pinawa. A basic requirement for such a club to be sanctioned by the American Contract Bridge League (ACBL) is a certified director. Under the tutorship of the directors in Deep River, Jerry studied for the test and passed successfully. He still has the original certificate signed by Easley Blackwood in May 1971.

Upon his return to Pinawa that summer, a group of enthusiasts got together and decided to start Pinawa's duplicate bridge club in the fall of 1971. The group consisted of Jerry Smee, Ken Dormuth, Bill Mathers, and Lorne Swanson to name a few. We applied to the ACBL, were duly sanctioned and started playing as a sanctioned club in September that year. We played in various facilities - the auditorium at the W.B. Lewis School, the cafeteria at Kelsey House – before we eventually struck a deal with the Pinawa Club in the mid-

70s to become a section. The annual spring tournament held for many years at the Pinawa Club or Kelsey House attracted many players from clubs in Selkirk, Winnipeg and the Kenora area.

The game fee at the first game was $0.50 – that's right, 50 cents! In addition to those mentioned above some of the regulars were Frank Barclay, Bob Pollock, Ralph Mills, Bob Lyon, Jim Beddoes, Hans Tammemagi and Gerry Rigby, David Bell, Agnes Swanson, Cheryl Holmlund, Alice Jones, Betty Smee, Virginia Schankula, Ronnie Walker, Bill Murray, Bill Kovacs, Don Cameron and Dave Faulkner, Jan and Dave Dugle, Donna and Ed Wuschke, Colin Brown, John Montin, Bill and Arlene Boivin, Ad Zerbin and Wally Dobush, George and Lyn Grant, Zona Dmytriw, Terry and Barb Andres, Marg Wikjord, Doug and Pat Blais, Blair Skinner and Leslie Strandlund. We usually had 4-5 tables so obviously we have forgotten many of the players. Apologies to those whose names have been missed.

Your Bid

In about 1975, Bill, Ken and Jerry thought why can't we use a computer to do the scoring instead of the tedious and error prone manual scoring? This was long before the days of personal computers and ACBL Score, so we wrote a program in Fortran, not the ideal language for a bridge scoring program but one we were all very familiar with. One Monday we arranged to borrow an acoustic coupler (identical to the one used by Mathew Broderick's character in the 1983 movie War Games), a keyboard and a monitor from the WNRE computer centre. We typed in the results, sent them off to the computer over the phone line and picked up the printout Tuesday morning. An interesting exercise but hardly practical. From the write-ups in the ACBL bridge bulletin about the early attempts to use computers for scoring games, I think we were among the first in the world to do so.

Richard Ferch, Virginia Schankula, Bill Murray, Doug Blais, Malcolm Sargent, Marg Wikjord and Jan Dugle have all served as director of the Club. Also serving the Club over the years are Ken McCallum, John Westdal, Lorne Swanson and Marg Stokes, as managers.

The first episode of a local Bridge column appeared in *PINAWA PRESS* on November 17, 1982. Named POLMABARMY'S Pathos, the column was the brainchild of four local bridge enthusiasts Bob *POL*lock, Bill *MA*thers, Frank *BAR*clay and Bill Murra*Y*. This was an outstanding column which was carried on until 1987. It dealt mostly with bridge hands which came up in our bridge club and at tournaments.

Jan Dugle started teaching a small group of interested players at the Pinawa Club in the late 1990s and developed the group into a regular Wednesday morning individual game. This group has thrived. The club still flourishes and regularly attracts many players to each of its two weekly games. The games now continue throughout the year.

Duplicate bridge is a thoughtful partnership activity and many Pinawa bridge players have done quite well in the bridge world outside Pinawa. Both Ed Wuschke and Lorne Swanson remember that Bill Mathers had a favorite ploy of announcing "That makes it" when the opening lead of a contract was first made, to unnerve the defence. On one occasion the regular partnership of Dormuth-Mathers was overheard discussing the Stayman Convention and Ken said "write an essay on the convention and I'll correct it!" This team was also observed bidding a hand when Ken doubled for penalties and Bill misinterpreted and took out the double. It came around one level higher and Ken carefully folded his hand on the table, backed out his chair, *stood* on the chair, raised his fist in the air and shouted DOUBLE to the immense enjoyment of all... must have been one of our "fun" nights! On yet another occasion, Bill was asked if his partner's 2D bid was weak to which he replied "Is it ever!"

In recent years many regular players travel to warmer climes in the winter months which limit game attendance somewhat, but at the same time we have an encouraging influx of new players from Pinawa and the communities surrounding Pinawa. Familiar names that are part of the Bridge Club include Ken McCallum and Chris Saunders, Bob and Betty Shewfelt, Ron and Sharon Brehm, Esther Wright, Fjola Davidson, Bud Biddiscombe, Carolyn Brady, Doug and Bonnie Edkins, Robert Hill, Marg Zach, Jerry Kozak, Joan Lidfors, Barb Zerbin, Glenna Zetaruk, Leon Clegg, Thea Anderstedt, Keith and Edith Olson, Wayne and Cathy Stewart, Fred and Edith Bousquet, Ann Duncan, Bev Stewart, Hazel Melnick, Gayle and Mike Rutherford, Ria Moreau. Again, please excuse errors and omissions!

Pinawa Minor Hockey
By Chris Saunders

Hockey has been a prominent game in Pinawa since the early 1960s. Pinawa's first rink was built in the fall of 1963 behind Gilbert School. A group of volunteers built a hockey rink, curling rink and tot rink. The town added a warming shack and lighting to round out Pinawa's first community recreational area. If you were not one of those who had dug out their old skates, you would at least have heard to the cries of the broom ball enthusiasts or the yelling of a curling foursome.

Pinawa's first rink committee was made up of Orville Acres (Chairman), Len Horn (Maintenance Committee Chairman), Ken Murphy (Programming Committee Chairman), Ray Sochaski (Curling Committee Chairman) and Don Green (Hockey Convener). The committee was responsible for the administration of Pinawa's three rinks. Minor hockey began in earnest in the winter of 1964. Pinawa had three minor hockey groups operating that first year, including a Girls League. Snow clearing was undertaken largely by the school children with the teachers capably filling the role of working foremen.

After 5 years of braving the elements, 1969 saw the formation of a Recreation Complex Advisory Committee. Fundraising began in earnest, with events such as a walk-a-thon held. The Lions Club donated over $14,000 to the cause and the newly formed NEWSSTAND committee donated money for the ice plant, bleachers and most of the other items in the building. The committee's success resulted in Pinawa's Arena officially opening on December 13, 1970.

Minor hockey thrived in the community for the next 30 years, thanks to the dedicated efforts of parents and volunteers who were coaches, referees, managers, drivers and fans. Throughout the 70s, 80s and 90s, Pinawa had a full slate of teams at

1974-75 Pinawa Bantam Team – Back Row: Walter Barnsdale, Doug Hollies, Gord Sochaski, Don Grant; Middle Row: John Montgomery (Manager), Mark McGinnis, Keith Montgomery, Neil Barrie, Mike Borgford, Wes Singbeil, John Bird, Len Williams (Coach); Front Row: Scott Williams, Marty Stanley, Cam Thomson, Terry Roy, Pat Critchel

all of the age groups. In the odd year where a particular team needed an additional player or two, communities around eastern Manitoba always stepped up. Tournaments were held, league playoffs were played and we even won a few provincial championship banners that hang from the arena ceiling. Many local players moved on to higher levels, including junior and senior hockey. Many of them can still be seen around the arena today as part of the local old-timer teams, recreational leagues, or as coaches and managers for their own children's' teams.

Long time coaches included names like Bill Hutchings, Orville Acres, Wayne Stanley, Dave Shoesmith, Garry Buchanan, and Bruce and Brent Donnelly. Referees seen at the arena for many years included Orville Acres, Len Williams, Ken Meek, Chris Saunders, Blair Skinner and Claude Deveau. Long time volunteers doing everything from skate sharpening to time keeping included Orville Acres (again), Tom McDougall, Cyril Clarke, Terry Reimer, Don Daymond, Peter Cliche and Hammy Carswell. Pinawa even had "super fans" that could be seen at almost all of the local games, no matter what the age group. These fans included names such as Marj Ehlers, Dolores Bird and June Hughes. All of these individuals, plus hundreds more, made the Pinawa Arena the place to be on a winter day.

Over the next decade, dedicated parents continued to support Pinawa's minor hockey program, even though participation numbers began to decrease. Today the association routinely has three or four local teams each winter. Recent key events have included honouring Orville's memory by renaming the arena the Orville Acres Arena (October 2003) and various major fundraising events to promote and improve the facility.

As part of the Kraft Celebration Tour, Pinawa hosted a special edition of TSN SPORTSCENTRE with anchors Jay Onrait and Dan O'Toole in August 2010. Pinawa also received a $25,000 community refresh grant from Kraft Canada that went towards renovations.

In 2011, Nestle Canada, in partnership with the Western Hockey League, presented a cheque to the Pinawa Minor Hockey Association as winners of the $50,000 WHL Delissio Hockey Challenge. The funds were used to upgrade the ice plant and to rebuild the outdoor rink.

Pinawa minor hockey continues to be a key winter activity for Pinawa's children. We would like to thank all of volunteers over the past 50 years that have helped make minor hockey such an integral part of Pinawa life.

Pinawa Panthers Intermediate Hockey Team
By Garry Buchanan

The Pinawa Panthers Intermediate Hockey Team began with the opening of the new arena in 1970. The Panthers were part of the new North Eastern Hockey League that was formed under the guidance of President Roy Barnsdale. Referee in Chief, Orville Acres, and league statistician Wayne Stanley, both from Pinawa, rounded out the new executive. The hockey club chose the Chicago Blackhawks as their team colours but a Panther head replaced the hawk logo. The coaching came from

1970/71 Pinawa Panthers - Back Row L/R Bill Hutchings (playing coach) , Dave Murray, Hosney El- Lakany(manager), Harry Backer, Elliot Alison , Jim Van Wart, Bob Donnelly, Ralph Moyer, Dale Graham, Garry Buchanan, Dale Easton. Front Row L/R Lloyd Dreger, Gary Tripps, Garth Hiltz, John Owens, Fred Legiehn, Lou Broulotte

player Bill Hutchings while Hosney El-Lakany managed the team. Ron Wiggins was trainer while equipment was handled by Tony Wiewel. Peter Cliche generally manned the clock with other budding volunteers. The referees were Orville Acres, Len Williams, Mike Schankula, Kent Truss and Jake Frederick. Encouragement was generally garnered from our top two fans; Gertie Gryseels and Dolores Bird. The Panthers' motto was "if the fans were having fun then so were the players".

Ice maintenance was done by hand scrapers and a 45 gallon drum of water pulled by hand using a finely-tuned spray bar. Of course a tractor replaced that and then it was replaced by the Zamboni.

The Panthers were successful in winning the NEHL championship that first

1976/77 Pinawa Panthers - Back Row L/R Bruce Rankin, John Owens, Doug Keith, Jamie Borgford, Ken Bush, Brad McCormac, Garry Buchanan, Rob Nerbas, Chris Hillier, Kelly Dereski, Mike Barnsdale, Dean Randell. Front Row L/R Bill Hutchings, Gord Lacquement (coach), Jeff Seifried, Jim Spencer (mgr), Ralph Moyer

season. They defeated a very good Pine Falls Juvenile team that represented Pine Falls, as the Paper Kings were still in the Interlake League. The Paper Kings and Beausejour Beavers joined the following season. The first goal scored by an intermediate player in our new arena was Ralph Moyer during an exhibition game against Beausejour.

The club made a donation to the Pinawa Minor Hockey Association in 1976 to adopt the Panther colours by giving a set of sweaters to the midget club. Eventually the Pinawa Collegiate also adopted the Panther logo and colours and continue to do so today.

At the end of the 1970s the older players began to call it quits and our coach moved to Neepawa. The desire still burned in the youth that remained and a new team was formed under coach Len Williams and manager Bill Ayres. The team chose popular New York Islanders colours to emulate their club. They played for five seasons before the league folded. The players then moved on to other teams. There were many other players, coaches and hockey personnel who are not listed above. Regrets to those not listed and thanks to everyone for the memories that you gave us.

Men's Fastball
By Marvin Ryz

Men's Fastball in Pinawa began in 1964 with the formation of the Pinawa Pioneers Fastball Team. The team was classified as Intermediate B Level according to the Provincial Fastball Classification and played in the Northeast Fastball League. Original league teams in addition to the Pinawa Pioneers were Lac du Bonnet, Pine Falls, Beausejour, Seven Sisters and Whitemouth teams. With an increase in interest in playing fastball at that level, a second team, the Pinawa Lakers, was formed several years later and the league expanded to include teams from Tyndall, Milner Ridge and McArthur Falls.

Weekend fastball tournaments were a favourite past-time during the 1960s and 70s with cash prizes awarded to the winning teams. At that time fastball teams were sometimes sponsored by brewing companies, a tradition the Pioneers willingly participated in. The Pioneers were sponsored by Molson's and in addition to a monetary contribution for sports equipment and uniforms, there also was a generous donation of the company's "product" which was great fully consumed after games, usually at the Bay House which was the residence of the Manager of The Hudson's Bay Store.

In the early years, games in Pinawa were played at the Gilbert School ball diamond. A couple of years later the Pioneers constructed a second diamond on the Secondary School grounds. This diamond was significantly improved from the earlier one and included a clay infield, home run fence and bleachers for the fans. Eventually, with the advent of a plant softball league, demand for ball diamonds increased and a third ball diamond was developed on the Lewis

First Pinawa Pioneers Team were: Front Row, left to right - Floyd Olson, Ted Deering, Jim Wallace, John Minton (coach), Al Roberts; Back Row, left to right - Sid Jones, Tom Boyle, Ray Andrews, Harry Backer, Al Rosser and Keith McIntyre

School property. The Pinawa Pioneers won the league championship on at least one occasion and went on to the Provincial playoffs that were held in Brandon.

Interest in playing fastball in Pinawa gradually began to fade in the 1970s (partly due to the demographic of the players) and partly due to the formation of an AECL Plant League and eventually a Slow Pitch League. By the 1980s there no longer was a fastball team playing in Pinawa.

Pinawa Plant League Softball
By Ken McCallum

Fastball was very popular in Manitoba in the 1960s. In Pinawa, the first senior team, the Pioneers, was formed in 1964, followed by a second team, the Lakers, in 1967. Both teams played in the North Eastern League for about ten years.

A recreational softball league was started at the Whiteshell Nuclear Research Establishment (WNRE) in 1965; that became known simply as the Plant League. Teams were organized around work units (typically plant buildings) and groups within the Pinawa town site. The league adopted one unique rule: no windmill or

Plant League's Pinawa Rebels –late 1970s - Back Row: Marvin Ryz, Roy Ticknor, Thor Borgford, Bob Bruneau, Barry Hood, Don Zetaruk, Don Bruneau; Front Row: Rick Murphy, Kevin Ticknor, Ward Wallace, Greg Brady, Ron Oberick, Wally Dobush

slingshot pitching was allowed so that pitching would not dominate play. Initially membership was limited to AECL employees and Pinawa residents but over the years membership rules were expanded.

In the early years, the Plant League competed for space at the one diamond at Gilbert School. A second diamond, built at WNRE, was used in 1967 and 1968. Play returned to Pinawa in 1969 with the building of the diamonds at Lewis School and at the current Burrows Road location.

In the first 12 years, there were typically 7 or 8 teams in the league. The league operated with two sets of communal equipment and used volunteer umpires. The league changed dramatically with the disbanding of the two senior teams. Play became much more competitive and recruiting crossed over the old work unit lines. Teams acquired their own equipment and new uniforms. Volunteer umpires were replaced with paid umpires in 1974.

In 1978, with the influx of new hiring at WNRE, the league began to grow. Over the next ten years, the league had between 10 and 14 teams. For several of these years the league operated in two divisions and began using three diamonds. By 1989 the league had returned to 6 to 8 teams and continued at that size until it ceased operation in 1997.

The Plant League lasted 33 years and created lots of enthusiastic competition and team camaraderie for hundreds of ball players. The league held a closed tournament (members only) from 1966 to 1988, an open tournament on the Pinawa Birthday weekend from 1973 to 1993, and held playoffs to declare a league champion from 1968 to 1997. The league was governed by a president and treasurer from the teams on a rotating basis. Thanks to the many people who held these positions over the years.

History of Pinawa Plant League

Year	Closed Tournament Winner	Open Tournament Winner	League Champion
1966	Chemical Engineers	-	
1967	400		--
1968	Teens		Stores
1969	412		Stores
1970	402		WR-1
1971	412		402
1972	400/401		300
1973	Hot Cells	412	Hot Cells
1974	Goldeyes	300	Goldeyes
1975	Goldeyes	River Hills	Goldeyes
1976	Foul Balls	Foul Balls	Goldeyes
1977		Barracudas	Foul Balls
1978	300	River Hills	Goldeyes
1979	Foul Balls	Barracudas	Guzzlers
1980	Bill's Boys	Guzzlers	Foul Balls
1981	Guzzlers	Guzzlers	Guzzlers
1982	Guzzlers	Old Gold	Guzzlers
1983	Guzzlers	Foul Balls	Guzzlers
1984	Rebels	Seven Sisters	Relics
1985	Teachers	Fouls Balls	Rebels
1986	-	No Names	Relics
1987	Relics	-	Relics
1988	Pirates	Miller Hi-Lites	Guzzlers
1989	-	Pirates	Rutamingos
1990	-	Woodticks	Guzzlers
1991	-	Guzzlers	Guzzlers
1992	-	-	Guzzlers
1993		Devils	Kaos
1994			Old Varmits
1995	--	-	Kaos
1996	--	--	Abe's Apes
1997	--		Guzzlers

Umpires-In-Chief: Ernie Muzychka (1974-78); Nat Fenton (1979-80); Ken King (1981); Dave Juhnke (1982-97)
Plant League Umpires: Orville Acres, Alex Ramsay, John Stefaniuk, Earl King, Dennis Klepatz, Chris Saunders, Blair Skinner, Sid Jones

Ladies Softball
By Shirley Pellow

Ladies softball was organized in 1967. The Atomettes entered the Northeastern Manitoba league, along with teams from Pine Falls, Great Falls, Lac du Bonnet, Milner Ridge and Seven Sisters – later on Beausejour and Powerview joined the league. First game played in 1967 was against Pine Falls. Brian Belinski was the first coach.

The Atomettes participated in the league from 1967-1981. In the early 70s the Atomettes had their signature uniforms of yellow/gold with red trim and red socks. There were many volunteer coaches during the 70s: Brian Belinski, Bob Komzak, George Duncan, Al Reich, Mac Pellow, Gord Oberlin, Ed Jacobs, Stan Dubeck, Gord Lacquement. Some of the team members in the 70s were Wendy Allison, Pat Duncan, Pat Bilinsky, Mavis Bollman, Karen Campbell, Linda McDaid, Dixie Jung, Ilona Komzak, Rita Pouteau, Alberta Fenning, Carol Moyer, Carol Morris, Judy Ticknor, Rita Oberlin, Judith Simpson, Merle Stepaniuk, Rose Thomas, Fran Otto, Marg Smith, Ann Sisler, Shirley Pellow, Vickie Shorrock, Karen Suchar, Carol Putnam, Eleanor Vanderweyde, Patti Vanderweyde, Farrell Rice, Jean Rennie, Lynda McCallum, Cathy Donnelly and Penny Spencer.

The Eastman Summer Games were hosted by Pinawa in 1976. The Atomettes had a new coach, Gord Lacquement, a no-nonsense coach and the 14 players were put into training doing pepper drills and a drill trying to catch a ball with a garden glove nailed to a board, resulting in the player having to catch a ball with both hands. The training paid off as the team won the regional summer final, winning over Powerview, Steinbach and a young team from Vassar.

1972 Pinawa Atomettes - Back Row L to R: Shirley Pellow, Pat Duncan, Carol Moyer, Carol Putman, Unknown, Eleanor Vanderweyde; 2nd Row l to R: Lynda McCallum, Unknown, Wendy Allison, Pat Belinski, Marg Smith; Front Row L to R: Carol Morris, George Duncan, Summer Student

1974 Pinawa Atomettes - Back Row: Al Reich, Eleanor Vanderweyde, Ilona Komzak, Alberta Fenning, Dixie Jung, Wendy Allison, AECL summer student, Karen Suchar, Gertie Zieske, Mac Pellow; Front Row: Lynda McCallum, Farrell Rice, Fran Otto, Unknown, AECL summer student, Pat Duncan, Patti Vanderweyde, Marg Smith

The Atomettes went on to compete in the summer games at Neepawa, MB. The team had great pitching from long-time player Eleanor Vanderweyde and Karen Campbell. No balls got by the team captain, Marg Smith. Marg had one of the best catching and throwing arms in the league. The team went on that year as well to the Provincials. The summer of 1976 was full of fun, fond memories and companionship.

In 1980 Don Daymond coached, followed by Frank Gryseels and Nigel Boulton in 1983-84.

During their history, the Atomettes represented the Eastman league many times at the Provincials. Although the Atomettes did not win any provincial titles they represented Eastman with pride and a competitive spirit (apologies for names forgotten).

1975 Pinawa Atomettes - Back Row L to R: Jean Rennie, Rose Thomas, Judy Ticknor, AECL summer student, Dixie Jung, Karen Campbell, Eleanor Vanderweyde; Front Row L to R: Vicky Shorrock, Penny Spence, Marg Smith, Farrell Rice, Ed Jacobs

1984 Pinawa Atomettes - Back Row: Frank Gryseels, Susan Reynolds, Ann Sisler, Jamie Holloway, Gertie Oliveira, Unknown, Cathy Abraham, Nigel Boulton; Front Row: Martha Laverock, Shelley Gillert, Karen Ross, Deb Brown, Unknown

Pinawa Co-Ed Fastball - 1981 to 1984
By Lloyd Dreger

The Men's Fastball team, the Relics were sitting around having a couple "Sociables" and someone said we should get a mixed team and go into the Whitemouth Mixed Fastball tournament. After a couple more games and discussing the topic it was decided to enter the Whitemouth Mixed Fastball Tournament. Lloyd Dreger (Lloyds Sporting Goods) said he would pay the entry fee and buy some sweaters for the team.

Tournament day went well, with some very, very good teams from around the area and Winnipeg. One rule was a woman had to pitch, and the men had to bat the opposite side. We picked up an Ace (Lefty) windmill pitcher in Jamie Holloway and needless to say not too many players got on base.

A highlight was Tom "Reggie" Boyle hitting a home run, opposite side, and when it cleared the fence and it the stage narrowly missing a couple band members whom were practicing. Someone said it almost hit the fiddle player, whom just carried right on playing. The team went on to win the tournament.

After another men's fastball game someone said "We should enter the Beausejour Tournament." Lloyd said he would phone around and see if he could get the team together and enter Beausejour. This Tournament had 16 teams entered, so some games were played on the High School diamond that had no fence. The semi-final game pitted Lockport Red Devils (Wpg. Sr. team) v. Lloyds Sporting Goods. Final inning Lloyds Sporting Goods were leading 5-4, Lockport got the winning runs on 2nd and 3rd base with 2 out. The Red Devils batter hit the ball to deep right field; Martha (Marvel) Laverock went back and caught the ball. The baserunners not thinking it would even be caught, had already crossed home plate, runners they tried to retracing back to 2nd. and 3rd, Martha rifled a perfect one hopper to second to get the player out before he could get back in time for the 3rd. out and Lloyds Sporting Goods advanced to the final and faced Beausejour. In a close, tight game the Lloyds Sporting Goods team won. The organizer of the Tournament, Mr. Shuster, could not find a place to sign the cheque ($300) for the winning team, Lloyd bent over and the cheque was signed on his back.

The next year the team again entered the Whitemouth tournament to defend its previous year's win. They now changed the rule that no Windmill pitchers were allowed and switched to Slow Pitch. That was just fine as Marg Smith, Merle Stepanik and Eleanor Vanderweyde did a great job pitching, and the team won, defending its previous year's win. The following year with players moving away and other commitments, the team retired undefeated in 3 tournaments.

After each tournament the team would meet at Lloyd Dreger's, and spend the winnings on a steak barbecue along with refreshments and rehash the games with the thinking, this was a very good team. And of course there would be beer bottle bowling tournaments using soft balls.

Lions Little League
By Judy Farr

The Lions Little League was organized by the Pinawa Lions Club in the mid-1960s, one of the Club's first projects. The first tournament was in April 1967 and was led by its first Commissioner, Bill Kovacs. Lions' ball started as a baseball league for boys only. Don Daymond was one of the umpires and coach and Howard Gilmour was involved as well. Before long, girls were included and there were co-ed teams. By the mid-1970s there were eight teams, 24 umpires and coaches and 120 children registered.

Most children who grew up in Pinawa remember playing Lions Little League during their childhood. Parents were willing to step up and take on the coaching and umpiring jobs. Fun was the main object and certainly was what you could hear for blocks Tuesday and Thursday evenings from the Gilbert School playground. The cheering was a wonderful, happy noise.

The Lions have always been fortunate to have community volunteers to assist with a variety of programs and one of those volunteers was Sid Jones, our very own Little League Commissioner. He took his job very seriously and the Lions appreciated all the time he put into this program. In the early days organizing the season was a time consuming task because it was before photocopiers, computers and e-mail. Diamonds had to be reserved, teams made up, as well as scheduling the games. While setting up the coaching schedule in 1978, there were rules to follow. "Two coaches are desirable, one may be a lady, one a teenager (along) with one a father," wrote Harry M. Johnson. T-Shirts, caps, bats and balls had to be ordered as well. In 1986, for instance, 128 T-shirts and 3 dozen soft balls were purchased.

Lions Club Little League

For the first three decades the Little League season always ended with a wiener roast. "The first one I saw was a never-ending line of kids who would get a hot dog and then go the back of the line ready for the next one, and so on," said Judy Farr. "The wiener roasts were for players, coaches and umps. Jerry and I held the end-of-year barbeque in our yard for five or so years. Once it was here we added chips and veggies along with the hot dogs, drinks and ice cream. Families were also included at that time."

Barbecues ended when the members of the Lions became too old and families were too busy at the end of June. In the early 2000s the wiener roast gave way to a treat at the end of each game. In recent years the Little League program has almost faded away because of fewer and fewer children in Pinawa and many other distractions such as Kids of Mud and video games. But, usually at the last minute they are able to gather two teams and continue to play ball.

So the Lions continue to give the children of our community the opportunity to "Play Ball" and have fun. The cost is minimal and the children have a T-shirt to keep at season's end along with memories of rounding the bases to the cheers of friends, parents and neighbours. Games are still being played in May and June on Tuesdays and Thursdays as it has for the past five decades.

As far as anyone can remember, none of the Pinawa Little League players ever went on to fame and fortune in the baseball field but according to Judy Farr they all were enriched with something more than fame and money. They learned team playing, understanding other's abilities and allowing everyone to try.

Pinawa Sailing Club
By Keith Reid

The Pinawa Sailing Club was formed in 1967, soon after the foundation of the town site of Pinawa, and has occupied the present site, next to the Pinawa marina, ever since its formation. In these early days the club's sailing activities included various recognizable and overlapping phases starting with Big Boats. An experiment with fast, deep fixed keel boats culminated in the incident leading to the naming of Sprungmann's Reef and Point on the East side of Sylvia Lake. Moral of this story: Try to screw up where no other sailors can see you.

The club was instrumental in the construction of the marina and town boat launch on the West side. Later, the club engineered the reinforcing the East wall of the marina. In the early 70s the club began hauling in sand to turn the swampy dinghy bay into a useable swimming area and improve launching and landing. During this time the club also constructed its own deep-draft boat launch. Around this time the Unicorn, cat-rigged catamaran, construction and sailing era was in full swing, thanks to John Walker, Roger Dutton and Frank Hughes. During this time the club engendered several Provincial Champions.

For the Lazy E era, beginning in the late 70s, the boats were again made in Pinawa by construction consortium including Frank Hughes. There could have been 10 or more of these plywood and fibre glass boats built by this group during the late 70s and early 80s. The moulds were later acquired by Egon Frech and a further 3 to 5 built in the mid-80s.

The next recognizable phase was windsurfing beginning in the early 80s. These boats reached their peak of popularity around the 1988 Games. We had had a group of young sailors that were also competitive at the provincial level including Dan Jung and Sheri Walton.

The Club started the Junior Sailfish Program in 1987, patterned after the Jackrabbit Cross-country Ski Program with various themes for each sailing day. These now grown-up sailors often speak of the skulduggery associated with "Spanish Armada Day". The program never was a formal sailing school - just good Saturday fun in boats for children aged 7 to 15. In 1988, a new clubhouse was built with the help of grants from the Manitoba government for the hosting of the sailing competition of the Manitoba Summer Games in 1988. The Rowing Club and the Sailing Club amalgamated in 1989 to form the Pinawa Sailing and Rowing Club. The often wildly independent nature of most sailors has been well complemented by the organizing ability and team spirit more characteristic of sissy rowers.

As windsurfing waned, it was followed by a laser phase. This led to the development of some young sailors that were very competitive at the provincial level, including Dave Westdal, Steven Cann and Scott Reid.

The Club purchased a Sabot ("Lake Lion") with funds from the Pinawa Lions Club in 2005. This boat and the purchase of 3 big, dilapidated "JY" dinghies with the help of MSA lead to our being able to teach our own CYA White Sail classes at the Pinawa Sailing Club. We have had one or two week-long sessions each summer training between 12 and 24 sailors each year.

Now the Pinawa Sailing Club seems to be back to a big boat phase with nine active big boats sailing of the Pinawa Sailing Club in the summer of 2012.

Young Sailors

Each year the PSC ran 2 annual regattas:

- Icicle Regatta (end of May), still the first regatta on the Manitoba Sailing Calendar.
- Pinawa Open (July) - regatta was dropped from the annual schedule in the mid-1980s because of low attendance and schedule conflicts with regattas hosted at larger clubs.

The club hosted the Western Intermediate Sailing Championships in 1987, the Manitoba Summer Games Sailing Competition in 1988, and the Manitoba Optimist Championships three times.

Past commodores of the Club have included Peter Dyne, Ian Peggs, Graham Strathdee, Frank Havelock, Jim Cafferty, Al Lane, Stu Iverson, Bruce Stewart, Mike Wright, Kurt Sprungmann, Bill Lavery, Egon Frech, Ted Melnyk, Keith Reid, Terry Solomon, Herman Saxler and John Trueman.

Sailors from the club who have sailed and won awards at the provincial level or above include Jim Cafferty, Stu Iverson, Egon Frech, Ian Peggs, Frank Walton, Dennis Chen, Dan Jung, Sheri Walton, Lisa Walton, David Westdal, Scott Reid, Steve Cann, Micah Melnyk and Adam Melnyk. Each year the Club gives out a number of awards and trophies - some of the more interesting trophies are the Dumpers Stump, the Big Crunch, the Golden Hook, and the Pinawa Icicle.

Pinawa Rowing Club
By Peter Vilks

When Derek Owen bought a recreational rowing shell in 1987, Peter Vilks and Jan Cramer were inspired to start a rowing club in Pinawa. In October of that year the Pinawa Rowing Club held its inaugural meeting, followed by a rowing clinic a week later. The clinic was run by the Winnipeg Rowing Club (WRC), who supplied coaches, athletes and two four person rowing shells. The original founding members included Jan Cramer, Derek Owen, Peter Vilks, Chris Moore and Ken Young. Rowing started in the summer of 1988.

The rowing club partnered with the sailing club to gain access to the river and to have a place to store their boats. The partnership was perfect since both sailors and rowers enjoy using the water with boats that do not require engines. An open air boat enclosure was built behind the sailing club in the spring of 1988, along with the first rowing dock. In 1988 the WRC donated two old four oared shells to the Pinawa Rowing Club (PRC). These boats, along with two privately owned singles kick started rowing in Pinawa.

The outdoor boat enclosure was replaced in 1995 with a three bay boathouse built with the help of a $64K matching grant from the Manitoba Sports Federation. Support for building construction was also received from AECL, the LGD of Pinawa, the Manitoba Rowing Association, the Pinawa Lions, and the Whiteshell Cross Country Ski Club. By 1990 the Pinawa rowing and sailing clubs had amalgamated into a single incorporated body, Pinawa Sailing and Rowing Club Inc., with rowing and sailing sections.

By 1990 club membership grew to 20, and by the mid-1990s it was up to over 50. The majority of rowing club members has been and continues to be recreational rowers, participating just for the fun of it and to enjoy the outdoors in summer. A few have been competitive, participating in regattas all across Canada and the United States. Some of these regattas included the Head of the Red in Winnipeg, the Canadian Masters, the U.S. Nationals (masters), the Regina Sprints, Royal Canadian Henley (1991 to 1999), Canada Cup in Montreal, the NWIRA championship regattas, and the Head of the Mississippi in Minneapolis. A few Pinawa athletes have participated with provincial rowing team to compete in the Canada Cup and the Canada Summer Games. During the 1990s the rowing club hosted a number of regattas in Pinawa, starting in 1993 with an informal competition with Winnipeg. In 1995 Pinawa hosted its first regatta on a fully buoyed, 2 km long course running parallel to Willis Drive. In 1996 Pinawa co-hosted the Winnipeg Invitational Regatta on its buoyed course, as well as the 3 day NWIRA Championship Regatta, which brought hundreds of athletes to Pinawa from Canadian and U.S. Clubs. An attempt was made to obtain the 1999 Pan Am rowing event for Pinawa, but it was not successful. After 2 years of using the buoyed course it became clear that

Kirk Vilks and Josh Bueckert rowing for Team Manitoba in 2005 Canada Summer Games

the current in the river was often too high to provide fair racing conditions. Consequently the regatta course was sold to Kenora, where it continues to be used for major rowing events on Rabbit Lake.

Over the years the rowing club has run a number of activities to promote rowing in the area. In 1994 the club ran an indoor rowing competition at both the elementary and senior schools, with most students participating, as well as a number of other community members. From 1998 to 2000 the club ran a Terry Fox row as a fundraiser for cancer, to parallel the Terry Fox run. A popular activity has always been rowing tours, which included trips to Otter Falls for breakfast, rowing to Seven Sisters or Lake Nutimik, rowing from Lac du Bonnet to Lee River, trips on the Whitemouth and Assiniboine Rivers, and the four day trip from Kenora to Pinawa.

Since 1992 the club has been running a learn-to-row program to introduce people to rowing. The rowing club has handed out awards on a yearly basis for a number of different accomplishments. For example, if you run your boat into a landmark you are eligible for the Peter Point trophy. If you capsize your boat you could get the Turtle award, or if you really mess up with your blade work you could earn the Crab trophy. Breaking equipment through efforts of great strength could merit the Cramer award. Other awards are awarded as new situation may arise.

Pinawa Rowing Club has grown over the last 25 years into a facility that provides a wonderful opportunity to experience nature and our local river through the sport of rowing, whether for fun, fitness or competition. The club continues to be the only rowing club in Manitoba outside of Winnipeg, and so makes up an important component to the Manitoba rowing community.

Whiteshell Cycling Club
By Frank Walton

Mountain biking started to become more popular with the opening of the Trans Canada Trail (TCT) in 2002. In the early years, group rides were loosely organized with no club structure. In 2006, Carol Randall (an ex-Olympic road cyclist), approached Frank Walton and suggested that Pinawa had the potential for forming a kids cycling program similar to those run by the mountain biking clubs in Winnipeg. In the fall of 2005 a group ride was organized to gauge local interest in the sport. Its success led to the formation of the Whiteshell Cycling Club (WCC) in the spring of 2006.

The WCC was initially directed by a group of parents and other adult cyclists. Kevin Dearing became the WCC's first certified coach. The WCC officially became part of the "Kids of Mud" (KOM) program in 2007. The first mountain bike races in Pinawa were also held that year.

The priorities during the early years were construction of biking trails and the training of coaches. With the support of the Pinawa LGD, the granite outcrop and open field behind Devonshire Park were transformed into a training and race facility. Trails were also developed across the diversion dam. A grant was used to build two wooden causeways over perennial wetland areas. The first causeway was built in the fall of 2007 and opened up the north side of the cross country Red Trail. The second causeway was completed in the spring of 2008 and eliminated another wet area on the Red Trail. A third project completed that year was a board walk in an eco-sensitive area in the Devonshire Park. Between 2009 and 2012 a series of biking trails were developed which complement the TCT. These bike trails take advantage of granite outcrops and game trails to traverse areas unsuitable for other outdoor recreational sports.

Kids of Mud

There has been a KOM series race (150 kids) in every year since 2007. By 2010 the WCC had developed from a small rural team to a successful provincial club. Talented young people have either won or placed in the KOM series races every year since they joined the WCC.

A long-standing tradition in Pinawa has been its ability to organize athletic events. The KOM races were no exception and feedback from parents in the major urban areas has been more than positive over the years. Two local innovations have now been adopted at other race venues across the province. Firstly, the WCC always provided lots of organizational staff, course marshals and other race officials. In this respect, the WCC is grateful to our partners the Wolseley Wheels and Bikes and Beyond. Secondly, the WCC developed shorter multi-lap spectator-friendly courses where parents can see more than the start and finish of the race. Much is made about fan support in professional sport and same can said to be true about the impact of a crowd of cheering parents, relatives and friends at different locations in mountain bike races. Pinawa is the only race venue where there is an organized team of photographers to record the event and to make these photos available to parents of all KOM clubs. Thank-you to photographers Stu Iverson, Derek Owen, Peter Taylor and Frank Walton. Finally, the history and success of any athletic club can be traced back its coaches who have dedicated their time to working with young people, including Kevin Dearing, John Buell, Jason Wu, Len Rasmussen, Mark Tinant, Dan Laliberte, and Vivianne Hayter.

Whiteshell Cross-Country Ski Club
By Dennis Cann

In the fall of 1973 thirty skiers and enthusiasts gathered at Gilbert School and formed the Whiteshell Cross-Country Ski Club. An executive of Herb Rosinger, Graeme Strathdee, Lyn Grant, Malcolm Sargent, Heiki Tamm and Walter Harrison was elected and set to work developing trails, teaching cross-country skiing and organizing ski races.

The Club's first trails were skied-in tracks on the rough and service roads of the Pinawa golf course. However, in 1974 there was little snowfall before Christmas and the golf club closed the course to skiers because of concern about possible damage. In response, scouting parties crossed the diversion dam and pieced together a ski trail from old roads, walking trails, swamps and ridges north of the Channel. This trail, now known as the Red Trail, was extended in subsequent years and has become the Club's most popular trail. An extension going east was started in 1976. The series of rock ridges on this trail often resulted in bruised skiers as they tumbled and made sitzmarks in the snow. This extension was consequently renamed the Blue Trail. In 1998, a log warming cabin was built on the Red trail by Larry Gauthier, Heinz Ehlers, Bob Jones, Bob Dick, Oliver Greenfield, Bruce Goodwin, Derek Owen, Roy Styles and Dennis Cann.

In the early years, off-trail tours were organized into the back country north of the Channel, to Pine Point Rapids and to the Agassiz Forest. By 1980, interest in these tours had dwindled and the Club decided to improve the local touring trails to old Pinawa and Otter Falls. The Old Pinawa trail, originally a favourite of Mike Tomlinson, Eric and Edna Graham and Bob Jones traversed marshes and forested areas along the Pinawa Channel to Old Pinawa. It was maintained until 2001 when low usage and the new Trans-Canada Trail to Old Pinawa no longer justified the effort required to maintain the trail.

The English River/Otter Falls area, first explored on skis by Jim Putnam, was a favorite destination of Walter Harrison and Bob Jones. Walter, Bob and Eric Graham marked and cleared the English River Trail on the peninsula jutting into the Winnipeg River opposite Otter Falls in 1979-81. The views of Margaret Lake and Otter Falls from this trail make it the most picturesque of the Club trails. In 1995 a log warming cabin was constructed on the trail by Larry Gauthier, Heinz Ehlers, Bob Jones and Bruce Goodwin.

In 1982, the Club decided to make a new, more challenging trail. Dennis LeNeveu and Derek Owen chose the route from aerial photographs and advice from hikers and back country skiers. In 1983, a cabin was built near the trail midpoint. It had an unusual shape, a polyhedral geodesic dome. By 2008, the dome cabin had suffered numerous bear attacks and needed replacement. Paul Chambers, Romeo Bernardin, and Oliver Greenfield with input from Larry Gauthier and Bruce Goodwin designed a new log cabin. Over the next three years, Paul led the cutting and peeling of 50 spruce trees, the hauling in of building supplies and the construction the new log cabin officially opened in 2012. The Jones-Graham-Gauthier Freeway trail provides a challenging but direct link between the Orange and English River cabins.

Ski Instruction

Eva Rosinger was the Club's first ski instructor and taught members how to tar and wax wood skis, many of which she and her husband Herb had sold from their basement business. In 1980, 35 juniors turned out for the first Jackrabbit program. The first leaders were Eva Rosinger, Mike Quinn, Don Ewing and Joe Szekely. This program continues to be a major success for the Club. In the past decade, many Jackrabbit coaches have completed the National Coaching Certification Program including current co-ordinators Susan Barnett and Kevin Dearing.

For the more competitive youth, Nick Scheier and Don Ewing started a Junior Development Program in 1984. By 1986, there were fourteen members. Sonali Bera, Tamara Ewing and Tanis Westdal made the Provincial A Team while Trudy Mills, Angela Moyer, Trevor Olson, Brad Ryz, Peter Szekely and Karla Wikjord were on the Manitoba Talent Squad. Later in the 1980s the group was renamed the Whiteshell Ski Team. For his knowledge and dedicated leadership Don Ewing was named Manitoba Cross-Country Skiing Coach of the Year in 1992. In March 2012, Ben Dearing competed with the Manitoba team at the Canadian National Championships in Quebec City. Graduates of the program have now entered coaching ranks. Karla Wikjord is qualified as the highest level Nordic ski instructor and both she and Jeff Hampshire have been presidents of the Canadian Association of Nordic Ski Instructors.

Rhys Hatherly – 2010 Loppet

Ski Competitions

The thunder of an RCMP shotgun or the blast of Martha Owen's air horn as she perched atop a step ladder usually signalled the start to ski races hosted by the Club. Its first Canadian Ski Association sanctioned race was run in 1976. The first loppet or citizen's race was organized by Herb Rosinger in 1977. This race, now called the Manitoba Loppet, has been held annually and regularly attracts over a hundred competitors from Manitoba and Northwestern Ontario. The Club has hosted many provincial cross-country ski championships and in 1987 and 2010 hosted Canada Cup races and Western Canadian Championships for elite skiers. In 2006, it hosted the cross-country ski competitions for the Manitoba Winter Games. To more easily handle the registration and result tabulation Peter Chernis developed the Race Wizard software program that was used for a number of years for managing races in Manitoba. More recently Paul Chambers played a key role in Manitoba in implementing the Zone 4 race management and timing program to meet the higher precision standards. More recently, Carol Randall started Racers and Pacers in 2009. This is weekly evening program allows skiers to race against others or themselves on a short set course.

Now and the Future

The Whiteshell Ski Club is a volunteer organization. With the exception of a few youth grants and government assistance in the early days, all the trails have been cut and improved and their cabins built by volunteers. Each fall members remove deadfall and new saplings from the 45 km network of Club trails. After snow arrives, members operate and maintain the Club snowmobiles and equipment to pack and set ski tracks and to cut and haul firewood to the cabins. The Club executive and many volunteers organize and run the Loppet and other race events as well as instructional programs. To gain additional funds to upgrade Club equipment, volunteers work bingos at Winnipeg casinos, a task organized for many years by Marj and Heinz Ehlers. One early Club member, Henry Kuehl, was such an enthusiastic volunteer in fund raising, trail clearing and maintenance that the Club now recognizes an outstanding volunteer each year by awarding them the Henry Kuehl Memorial Trophy. In total, it is estimated that volunteers put in 3000 to 5000 hours each year to provide the excellent trails, facilities and events enjoyed by members, area residents, and skiers from further afield in Manitoba and elsewhere. The Whiteshell Ski Club has been a strong and vibrant part of the recreation scene in Manitoba for 40 years.

1980-81 Whiteshell Jackrabbits 1 Erica Greenstock; 2 Tammy Ohta; 3 Andrew Chambers; 4 David Mayman; 5 Peter Szekely; 6 Unknown; 7 Alaina Bridges; 8 Janet Bird; 9 Sowmil Mehta; 10 Graham Wright; 11 Jay Bridges; 12 Alison Ritchie; 13 Carol Schatzlein; 14 Karen Harrison; 15 Joseph Szekely; 16 Andrew Simpson; 17 Todd Bridges; 18 Sonali Bera; 19 Keri-Lyn Bailey; 20 Glenn Bailey; 21 Anna Chambers; 22 Helen Ritchie; 23 Unknown; 24 Jane Simpson; 25 Eva Rosinger; 26 Sandra Wright; 27 David Johnson; 28 Unknown; 29 Mike Quinn

Triathlon in Pinawa
By Don Ewing

The first "Gamma Man" Triathlons in Pinawa were two small gatherings of enthusiasts in 1986 and 1987. The success of these first events encouraged Ken Young, with the urging of David Markham and Brian Payne, to organize the first Free Spirit Triathlons in 1988 and 1989. David Markham then put on a series

of races called the Prairie Sun Triathlon from 1990 until 1994. Cameron Gray from Winnipeg organized the next series of races called the Raivo Tamm Triathlon in memory of Raivo who was a local resident and athlete.

When Cameron moved to Calgary, Don Ewing and Martha Laverock became the new race directors resurrecting the name Free Spirit Triathlon. It has remained so to this date. Clay McMurren ran the race in 2007 and Kyle Wilken has been the

race director since then.

Getting ready for the start

Our local group, Pinnacle Triathlon/Duathlon Club, was formed in 2001 for two major reasons. It gave us a vehicle to register and organize the Free Spirit Triathlon and it allowed us to put structure into our small group of enthusiasts. The first executive was made up of Don Ewing (President), Keith Olson (Vice-President) and Martha Laverock (Secretary/Treasurer). The Pinnacle Club has also run a Kids of Steel Triathlon on the same weekend as

the Free Spirit Triathlon. One of the goals of the club has always been to encourage Triathlon as both an individual and a family sport.

We have always had tremendous help from the people of Pinawa and the LGD. We would not have been able to continue year after year without the volunteers and their efforts before, during, and after the race. They have made the Free Spirit Triathlon one of the best organized races in the province.

Agniesika "Aggie" Gigiel - Free Spirit
Triathlon Pinawa August 25, 2013

Members of our group have had some success in the sport. Ken Young and Dave Locke both completed the Ironman Canada in Penticton BC. Don Ewing won his age group for both Manitoba and Canada. Don also was a member of the Canadian Triathlon team as an age group athlete in Cancun, Mexico and Perth, Australia. Martha Laverock won her Duathlon age group for Manitoba for two consecutive years, and was a member of the Canadian Duathlon Team which competed in France.

Don Ewing also became a level III official and worked as an official at several Canadian Championships, ITU races in Edmonton and also was a triathlon volunteer at the Athens Olympics.

Manitoba Provincial Summer Games – 1988
By Chris Saunders

The idea of Pinawa and Beausejour hosting the Manitoba Summer Games came from Marion Mitchell, Eastman's Sport Directorate Coordinator in 1986. Marion laid forth her vision to her ad hoc committee of what could be accomplished by a successful bid to host the games. The committee quickly determined that for Eastman to host the Games, Pinawa needed a partner community to ensure we had the facilities to house, feed and entertain 1800 athletes and coaches. Marion took her plan to Beausejour and the team of two communities, under the chairmanship of Archie Warren, took their plan to the provincial selection committee. In February, 1987, we were told that our bid was successful and the 1988 Manitoba Summer Games would be from August 16 to 21, 1988. Three key Pinawa residents acted as vice-chairman: Bob Jones, Bruce Stewart and Roger Smith. Don Roy was also on the original Steering committee. The Steering Committee was strongly supported by the local Councils led by Mayor Marvin Ryz (Pinawa) and Don Mazur (Beausejour). Pinawa was well represented in the eleven individual sports, with 65 athletes and coaches. Sheri Walton, Jennifer Miller, and Mark Sprungmann brought home medals in sailboarding. Lawrence Johnson medaled in tennis.

Viv Thomson designed the games logo.

Sports with Pinawa Participation	Pinawa Athletes
Sailboarding	Luke Sprungmann, Rick Voelpel, Sherri Walton, Lisa Walton, Jennifer Miller
Tennis	Lawrence Johnson, Vaughn Thibault, Paul Buchanan, Ron Fung, Alka Mehta, Jeanette LeBlanc, Harris Vikis, Anousch Mathew, Sandra Wright, Judy Tamm, Anne Lang, Marnie Melynk, Colin Dormuth, Sowmil Mehta, Kala Sridhar, Fariel Hosein
Golf	Heather Grant, Derek Honky, Iowna Meek, Ruth Dobbin, Des McCormac, Edna Graham, Margaret MacLean, Faye Campbell
Swimming	Frank Jacobs, Mark Hembroff, Kendra Cann, Dhenuka Tennankore, Steiner Cramer, Peter Stam, Corry Sterling, Sean Middleton, Jayson Abraham, Stewart Galay, Erin Bell, Lauren Corman, Beckie Plunkett, Kimberley Mills
Track and Field	Jonathan Delanney, Cindy Hembroff, Sean Corman, Lesley Zetaruk
Men's Soccer	Paul Ingham, Laurie Frost, Mike Kerr, Kevin Henschell, Fred Kuziarz, Marcello Chuaqui, Todd Meek, Bob Dixon, Paul Amos, Todd Hawton, Ryder McRitchie, Ian Dixon, Kevin Ticknor, Art Holloway, Kelly Snider, Jim McDowall, Steve Schankula, Dave Shoesmith

Pinawa Ballet Club
By Rachel Dutton-Gowryluk

Yvonne Oldaker opened the Pinawa Ballet Club in 1967 (September), with an enrollment of 25 girls who came to her for ballet lessons once a week. This grew to 80 kids twice a week by the time she left the community in 1980. Yvonne was an examiner for the Royal Academy of Dance so brought with her excellence in the technicality and artistic elements of ballet. She was assisted by Dawn Opie who kept the club organized and running smoothly – they would work together until Yvonne left the community. Ballet provided girls in the community, as young as 5 years of age (and a couple of boys); an artistic outlet and an opportunity to develop and perfect their ballet skills until they reached grade 12. For some, such as the notable Karen Unsworth and Alana Shewchuk, this dream would continue as they reached heights with the Winnipeg Contemporary Dancers. And Lara Peggs who continued later in life and accomplished a dancing career in San Francisco. We all had these dreams but most of us were content with just living the fantasy of "making it big" in the dance world. However these great dancers provided much inspiration to us all!

The club operated out of "the kitchen" (now converted space that occupies a small custodian office and to a large extent part of the library expansion) of the community centre where it was retro-fitted with full length mirrors on the south walls, hand rails along the west and south walls and wooden partitions blocking the windows that looked into the courtyard (as passers-by in the library were a distraction!). A piano was rolled into the kitchen and carefully positioned in one corner of the room where piano accompaniment was provided for each of the classes. Some of the pianists were Phyllis Gillespie, Heather Petkau and Val Kidson.

Pinawa Ballet Students

Yvonne ensured that the dancers set personal goals and many of us were given opportunities to challenge ourselves through the experiences of Royal Academy Exams. I remember the copious amounts of hairspray that were used minutes before our exams that was not limited to perfecting our "up-do's" but also securing the ribbons of our ballet slippers as we were not to be seen as unprofessional with wispy hair or uncontrollable ribbons! However, the lessons learned about how to manage stress and at the same time perform to the best of our abilities would prove beneficial as we journeyed down life's path.

With the serious came opportunities of fun in performing on stage that included dancing, acting, spotlights and curtain calls, as Yvonne directed and choreographed productions such as Snow White, Alice in Wonderland, Peter Pan, Cinderella and the herculean performance of the musical, Annie Get Your Gun, which I remember to be a true collaboration of community artistic extravaganza! As these productions consumed a lot of resources and time, Yvonne wisely sprinkled year-end ballet recitals between the biennial productions.

But when 1980 swung around, Yvonne and her family left Pinawa for the big city of Toronto. At that time the Pinawa Ballet Club continued through dance instructors from the Royal Winnipeg Ballet and Winnipeg Contemporary Dancers (Karen Unsworth, Debbie Delvechio). From 1987-1996, Susan Opie was the ballet instructor continuing the tradition of ballet classes in the "kitchen" of the high school until the library expanded around 1995 and the kitchen became smaller and no longer viable to hold ballet classes. At that time Susan moved the club to the W.B. Lewis School, which lasted a year until the regional health authority expanded their office space. So 1996 was the last year the club operated and then closed its doors.

Pinawa Figure Skating Club
By Holly Parcey

January 4, 1965, saw the start of yet another club in town, the Pinawa Figure Skating Club. Founding members were: President Mr. J. McLeod, Vice-President Mrs. H. Grant, Secretary Mrs. B. Carswell, Treasurer Mrs. T. Morecraft, Period Practice Convener Mrs. J. McLeod, and Assistant Convener Mrs. M. Mayman. The Club was created "to encourage the instruction, practice, enjoyment and advancement of its members in all aspect of figure skating in accordance with the rules and policies of the C.F.S.A." Forty-six children registered immediately. The first skating instructors were Margaret Carswell, Lynn McLeod and Wendy Ann Torresan. Mrs. Hawton was the instructor for the preschoolers. Mr. H. Carswell was the consultant instructor.

1974 Salute to the Sea Carnival

The first ice carnival, 'A Winter Wonderland', complete with spruce trees, park benches, outdoor lighting and taped music, was offered as community entertainment the evening of February 26, 1965. Sixty-three skaters displayed their skills, dressed as clowns, nursery-land and toy-land characters, skating through winter snow scenes and park settings.

In 1966, the ice carnival scheduled for March was cancelled due to the worst winter storm since 1902. Thirty-five cm of snow with 120 km/h winds proved too difficult for even the most die-hard skaters or dedicated parents.

The skating club was referred to as the Pinawa Figure Skating Club and the Whiteshell Figure Skating through the 1960s, but officially became the Pinawa Figure Skating Club in the early 1970s. The Club was well established with over a hundred figure skaters receiving lessons from amateur Club instructors and professional instructors.

The Club's success was reflected in the review published by the regional paper, The Beaver, March 19, 1974, for the ice carnival "Salute to the Sea":

Large crowd enjoys figure skating carnival at Pinawa on Saturday evening

One hundred and ten members of the Pinawa Figure Skating Club took to the high seas Saturday evening and 725 passengers were carried off at the most successful carnival ever staged in that community. On the horizon was a genuine sail boat with billowing sails. Silver gulls soared in the 'breeze' and hundreds of yards of waves lapped at the sides of the frozen sea. All members of the crew (from the tiniest starfish to the biggest octopus), put on a good performance. Parents and members of the teen centre set the stage for the carnival with 97 feet of decorative waves, 40 sea animals, 6 seagulls with 4 foot wing spans, fishnet back drops, yellow submarine, giant pearly shell, treasure chest, two oversized lily pads and full size sailboat.

1997 Regionals Team: Front – Janice Ikeda, Kristin Ikeda, Senem Ates, Sheena Turner, Sunita Mulpuru; Back – Jason Kaczanowski, Sujin Wren, Sumi Wren, Sara Coleman

The Club registered close to 150 figure skaters each year through the 1970s and 80s. The Pinawa Figure Skating Club provided opportunities for skill development for the children of Pinawa thanks to those who imagined early on what could be and those who supported the Club until it packed away its skates and costumes 40 years later.

Pinawa Gymnastics Club
By Wendy Gibson

In the fall of 1973, the Recreation Department offered an Olympic Gymnastics program under the leadership of Judy Tamm. Classes were held in the auditorium of the Community Centre. On April 4, 1974, a "Gymnastics Display" was offered to the public. These 'Year One' gymnasts were JoAnne Williams, Kelly Howe, Shari Hart, Jeanine Cadoreth, Z'anne Peterson, Dianne Parent, Maureen Krupka, Cathy Smee, Shannon Lidfors, Sue Jeffries, Dianne Cadoreth, Cheryl Lidfors, Barb Sawatzky, Marg Kroeger, Terry Reimer, and Alain Parent.

The 'Pinawa Gymnastics Club' name was used in 1975 for the first time. Hal Peterson, Helen Tomlinson, Eleanor Dean, Bob Hart, and Dale Lidfors formed the first executive. Activities were expanding and with

an interest free loan from Bob Hart (ref. H. Tomlinson), uneven parallel bars were acquired in November 1976. The newly formed club had thirty-eight gymnasts.

The 1976 program was now under the direction of Valerie Tammemagi. New floor mats were purchased under an equal cost sharing agreement between the Club, the Rec Department, and the School Division.

In 1979, horizontal parallel bars (complete with fitted mats) and a high bar were added with the financial help of the Manitoba Gymnastics Association. Don Ewing volunteered to coach the Clubs first group of boys. Don continued coaching through 1983. The club was growing and many of the older gymnasts became assistant coaches (Lisa Zerbin for example made a significant contribution during this time), with parents continuing as spotters.

JoAnne Williams, Sheryl Meek, Jo-Anne Kelly, Kerri Bailey, Kelly Howe, and Coach Judy Tamm - Gymnastics Demonstration. (1976)

Records (and memories) are rare for most of the 1980s. In 1988, five gymnasts represented Pinawa at the Eastman Regional competition. These were Heather Butterworth, Jeannette LeBlanc, Dhenuka Tennankore, Brandi Smith, and Andrea Greenstock. They were supported by student coaches Nicole Roy and Karen Harrison. Some of the volunteers who helped drive the club at this time were Barb Sabanski, Barb Andres, Noreen LeBlanc, Rich Hamon, Frank Walton, Lyn Ewing, and Ruth Harrison.

David Mayman went on to join competitive gymnastics teams in Winnipeg and Ottawa, as well as at the University of Western Ontario and Queen's University after getting his start with the Pinawa club in 1978. David Mayman also coached gymnastics at the University of Western Ontario. Michelle and Brandi Smith went on to become coaches for competitive clubs in Winnipeg during their university years. Travis Law joined the Club in 1990, and by March of 1992 at the age of ten, Travis was invited to enter the Men's Closed Gymnastic Competition where he won

Stacey Smith, Amy Smith, Maureen Perzan, Sarah Gibson show their results from the Eastman Winter Games in Ste. Anne (1994)

bronze and silver and placed 8th overall. He was the youngest competitor at the competition. Based on these results, Travis was chosen to be a part of the training squad for the 1995 Canada Winter Games as well as for the Manitoba Provincial Team. In March 1995, Travis won the trophy for 1st All Around in the

Manitoba Open with four silver medals and two gold medals. He also participated in the Western Canadian competition in April and the National competition in May.

Through the 1990s, the club was thriving. There was an average membership of forty gymnasts. The club had an active Board and numerous coaches and always had a supply of upcoming student coaches. Pinawa hosted many competitions, coaching clinics, spotting clinics and sports days. This included hosting the Eastman Regional Winter Games in 1995. Important volunteer personnel during these active times were Trudy Dueck, Rob Smith, Wendy Gibson, Florence Vilks, Peter Vilks, Maureen Bychuk, and Rudy Klassen.

Through 2000-2005, the interest in gymnastics began to drop off. By 2007 the Club had only seven members. The Board made the painful decision to shut down the Club and sell the equipment. The funds from the sale paid the final bills and left $5,000 that was donated to the Pinawa Foundation to be used for the support sport in our community. This description necessarily omits many, many people who must have helped form, operate, and support what became the Pinawa Gymnastics Club through thirty-four years. We have included names here not because they were most important, but because they are the ones preserved in the available records. We wish to sincerely acknowledge everyone who contributed effort to the sport of gymnastics in Pinawa.

Pinawa Rhythmettes
By Barb Zerbin

Rhythmic gymnastics is a sport that combines elements of ballet, gymnastics and dance movements. Individuals use pieces of apparatus such as the ball, ribbon, rope, hoop, scarf, and club. Free style uses no apparatus. The Pinawa Rhythmettes had its beginnings in the early 1970s after Mrs. Judy Tamm moved to Pinawa in 1973. She convinced the recreation director, Mrs. Kathy Woodbeck, to let her start a ladies exercise group and later a rhythmic gymnastics class for girls and an artistic gymnastic class for boys and girls.

The ladies exercise group was formed and with Judy's background in rhythmic gymnastics as a guide, the women were soon learning basic rhythmic skills. Chris Shoesmith and Barbara Strathdee soon agreed to take training and join in the coaching. The ladies learned a ribbon routine which they performed for the opening ceremonies when Pinawa hosted the Eastman Summer Games in 1976. Some of the performers were Barb Strathdee, Chris Shoesmith, Eva Rosinger, Val Tammemagi, Fiona Wright, Joyce Hampton and Joan Lidfors, to name a few. When older teen aged girls joined the group, a division between the exercise and gymnastic group was the beginning of the Pinawa Rhythmic Gymnastics Association.

1980 Rhythmic Gymnastics Team: Front Row-Judy Tamm, Barb Strathdee, Alanna Hawkes, Sheryl Ramsay, Shannon Swiddle, Elisabeth Aitken, Alanna Reykdal; Back Row-Maureen Krupka, Judy Hart, Jayann Hawton, Elinor Aitken, Alanna Lidfors, Shelley Ramsay

The girls worked very hard for their coaches and parent helpers, who also acted as club executive, equipment managers, music co-ordinators, and chauffeurs. They practised twice a week and performed many times in a number of events in Winnipeg. The group also toured Western Manitoba where they performed in high schools and gave clinics to the students. In 1977 the group attended the Manitoba Provincial Gymnastrada for the first time and attended annually for many years. A highlight for the club was travelling to Montreal for Canada's first National Gymnastrada in 1980. Eleven of the elite group of girls, Elinor and Elisabeth Aitkens, JayAnn Hawton,

Maureen Krupka, Sharon Swiddle, Shelley and Sheryl Ramsay, Alanna Reykdal, Alanna Hawkes, and Alanna Lidfors were accompanied by their coaches Judy Tamm and Barb Strathdee. The girls learned a routine which they performed with gymnasts from across the country in Montreal's Olympic Stadium. The display team represented Manitoba at the annual Manitoba Gymnastrada held in Winnipeg each year and at the nationals in Toronto in 1985. When Barb Strathdee moved, Joyce Hampton joined the coaching team. The name Pinawa Rhythmettes was adopted in the 1980 season and the club colours of black, red and yellow emerged in 1982.

While the Rhythmettes originated with teen aged girls, the club soon included girls as young as six. In 1983 at the 7th Annual Provincial Gymnastrada, the Pinawa Rhythmettes were represented by Alanna Hawkes, Alanna Lidfors, Nicole McAuley, Eileen McKay, Kim Molinski, Lynn Molinski, Tara Rummery, Muffy Snider, Leanne Snider, Liane Steinleitner, Shannon Swiddle, Tracey Turner, Carmen Turner, Karla Wikjord and Michelle Zerbin. The number grew to about 50 members in the later years. There were two displays a year for Pinawa - the first at Christmas for the benefit of parents. At the windup each April the club hosted a display for the benefit of the whole town and always received a great deal of support from parents and townspeople.

In 1982, Judy Tamm retired from coaching and Chris Shoesmith carried on for a number of years with the help of junior and senior coaches who had come up through the system. Alanna Lidfors was a senior coach until she graduated in 1985. The club suffered because of moves and retirements. Alanna returned to Pinawa and coached through the 90s, but after the senior girls graduated in 2000, the club soon disbanded and the equipment was given to the Rhythmic Gymnastics Association in Winnipeg.

Scouting and Guiding
By Barb Sanipelli

Scouting began in 1907 when Lt. Gen. Robert Baden-Powell took a group of youth to a camp on Brownsea Island in the United Kingdom. The Canadian General Council of the Boy Scout Association was incorporated by an act of the Canadian Parliament on June 12, 1914. Today, Scouts Canada is a highly diverse organization with over 100,000 members nationwide representing every faith and culture. Scouts Canada offers programming in more than 19 languages reflecting Canada's multicultural landscape and communities.

In 1909 Lord Robert Baden-Powell, the founder of Scouting, when faced with an increasing number of girls wishing to take part in Scouting, decided that girls should have their own separate movement, and the Girl Guides were founded in the United Kingdom in 1910. Many, though by no means all, Girl Guide and Girl Scout groups across the globe trace their roots to this point. Agnes Baden-Powell, the Baron's sister, was in charge of Girl Guiding in UK in its early years. Other influential people were Juliette Gordon Low, founder of the Girl Scouts of the USA, Olga Drahonowska-Małkowska in Poland and Antoinette Butte in France. The name "Guides" was taken from a famous frontier regiment in the British Indian army, the Corps of Guides, which was noted for its skills in tracking and survival.

Barb Sanipelli

The Pinawa Boy Scout Troop was formed September 1963, with a registered membership of nine boys and three leaders. Bruce Smith and David Robertson were patrol leaders of the Otter and Bear Patrols respectively. Mr. R. Woods, Mr. G. Hyman and Mr. W.D.C Fitzsimmons were the adult leaders of the Troop. The 1st Pinawa Wolf Cub Pack was also formed in the fall of 1963 with 10 boys. Cub leaders were: Akela - Tom Lamb; Bagheera - David Robertson; Balso – Marion Lamb. In just one year, membership rose to 35 Cubs. The local pack even had a waiting list of boys.

The 1st Pinawa Girl Guide Company was formed on October 17, 1963. At this time we had three girls who had been enrolled as guides shortly before coming to Pinawa, the rest were new to the guide movement.

Three days later we joined with the Brownies, Scouts and Cubs, and had a marvellous and tiring time washing Manitoba gumbo off Pinawa cars. We made lots of money and for one whole day we could tell the colour of our neighbors' cars.

Pinawa's Wolf Cub Pack – mid 60s

The Guiding movement, including Pinawa, has many universal themes:

The Guide Promise – Girls become Guides by making their Promise. The Promise has three parts: duty to God or to your religion, duty to your country and keeping the Guide Law.

The Good Turn – Each Guide tries to do a kind thing for someone else, without payment and without being asked, every day.

The World Badge – This can be worn on a uniform or ordinary clothes. The three leaves of the trefoil stand for the threefold Promise. The vein in the centre is a compass needle, pointing the way and the two stars stand for the Promise and the Law. The colours stand for the golden sun shining over all the children of the world, from a blue sky. This badge is a guiding symbol that can be recognized all over the world.

The World Flag – This is in the same colours as the World Badge and can be carried or flown by any member of the movement. It is often used as the Unit Flag. The three yellow blocks represent the threefold Promise and the white corner represents the commitment to peace.

Girl Guides and Brownies in the 50th Parade in 2013

The Guide Sign – The three fingers stand for the three parts of the Promise. The Guide sign is used when making or renewing the Promise and can be used when meeting other Guides. It may also be used when receiving a badge or at the end of meetings.

The Motto – "Be Prepared" – This means that Guides are ready to cope with anything that might come their way.

The left handshake – This is the way members of the Movement greet each other. The left hand is the one nearest the heart, so symbolizing friendship. Additionally, warriors held their shield in the left hand, so putting down your shield means that you are vulnerable, making it a display of both bravery and trust.

Thinking Day – On 22 February each year, Guides think of their Guide sisters all around the world. The date was chosen at a World Conference because it was the birthday of both the Founder and the World Chief Guide.

The World Centres – There are five World Centres in different parts of the world: Our Chalet in Switzerland; Pax Lodge in London; Our Cabana in Mexico; Sangam in India; and Kusafiri in Africa.

The World Chief Guide – Lady Baden-Powell is the only person ever to have been World Chief Guide. She was the wife of the Founder, Lord Baden-Powell of Gilwell, and lived from 1889 to 1977.

Two central themes have been present from the earliest days of the movement: domestic skills and "a kind of practical feminism which embodies physical fitness, survival skills, camping, citizenship training, and career preparation".

Hundreds of Pinawa girls and boys have participated in the Guides and Scout Movements since 1963. Some of the highlights over the years have included:

On January 16th, 1964, parents and friends participated in Pinawa's first enrollment ceremony for both Guides and Brownies. Miss Hoskin, Provincial Administrative Secretary for guiding in Manitoba enrolled five new guides and presented the Company with its Certificate of Registration. The first leaders to work with the Pinawa Brownies included Fran Dalby, Isabel Acres, Arlene Boivin, Marg McLean, Marg Baker, and Juanita Williams. For the Guides, the first leaders included Jane Petkau, Darlene Archinuk and Judy Coleman.

Around 1967, Helen Olchowy, Maureen Lyon and Lynn Stevens, with the help of Guide Leader Sue Morgan, started another Brownie troop at the Lewis School. An early memory was the detailed exams the troop leaders had to take to allow them the take the girls camping. No Brownie camping outside houses or cottages was allowed until the Lewis School Brownies pioneered it.

Camping became an important part of the Pinawa Brownie history. Their first trip was to a farm outside Beausejour. The girls, their leaders, and parent helpers, including Marg Reimer and Marilyn Cadoreth, slept in a granary. The second camping trip was the spring of 1968, when the troop stayed in tents at a farm across the river from the AECL plant site. This trip was memorable because of the snow. Imagine as many as 20 Brownies in snow-covered tents. Other camping adventures over the years included trips to Caddy Lake and Falcon Lake.

Another fond memory from the Lewis School Brownies was in 1969 when they won the Thompson Toadstool Award for their toy making skills. This provincial competition had Brownie troops demonstrating both their artistic and practical skills. The Brownies were also proud that the toys were donated to kids with developmental disabilities and autism at the St. Amant Centre.

In March 1972, the Boy Scout Stampede was held in Pinawa, including the Manitoba Chuckwagon Championship.

In the spring of 1972, Pinawa Scouts won the top awards at the North Dakota Scout Expositions.

Members of Pinawa Girl Guides and Pinawa Scouts carried the flags at the 2007 Remembrance Day Ceremony.

Kirsten Ramsay, of Pinawa, has had a variety of roles within the Girl Guides of Canada, including as a Vice Chair of the Western Hemisphere Committee of the World Association of Girl Guides and Girl Scouts (WAGGGS). Kirsten is currently a member of the Nominating Committee of WAGGGS. Kirsten also worked at Two World Centres: Our Cabana and Pax Lodge.

The annual cookie sale is a highlight for Pinawa residents. Girls still blitz the town, twice a year, in April and October, knocking on every door to sell their cookies. Pinawa residents are very loyal to their cookie sellers. Recently, a leader from another town recited an incident where one of her Guides approached a couple in a shopping mall to sell them cookies. The couple informed her that they could not buy from her, because they lived in Pinawa, and they had to buy their cookies only from the Pinawa girls!

Pinawa had 3 Brownie packs and 3 Guide companies for many years, when there was a large population of school-age children in Pinawa. Over the years, Guiding added new age-groups to the Guiding Structure. In 1979, Pathfinders were added (girls ages 12-14). Pinawa immediately started up a Pathfinder unit, with 12 girls joining in the first year.

In 1988, Pinawa's 25th anniversary, our Guiding units each had a float in the Birthday parade. At the end of those floats, a Guide pulled a wooden wagon with two five-year-old girls in it. On the side of the wagon was a sign, "Five-Year-Old Program". This was the beginning of Sparks (age 5) in Pinawa. Nine girls joined the group in 1988.

We currently have five units in Pinawa: Sparks (ages 5-6); Brownies (ages 7-8); Guides (ages 9-11); Pathfinders (ages 12-14); and Rangers (ages 15-17).

Brownie troop making flags

Prior to 1979, the Guides spent a week every summer camping at Camp Alloway, the Scout camp situated on Big Whiteshell Lake. Starting in 1980, groups switched to having two weekend camps each year, in the spring and fall, usually camping in Whiteshell Provincial Park or at other local camping areas.

The Pinawa Parent Group Committee is the sponsor for Scout groups in Pinawa, and a fundraising body for both Guiding and Scouting. The idea was to free the leaders up from fundraising chores in order to give them more time and energy to run their units. Parent Group organized bottle drives twice a year to raise funds for camping equipment, leader uniforms, training fees and leaders' membership fees. This group also gives a donation to Scout or Guide members attending special international events. After bottle drives were no longer viable, Parent Group started delivering phone books twice a year. This continued until 2015. They also raised funds with many other campaigns over the years. Parent Group still continues to supply camping equipment for the Guiding groups (there have been no open Scouting units since 2008), but due to falling numbers of school-age children in Pinawa, it has been impossible to find parents willing to help with Parent Group. One parent and one Guide leader now run Parent Group and take care of the equipment.

Parent Group organized "Baden-Powell Night" every year during Guide-Scout Week, around February 22 (Thinking Day). This was a night for all the Guiding and Scouting groups to get together to celebrate our joint history and pay our respects to the Founder, Baden-Powell. Some years this was a more formal ceremony, with each group parading in with our unit flag, and all the parents invited to attend. Other years it was a "fun" night, with a round-robin of international games and a campfire. Regardless, we always ended the evening with birthday cake (for Lord and Lady BP) and juice.

Pinawa Guiding and Scouting (both children and adult leaders) have had a proud heritage of attending numerous camp and events organized at the local, district, area, provincial, national and international levels. Scouts attended Jamborees across the country, as well as Service Area 6 camps held throughout Eastman and the Interlake. Guiding units, in addition to camping with their unit at least once a year, have sent girls and Guiders to district, area, provincially and nationally organized long-term camps (4-12 nights).

Area long-term camps attended:

1995: Looking Outward (Turtle Mountain Provincial Park)
1998: Holiday Magic (Spruce Woods Provincial Park)
2005: Our Native Land (Falcon Lake)
2008: Beyond the Horizon (Caddy Lake Girl Guide Camp)
2012: Under the Sea (Caddy Lake Girl Guide Camp)

Provincially-sponsored camps attended:

1989: Pack and Paddle ((Caddy Lake Girl Guide Camp and Rushing River, ON) International Event
1991: Camp Kiche Manitou (Spruce Woods Provincial Park) International Event
1992: I Survived (Caddy Lake Girl Guide Camp) National event (Guider Training Camp)
1997: Under the Open Sky (Caddy Lake Girl Guide Camp) International Event
2002: Packs, Paddles and Pals (Caddy Lake Girl Guide Camp) International Event
2009: Keystone Quest (Caddy Lake Girl Guide Camp) International Event

Nationally-sponsored events:

1988: Echo Valley (Qu'appelle, SK) International Event
1996: Camp Blomidon (Blomidon Provincial Park, NS) in conjunction with the World Conference of WAGGGS
1999: Canadian Mosaic (St Malo, MB and Yukon) International Event
2006: Guiding Mosaic (Guelph) International Event
2010: Guiding Mosaic (Guelph) International Event

Girls and Guiders have also attended events sponsored by other provinces in BC, Alberta, Saskatchewan, Ontario, Quebec and New Brunswick, and attended International events in other countries including Netherland Antilles, Jamaica, Mexico, England, Belize and Switzerland.

In many of these events, Pinawa Guiders were involved in the planning and running of these events. Our Guiders have held numerous positions at district, area and provincial levels, and also have been assigned to National Task Forces.

Our units have helped with many local service projects over the years including highway clean-up (ongoing), White Gift Sunday (sorting, wrapping, making doll clothes), Pinawa Triathlon, Manitoba Loppet (aid stations), Health Auxiliary booth at the beach during Birthday celebrations, Relay for Life (putting out luminaries), and delivering door-to-door for various groups like Two Rivers Seniors Services.

Pinawa girls and Guiders have had a long involvement with Caddy Lake Girl Guide Camp. Many of our girls attended the camp during the regular summer session, and then went on to become staff members for several years. Pinawa units frequently use the camp in June to hold their spring camps. Many lasting friendships have been made at Caddy over the years with girls and Guiders from other parts of the province, and across the country.

For over 15 years, Rick Backer has allowed the Guiding units to use Pioneer Bay Campground for their annual Bike Hike and Wiener Roast. All the girls gather at W.B. Lewis Business Centre, and then ride their bikes to the campground. Rick provides us with the wood, and the Guides start one or two fires, then everyone roasts wieners and smokies over the fire, with s'mores for dessert. The girls play on the play structure, take part in various nature observation activities, perform skits and sing songs, before returning to town on their bikes. A great time is had by all!

Pinawa Square Dancers
By Pat Ramsay

Howard and Gail Gilmour introduced square dancing to Pinawa in 1965. The first square dance club was called the "Up 'n' Atoms". Their patient and enthusiastic instruction started the small group dancing in a classroom at Gilbert School, later moving to the newly-built Lewis School auditorium. The club badge featured a gold square dance couple inside a nuclear atom symbol. Around 1966/67, Phil and Marilyn Roy joined the club and, within a short time, were calling for the beginner square dancers. Phil provided excellent calling and instruction.

In March of 1968, the Up 'N Atoms hosted a large Square Dance Jamboree with over 20 squares of dancers coming from out of town for the weekend. This was a huge undertaking in those days considering the facilities available. Gail was an exceptional organizer, and everything came together remarkably well. There was no accommodation in town, so Pinawa dancers billeted people for the weekend and provided all the meals. The three-day program started with a dance Friday evening, a tour of the Whiteshell Laboratories Saturday morning, followed by a dance workshop in the afternoon. The supper dance, "Foolish Frolic", was a memorable night with Joe Johanson from Winnipeg doing the calling. The weekend concluded with a pancake breakfast Sunday morning. It was an exciting event for our small town and is remembered by many.

As well as our weekly dances, the Up 'N Atoms enjoyed hilarious Halloween dances, family Christmas parties, and family camping trips. Fun was the top priority, and everyone still talks about getting Howard and Gail out of bed one night to come out and call a square dance. Earning silly "badges" was fun, and some of the badges earned were the "Sand Flee" badge for dancing in the sand at the beach and the "Idiot's" badge for one whole square (eight people) that danced in a very small bathroom. One favorite memory was being invited to dance in the Pinawa Jail thus earning our "Jailbird" badge. We also hosted another large Jamboree in Pinawa which was a huge success. In the early 1970s, many in the club went to an International Jamboree held in the Marlborough Hotel in Winnipeg. The club was very fortunate to have such an enthusiastic couple as Gail and Howard who introduced us to such a fun recreation.

March 1968 - Back row: Phil Roy, Lorne Swanson, Gordon Murray, Al Reich, Lloyd Sterling, Ky Kubota, Ted Deering, Grant Bailey, Rosemary Ralph, Mike Ralph, Norm Roy, Gord Murray; 3rd row: Bev Banks, Marilyn Roy, Agnes Swanson, Grace Murray, Ethel Reich, Lois Sterling, Fran Kubota, Laraine Deering, Bonnie Bailey, Barrie Banks, Larry Ramsay, Pat Ramsay, June Roy, Gayle Murray, Joanne Hawton; 2nd row: Jim Harding, Shirley Harding, Ad Zerbin, Barb Zerbin, Elizabeth Turner, Dave Turner, Gail Schatzlein, Erwin Schatzlein, Gail Gilmour, Jay Hawton; Front row: Jack Remington, Barb Remington, Garry Buchanan, Faye Buchanan, Penny Faye, Ken Faye, and Howard Gilmour

In the fall of 1970 or 71, another club was formed with Phil Roy calling and they called their club the Whiteshell Whirlers. Both clubs continued to be active through the 1970s when the Pinawa Up 'N Atoms folded with Howard Gilmour becoming very busy as Mayor of Pinawa. Phil and Marilyn Roy moved away and Norm Sagert, who had been going to both clubs, took over calling for the Whiteshell Whirlers. He did this for a few years and in the early 1980s moved to Winnipeg.

On March 5, 1997 a group from the original clubs, Up 'N Atoms and Whiteshell Whirlers, started up. Dancers that night were: Viola and Jim Mark, Barb and Jack Remington, Dianna and Derri Evans, Barb and Ad Zerbin, Agnes and Lorne Swanson, Gail and Howard Gilmour, Sue and Lloyd Rattai, Chris Shoesmith, Ethel Hunter, Harriet Guibache, Betty and Alf Chester, and Joan and Dale Lidfors. They again called themselves Whiteshell Whirlers.

The group was fortunate to find caller Lorraine Lutz from Winnipeg who was willing to come to Pinawa. Lorraine and husband Ernie drove out every week and the club enjoyed their leadership for several years. We danced every Wednesday at the Lutheran Church from 7 to 9 p.m. followed by coffee, snacks and a visit. Square dancing is a great activity, providing a good physical and mental workout as well as many laughs and good memories.

Whiteshell Toastmasters Club 1980-2003
By Mike Luke

In March 1980, Bill Morgan approached Don Gregg for help start a Toastmasters club at Whiteshell Nuclear Research Establishment. They approached potential members and held demonstration Toastmaster meetings. The Whiteshell Toastmasters Club was established in March 1980. Within a few weeks, 20 members, the minimum required to charter a new club, had joined and the Club applied for its charter on June 20, 1980. The official charter was presented to the Club on Dec. 10, 1980. Joseph Szekely remembers it as a time of great excitement and tension.

Throughout its history the Club has usually held its meetings at lunchtime in the Public Affairs Theatre/Conference Room in Building 401 at Whiteshell Laboratories. The format for regular meetings consisted of a ten minute business session, table topics, prepared speeches and evaluations, reports by the timer, grammarian, parliamentarian and ah counter, and, finally, a general evaluation of the meeting. The goal was to do all this within one hour. The Pinawa Evening Group was started by Alan Gibson in October 1983 but lasted only a year.

Some Club members have enjoyed testing their speech making against those of Toastmasters from other Clubs by entering speech contests. Among the first of these was Tjalle Vandergraaf who represented the Club at the Area contest in 1983 with a speech entitled "Ghosts of Prosperity Past" while Rogan Watson spoke on "Lies, Damn Lies and Statistics" at the Area contest in 1984. Calvin Chan has represented the Club well at many speech contests. In 1988 he won the Club, Area, and Division Humorous Speech Contests with his speech "No Job is Too Big". In 2003 he again reached the Division Level with a speech about one of his beloved Volkswagens. In 1992, his speech on "Travel in China" again won the Club, Area, and Division Humorous Speech Contests and came third at the District level. Other members who have competed at the area level include Joe Szekely, Dennis Cann, Heidi McIlwain and David Bray. Lloyd Penner and Nithy Nitheanandan won the Area Junior Speech Contest in 1999 and 2000 respectively.

Words were introduced by the Wordmaster or

Receiving the Club Charter, Dec. 10, 1980- Standing: Ethel Hansen (Sherman), Mike Luke, Joe Szekely, Jack Gillespie - District 64 Vice-President, Patrick O'Connor, Alan Gibson, Bernie Bjornson, Al Lane, Joe Frechette - District 64, Alex Ramsay. Sitting: Alf Wikjord, Gus Powaschuk, Gladys Gibson, Don Greig

Grammarian at the start of each meeting to help Toastmasters expand their vocabularies. Rogan Watson introduced this feature to meetings in 1985 and using the "Word of the Day" has been a regular part of the meetings since then. Ah Counters and Timers are other jobs that have been performed at every meeting since the Club began. More memorable Ah-Counter reports over the years include those of Deb Brown and Janet Losel Sitar. These members excelled at accurately numbering the uttered "ums", "ahs" and "ers" and "non-dramatic" pauses and their reports were very helpful to speakers.

The Goblet, the Club newsletter was started and first sent to members in April 1983. The editor, Rogan Watson, chose as its name a drinking cup, a necessity for a toast. The Goblet was published on a regular basis until September 1994 when a reduced Club size and the advantages of e-mail for distributing schedules and other information made it no longer necessary.

Members of the Whiteshell Toastmasters Club June 2003. Back Row: Myles Drynan, Bellamy Bakosti, Laverne Wojciechowski, Heidi McIlwain, Janet Loesel Sitar, Calvin Chan, Tom Town, Dennis Cann. Seated: Mulugeta Serzu and Keith Reid

An early meeting that still brings smiles to many of the early Toastmasters was the special debate meeting on the motion that the capital of Manitoba be moved to Pukatawagan. Alf Wikjord, a native of that village, and Gwen Greenstock were to speak in favour of the motion while Barrie Banks and Joe Szekely were to argue the negative. Barrie liked to wing everything. Joe gave up planning and, out of desperation, decided to be silly and make use of his debate time to give a humorous talk against the motion. Barrie picked up on it and as the last speaker used his rebuttal time to tell a joke that brought down the house and carried their team to victory, all without making any debating points, somewhat to the chagrin of the other team.

Pinawa Friendship Block Quilters
By Linda Huisman, Ann Oravec and Marilyn Berry

Eleanor MacMillan began teaching quilting classes in the early 1990s. The quilting group was formed in 1993. Some of the original members included: Marilyn Berry, Ann Oravec, Pam Haugen, Lori Graham, Myrna Suski, Sandy Demoline, Brenda Morash, Cathy Harding, Debbie Smith, Marg Wikjord, Glenna Zetaruk and Emily Wooster. Eleanor taught hand quilting, graphing patterns for blocks and making your own templates. The guild worked out of homes and basements, schools, churches and local businesses.

In 2005 Teresa Frey worked with Marilyn Berry teaching the guild members different blocks or patterns each month. Marilyn ran the guild for five years up until the spring of 2009 when she handed the reins over to Linda Huisman. Linda remains President of the Guild. The Guild meets Tuesday evenings from September through May.

Seated – Lori Graham, Marilyn Berry; Standing - Sandy Demoline, Ann Oravec, Eleanor McMillan, Emily Wooster, Glenna Zetaruk, Judy Chernis

Major accomplishments over the years for the Guild include:

Early members made our "Welcome" wall hanging.

2006 - Individual members sewed lap quilts for the Pinawa Cancer Care ward.

2007 - Guild completed a raffle quilt for the Pinawa Health Auxiliary.

2006-2010 Guild invited guests or members to teach classes, including Adienna Boschman (Oma's Quilt Shop), Marilyn Berry, Gertie Wilton, Linda Nickel, and Teresa Frey.

2009/2010 – Members made 30 baby charity quilts, using donated fabric. Fourteen quilts were given to the Women's Center at the Health Science Centre and the rest were divided between the two women's shelters for Eastern Manitoba.

In September 2009, Linda Huisman created "Quilter's Corner", available on-line as part of the monthly Pinawa Life Newsletter.

On Sept. 22nd 2009, the guild held their first yearly Fall Tea – an open house event to share their quilting endeavors with family, friends and neighbors.

In July 2010 the guild joined the Pinawa Birthday Parade and rolled their quilting rack down Burrows. The walkers remember the fast pace they held to keep abreast of the horses coming up behind them!

2010/2011 - Members made 13 baby quilts and 8 receiving blankets for Villa Rosa in Winnipeg. Several members also donated baby quilts for the Christmas hampers. In May 2011 members held a spring tea and invited the public to see their 3rd

Glenys Perry, June Roberts, Elaine Strandlund, Ann Oravec, and Leslie Strandlund

"Mystery Quilt" challenge – quilts made from a variety of floral and insect fabric.

2011/2012 – Members made 27 baby and large quilts and 5 receiving blankets, divided up for: Nova House, Agape House and Villa Rosa. Members completed 15 "Touch Quilts" for the Alzheimer's Society, which were presented to Kin Place in Oakbank. This was the 6th year that several guild members joined up with ladies from the Whiteshell to sew lined fleece mitts for Siloam Mission (92 pairs Oct. 2012)

The guild presently has 24 members, who continue with community service work, teaching and sharing ideas. We're working on our 4th Mystery challenge in blue batiks. Once a month members design lessons for Teaching Tuesday. One Saturday a month is booked for "UFO's" or "unfinished objects", where members get together to work on projects, have pot-luck lunches and enjoy a day of quilting.

Pinawa Recycling
By Derri Evans

Pinawa Recycling Inc. was established in early 1989 as a non-profit, fully volunteer organization in response to concerns over environmental issues. It has grown from a "back of a pick-up truck" operation to one that occupies two buildings that processes tons of recyclable material. Pinawa Recycling is the story of many a volunteer's persistence, sacrifice, skill and dedication combined with the support and cooperation of the people and the employees of the Local Government District of Pinawa.

Pinawa Recycling – 1992-1998

Alice Chambers, Sharon Taylor, Steve Ryan and Anne Knight comprised the start-up committee, joined later by Morgan Brown. The first receiving depot consisted of an area of the Pinawa Mall parking lot. Once a month, Mike Quinn's pick-up truck made the trip to Manitoba Soft Drink Recycling in Winnipeg.

Pinawa Recycling was incorporated in 1991 on the advice of Anne Knight, Treasurer, and Morgan Brown, President from 1991 to 1992. Alice Chambers assumed the President/Secretary positions in late 1992 and Cyril Clarke took on the Treasurer/Materials jobs.

In 1996, Pinawa Recycling began shipping fiber materials to Environmental Options in Lac du Bonnet. Newspapers, magazines, catalogues and magazine-quality flyers were tied into bundles and sent to Lac du Bonnet for compacting into 600 to 700 kg bales, destined for the paper mill in Pine Falls. The summer of 1998 saw a new building completed, mostly by volunteer labour. The 1999 Pinawa Recycling crew consisted of Mike Duclos, Cyril Clarke, Steve Ryan, Wayne McLeod, Nat Fenton, Al and Shirley Nelson, Dan Butler, Derri Evans, John Gmiterek and Herb Brown. Operational streamlining and technological modernization have taken several paths over the years.

New Pinawa Recycling Depot – 2002

Giving Back to the Community

With the major capital expenditures completed, Pinawa Recycling began "recycling" part of its revenues back to the community in 2000. The depot donated $5,200 in October 2000 to the Pinawa Hospital. Pinawa Recycling purchased benches for the Ironwood Trail along the Winnipeg River. In keeping with its mission, the benches were constructed from recycled mixed plastics. Two benches were dedicated to the memory of Alice Chambers. Charitable groups began working at the depot in November 2000 to raise money for their organizations. This was also an extra source of funding for some extracurricular activities at Pinawa Secondary School. Since 1995, grants from the Manitoba Green Team allowed us to support one or two Pinawa Secondary School students planning on post-secondary training.

On to the Future

In April 2002, Pinawa Recycling ceased to be a volunteer-run venture. The LGD took over the administration of the depot and assigned one of their employees to the recycling depot full time. This took a lot of pressure off the volunteers. The future of the recycling business depends on a number of variables, not the least of which are labour and money. One of the characteristics of the past that will surely endure is the spirit of cooperation between the LGD of Pinawa administration, the people of the District, Environmental Options and Pinawa Recycling, Inc.

Pinawa Land Development Group
By Marsha Sheppard

When the dust of rallies, petitions and media features settled after the announcement that AECL intended to close Whiteshell Laboratories, Pinawa's citizens got down to the serious business of re-inventing the community. Part of the re-grouping was the formation of "Citizens for Change" spearheaded by Marsha Sheppard and Judith Simpson. The group's mission was to "make things happen for Pinawa". In its early days the group, now known as the Pinawa Land Development Group (PLDG) spent many hours brainstorming to develop a plan and a means to equip Pinawa for independent survival and prosperity. The initial result was a report, presented to the Whiteshell Task Force in June 1996. The report requested the Task Force to present a request for transfer of land and funds from AECL, the Federal and Provincial governments and the Western Economic Diversification Fund. Nearly seven years later the lobbying continues.

A rest place at the suspension bridge

Meanwhile the PLDG decided to focus its energies on making Pinawa a better place. What would entice visitors to want to come to Pinawa? Pinawa is known for its challenging golf course and beautiful ski and snowmobile trails but the objective was a year round tourist attraction; something that visitors could enjoy without having to haul equipment or be particularly athletic to enjoy. The answer was a walking trail. The initial plan was to create a loop of about 8 kilometres around Pinawa to be known as the Pinawa Heritage Walk and by June 1997 the trail was marked out and ready for brushing. The trail would initially cross the Pinawa Channel at the Diversion Dam and continue along the north side of the channel. The problem was that unless the walkers doubled back they had no way to get back across the channel. The obvious solution was a bridge crossing the channel further along the trail to form a continuous loop. Long-time Pinawa resident, Ray Sochaski took up the challenge. With his expertise, the surveying know-how of Barrie Burnett, the rock mechanics expertise of Peter Baumgartner and several volunteers from the community, the Suspension Bridge was born.

Pinawa Channel Heritage Walk

Funding for the project came from a grant from the provincial Sustainable Development Initiatives Fund with matching in-kind donations of material from Tantalum Mining Corporation (TANCO), equipment from AECL, gravel from Al Meisner Limited and equipment and labour from the LGD of Pinawa. The sheer determination of construction foreman Al Hampton and right-hand man Kirk Haugen saw the job through. Some 60 community volunteers and PLDG members put many an hour into this major infrastructure project. The community also contributed through the "buy a board" campaign initiated by Carl Sabanski.

Following completion of the bridge, work started in earnest on developing the walking trail. The PLDG quickly affiliated with the Whiteshell Cross Country Ski Club (WCCSC) and decided to reroute the Trans Canada Trail (TCT) into Pinawa. With funding from the province through the Manitoba Recreational Trail Association (MRTA) volunteers blazed a route from Old Pinawa to the Seven Sisters Falls Generation Station dyke.

As volunteers continued upgrading the trail, work began on a pavilion at the west end of the suspension bridge. The Bridge Pavilion was designed by Carl Sabanski. Once the Group had the design Jeff Harding produced a detailed construction plan based on the architect's work while Barrie Burnett surveyed the property to determine proper placement. Another great crew of volunteers put the finishing touches on the project.

Ironwood Trail

It took five years, 2500 hours of volunteer labour and grants totalling $216,890 to build the bridge, trail and pavilion. Upgrading of the trail continues to this day. On April 11, 2000 the Province of Manitoba recognized the Land Development Group and its volunteers with the Premier's Volunteer Service Award in the Community Group Category. Marsha Sheppard accepted the award on behalf of the Group. The PLDG also received the "Trans Canada Trail National Trail Builders Award" from the Trans Canada Trail Foundation. The Pinawa section of the Trans Canada Trail and the Bridge Pavilion officially opened August 11, 2002.

Friends of Old Pinawa Cooperating Association
By Vivian Thomson and Richard Thomson

The Friends of Old Pinawa was formed in 1996 as a non-profit association working to improve and promote the historic Old Pinawa Dam Heritage Park. The Friends have a strong community commitment.

Because this historic local site is located midway between the two communities, the Friends of Old Pinawa have partnered with many local groups and organizations, including local LGDs and Chambers of Commerce, Conservation Manitoba, Manitoba Hydro, tourist associations including the La Verendrye Trail Association, the Pinawa Community Development Corporation, the Heritage Advisory Committee of Lac du Bonnet, Trans Canada Trail Association and the Manitoba Recreational Trails Association.

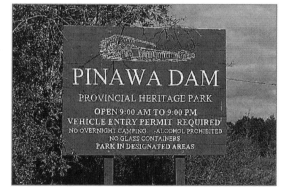

Old Pinawa Provincial Heritage Park

Some of the key accomplishments for The Friends over the years have included:

- Building an Amphitheatre. This facility has a seat capacity of 3000, a concrete stage and all needed services.
- The Friends developed the Heritage Walk that winds through the old town site, including all signs. A bridge was built to span the channel at the back of the dam to give alternate access to the dam and nature trail. The Trans Canada Trail has also been incorporated into the historical walk.

- In 1998, we created a Nature Trail to show ecological areas of interest and provide views of the dam from a different perspective. This trail was expanded in 2006.
- In 2001, the Friends of Old Pinawa were presented with the Prix Manitoba Award
- An archive of items pertaining to Old Pinawa has been collected.
- The Friends of Old Pinawa hosts a family event with music, children's events and other activities each year. This is a very large undertaking for such a small group. We are looking for organizations to partner with us.

SnoPALS
By Roy Ticknor

Eastman SnoPALS is a snowmobile club formed in 1996 by the amalgamation of three smaller, local clubs from Pinawa, Agassiz (Seddon's Corner) and Lac du Bonnet. This is how the acronym PALS originates. The SnoPALS is presently comprised of members from Lac du Bonnet, Seven Sisters Falls, Pinawa, Whitemouth and Elma. Many members are also from outside the immediate area with many coming from Winnipeg. The club objectives are to promote safe, high-quality recreational snowmobiling, to develop and maintain snowmobile trails, to foster good relations with the non-snowmobiling public, and to take collective action on matters concerning the membership.

The SnoPALS club maintains approximately 300 km of trails, stretching from Red Deer in the Brightstone hills in the north, Elma to the south, Seddon's Corner to the west and Pinawa in the east. The trails connect with trails maintained by our neighbouring clubs, all part of the provincial trail network.

The SnoPALS have always been safety-oriented with their trails cleared, signed and groomed annually. The trails range from a nice flowing ride through a pine forest in the Canadian Shield to a straight line over an old rail bed through swampy and sandy pastureland. Every season, the volunteer crews clear debris and fallen trees off of the trails. The club also has five warm up shelters along our network. They are open anytime to allow snowmobilers to stop and rest, build a fire, and enjoy a quick meal on the trail. Services are available in various locations along our trail system which are marked on our maps and signs. We also obtain permission from landowners where our trails use private property to link between trails on public land.

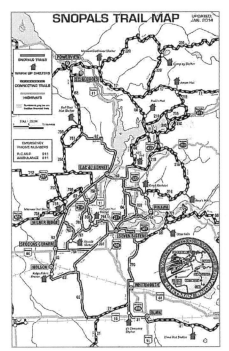

Eastern Manitoba Trails

The club has three groomer units, which are farm tractors converted to run on tracks. The club stations all equipment in our groomer building in Seven Sisters. Everything done by Eastman SnoPALS would not be possible without the core group of dedicated volunteers that work on our trails for the love of it and the desire to see safe, groomed trails to ride on themselves.

As a club, we think of ourselves as a social network as well. We are online and we have fundraisers to help promote the club and safe riding habits. For the past several seasons the club has held an appreciation Bar-B-Q at one of our warm-up shelters. We have also had several wrap-up dinners at one of the popular eating spots to thank all those who have worked on the network each year.

We hope you enjoy our trail system as you pass through our communities and make use of our services and facilities. Club membership and volunteer participation are always encouraged.

Chapter 5
Do You Remember?

Pinawa, like all communities, has experienced events, milestones and accomplishments that have helped define us as a community. This section is just a snapshot of some of these memories, randomly selected from newspaper articles and public submissions. The walk down memory lane is meant to help you remember your community and the extraordinary people that have been part of living in Pinawa.

1960s

In 1962 the first elementary school (F.W. Gilbert) was constructed, opening in the fall of 1963. Senior high students were bussed to Lac du Bonnet, pending the completion of the High School.

The Bank of Montreal, under the management of Jim Gormican, opened its doors to Pinawa residents in 1963. It was situated in a trailer which was opened twice a week. The bank was located on the site of the Pinawa Club.

The Pinawa Club was created by AECL in 1963 as a non-profit corporation to hold the assets of the newly constructed Curling Club/Clubhouse, the Golf Course, and whatever other Sections evolved in the future.

Pinawa Pioneers playing at Burrows Field

Pinawa's first RCMP officer, N.C.J. Searle arrived in 1963. Over 30 officers have called Pinawa home over the years.

The first outdoor ice surfaces were built by the Rink Committee in the fall of 1963 next to Elementary School No.1 (F.W. Gilbert School).

In October of 1964 the stainless steel calandria arrived at WNRE from the Peterborough Works of General Electric via truck.

The Lions Club, through the sponsorship of the Beausejour Lions, was chartered in 1964.

In 1964, permanent office space was constructed and allocated to the municipal and commercial concerns (i.e. LGD, RCMP, Fire Department, Bay, Drugstore, Beauty Salon, Post Office, and Gas Station).

Pinawa Club - 1964

The Pinawa Curling Club officially opened December 11, 1964.

Men's Fastball in Pinawa began in 1964 with the formation of the Pinawa Pioneers Fastball Team.

In July of 1964, Pinawa celebrated its first anniversary.

The first elections were held in Pinawa, those being the election of the Library Board.

The hospital was formerly opened in December of 1964.

Pinawa Figure Skating Club began in January, 1965. The first ice carnival, 'A Winter Wonderland', complete with spruce trees, park benches, outdoor lighting and taped music, was on February 26, 1965.

The tennis section of the Pinawa Club was founded in 1965 under the presidency of John Boulton.

The first Pinawa Birthday Celebrations were held in July of 1965, under the guidance and support of the Pinawa Lions.

Pinawa's First Wedding
Maureen Dobbin and Garth Mitchell
July 30, 1966

The first local Christmas Bird Count was held on 2 January 1965 under the leadership of Bruce Stewart.

Pinawa experienced its coldest recorded temperature -47.8ºC on February 19, 1966.

1966 was the year of the big blizzard in March.

August 27, 1966 was marked sadly by the passing of F.W. Gilbert, WNRE's first general manager.

The Pinawa Club was completed in 1966.

Pinawa Collegiate opened, with Mr. G.W. Hanna Principal, in 1965.

The Pinawa Health Auxiliary began in 1966. Since inception, they have donated over $300,000 in equipment to the Pinawa Hospital.

The official openings of the golf course and the new marina were in 1967.

The teenagers welcomed a new drop-in centre in 1967, located in trailers adjacent to the high school.

The elementary schools were named for F.W. Gilbert and W.B. Lewis in 1967, and excavation began for the addition of the Junior High to the Collegiate.

Yvonne Oldaker opened the Pinawa Ballet Club in 1967 with an enrollment of 25 girls.

Pinawa's Goose Sanctuary began when Gerry Smith brought two hatchlings to the site in the late 1960s

The Pinawa Sailing Club was formed in 1967 and has occupied the present site, next to the Pinawa marina, ever since its formation.

Ladies softball was organized in 1967 when the Atomettes entered the Northeastern Manitoba League.

The first School Board was elected in 1968.

The Motor Inn opened officially in 1968, owned and operated by Mr. Bill Chyzzy.

Pinawa's First Family, the Ben Banham's left in 1969, giving Mr. Banham the distinction of being the first retired employee of WNRE.

Tragedy struck our town when a 3 year-old boy drowned at the beach in September of 1969.

The Pinawa Dental Clinic opened with Drs. Cross and Derksen accepting patients in April of 1969.

Blizzard in March 1966 - Gerry Nayler and his daughter Laurie in front of F.W. Gilbert School

1970s

The Credit Union opened its doors at WNRE in 1970, under the direction of W.J. Baker. After relocating at the Shopping Centre, it underwent two name-changes and two managers: Jim Spencer and Bill Barkman.

The Pinawa Panthers Intermediate Hockey Team began with the opening of the new arena in 1970.

In January of 1970, the Pinawa Public Library and the High School Library amalgamated to become the first library of its kind in Manitoba.

The Pinawa Centennial Committee, including Mrs. Chris Gilbert, published a history of Pinawa in 1970.

Ed Ingersoll

1971 saw the opening of the Junior High, with Mr. Fred Olson, Principal. Parents of Prescott Crescent began the first of several petitions requesting that their children be allowed to attend Lewis School. The School Board denied this request.

The long-awaited opening of the new Pinawa Arena was held on Sunday, December 13, 1970.

The first goal scored by The Pinawa Panthers Intermediate Team in our new arena was Ralph Moyer against Beausejour in 1970.

Dennis Fitzsimmons retired as the Agassiz District Commissioner of Scouting in 1970. Mr. Fitzsimmons had been involved with the Scouting movement in Pinawa since 1963.

Mr. Ed Ingersoll, the manager of the Bank of Montreal since the bank opened in the shopping centre, retired

Remember when Tony Sawatzky built a glider in his basement?

136

in 1972. His duties were assumed by Wayne Goodman.

1972 will be remembered for the August 12ᵗʰ hail storm. Among other things, the wedding party for the newly-wed Jerry and Connie Plunkett was interrupted by the storm, and guests had to run for the nearest shelter.

Pinawa experienced its largest single day rainfall of 168.4 mm on June 14, 1973.

Rain storms in 1973 caused 107 Pinawa basements to be flooded.

Orville Acres (1932-2002)

Orville Acres was born in Kars, Ontario and spent his early years growing up on the farm. He attended Kemptville Agriculture College. Shortly after graduation, Orville married Isabel Coleman and spent seven years working in Ottawa at the Department of Agriculture Experimental Farm. In 1963, Orville and his family moved to Pinawa where he spent the next 35 years with Atomic Energy of Canada. Orville will be fondly remembered for his dedicated volunteer service. He was a member of the Pinawa Christian Fellowship and contributed almost 40 years to the Pinawa Volunteer Fire Department where he served in many capacities, including his final years as Fire Chief. His dedication to amateur sports included many years umpiring softball but his true passion was hockey where he served at the local, provincial and national levels in many capacities. Fairness in sport was his guiding principal. In 2001 he received the Manitoba Lieutenant Governors Make a Difference Community Award. Orville was a man of great integrity, with a kind and gentle nature.

Three new clubs were formed in Pinawa in 1973, those being the Eastern Manitoba Concert Association, the Cross Country Ski Club and the Pinawa Co-op Nursery School.

The Pinawa Nurses, along with nurses from the surrounding region, formed a chapter of the Manitoba Association of Registered Nurses in 1973.

Adrian Hatcher won the Gold Medal at a Science Symposium in 1973. Pinawa students won a total of 22 medals at the Provincial Symposium held in Winnipeg.

In the fall of 1973 thirty skiers and enthusiasts gathered at Gilbert School and formed the Whiteshell Cross-Country Ski Club.

In 1974 the Ladies Auxiliary to the Pinawa Fire Department presented Fire Chief Tom Lamb with the keys to a new rescue wagon. The rescue wagon was named Olive, after Mrs. Olive Taylor, President of the Ladies Auxiliary.

Do you remember when the moose walked down Devonshire

Bruce Nerbas made the Provincial Junior Men's Golf Team in 1974. His brother Robert Nerbas repeated the feat in 1976.

In 1975 the Pinawa Volunteer Fire Department was awarded first place in the national fire prevention contest, out of 177 other entries in its class.

On November 1, 1975, WR-1 celebrated its tenth anniversary.

The Eastman Community Band began as a pick-up band formed by Heiki Tamm to provide the music for the Pinawa Player's production of "Annie Get Your Gun" in 1977.

In 1977, the Pinawa Rhythmettes attended the Manitoba Provincial Gymnastrada for the first time. The club also travelled to Montreal for Canada's first National Gymnastrada in 1980.

The Pinawa Cross Country Ski Club's first Loppet or citizen's race was organized by Herb Rosinger in 1977.

Peter Cliche becomes the new hospital administrator in 1978.

Peter Cliche - Fire Services Exemplary Service Medal from Governor General of Canada - 1990

The Fire Services Exemplary Service Medal, created on August 29, 1985, honours members of a recognized Canadian fire service who have completed 20 years of service, ten years of which have been served in the performance of duties involving potential risks, and were employed on or after the date of creation of the Medal. Recognized fire services include Canadian fire departments, fire marshals' offices, fire commissioners' offices and the Canadian Forces fire services. Exemplary service is characterized by good conduct, industry and efficiency.

Consideration is given only to periods of service for which no other long service, good conduct or efficiency decoration or medal has been awarded by the Crown.

1980s

The Pinawa Press published its first Issue on November 11, 1981. The town had been without a paper of any kind since the late 1960s. The Pinawa Press was the first registered newspaper in Pinawa. The editor was Mrs. Pat Roy.

Karen Kovacs became the first woman employed in the WNRE apprenticeship program, as well as the first in Trades in July of 1982.

The Whiteshell Toastmasters received their official charter on Dec. 10, 1980.

Vanier Community Centre was officially opened on December 16, 1981 by Mayor Howard Gilmour.

Pinawa establishes a Chamber of Commerce in January, 1982, with Don Roy as the first President.

In 1982 the Assiniboine Credit Union closed its doors in Pinawa.

Pam Tymko and Patrick Woodbeck qualify for the Canadian Figure Skating Championship in Dance in 1982.

On February 5, 1982, WR-1 Reactor completed its 100,000th hour of operation.

The Bank of Montreal announces its plans to close in October, 1982.

Pinawa got its first propane-powered car, owned by Cyril Clarke, in October, 1982.

Peter Cliche was named President of the Manitoba Association of Fire Chiefs in April 1983.

Pinawa Secondary School Men's Soccer Team, coached by Dave Shoesmith and Paul Ingham, won the Provincial Rural Soccer Championship in 1984.

On February 04, 1984 the Pinawa Business Women's Association (PBWA) was born.

A forest fire threatened Pinawa in May 1984.

The Underground Research Laboratory opened on May 26, 1984.

Paul Nuttall and Sandra Wright made the Manitoba provincial tennis team in 1984.

The expansion of Highway 44 in eastern Manitoba begins in August 1984.

The Pinawa Panthers, coached by Dave Shoesmith and Chris Saunders, won the Provincial Midget Hockey Championship in Souris in 1985. This was Pinawa's first minor hockey provincial title. The 1986 Midget team, coached by Bill Hutchings, repeated as Provincial Champions in Carman.

The new road construction to connect PTH 211 and PTH 313 began in April 1986.

A renovated Old Pinawa Heritage Park opened to the public in May 1986.

May 1984 – Fire near Pinawa

The new gates to the Pinawa Cemetery, donated by the Pinawa Lioness Club, were installed in July 1986.

Pinawa Recycling Inc. was established in early 1989 as a non-profit, fully volunteer organization in response to concerns over environmental issues.

The Pinawa Cross Country Ski Club hosted the 1987 Canada Cup races and Western Canadian Championships.

Gary Hanna became Pinawa's Resident Administrator in January 1989.

1990s

The Pinawa 50+ Club was officially incorporated on February 13, 1990.

The Pinawa Panthers win the Manitoba Midget B Hockey Championship at home in March 1990.

Minister of Energy Jake Epp announces long-term funding for AECL in April, 1990.

Pinawa School Board gives notice of the closure of W.B. Lewis School on March 26, 1991.

Peter Taylor is awarded the Ernest Thompson Seton Medal by the Manitoba Naturalist Society in April 1991.

On December 20, 1992, the Lutheran Church had their first services in Pinawa's first church building.

Don Ewing was named Manitoba Cross-Country Skiing Coach of the Year in 1992.

Pioneer Bay Campground was proposed for Pinawa in April 1992.

Seven charged in Pinawa Service Station thefts in August 1992.

The Whiteshell Campus of the Deep River Science Academy was officially opened on June 28, 1993.

AECL sells the Shopping Centre and the Pinawa Motor Inn to John McPherson in June 1993.

Thelma Boase, kindergarten teacher at F.W. Gilbert School for 25 years, retires in June 1994.

Software Solutions is the first business to occupy space in the W.B. Lewis Business Centre, January 1, 1995.

The Pinawa Pharmacy relocates to the hospital in February 1995.

The new Alliance Church was dedicated on February 5, 1995.

In March 1995, Travis Law won the trophy for 1st All Around in the Manitoba Open Gymnastics Competition with four silver medals and two gold medals.

Remember when CBC filmed an episode of "On the Road Again" featuring Barrie Burnett.

Pinawa experienced its warmest recorded temperature 37.5°C on June 17, 1995.

Pinawa hosted its first rowing regatta in 1995.

Beauday Publishing launches a weekly newspaper, The Paper, November 28, 1995 (Editors Cathy Beauchamp and Louise Daymond).

*The **"Save Our Site"** Rally was held on December 7, 1995.*

The Whiteshell Task Force, formed to examine business opportunities for AECL's Whiteshell Laboratories, meets for the first time on February 12, 1996.

Leyton Roe wins the first Pinawa Curling Club Car Raffle on April 20, 1996.

Pinawa's "Reach for the Top" team of Scott McCamis, Riley Kearns, Barrett Miller and Jennifer Vandergraaf win the Manitoba Championship on April 23, 1996.

Pinawa co-hosted the Winnipeg Invitational Regatta, as well as the NWIRA Championship Regatta, in the summer of 1996.

Pinawa experienced its largest single day snowfall of 48 cm on April 4, 1997.

Ann Portman (1943-2010)

Ann Portman (nee Vlemmiks), born in England in 1943, was a war baby. She and her husband Roger sailed to Canada on the Empress of Canada in 1968 and built a life in Pinawa for 40 years. After a 25-year career she retired from AECL as Human Resources Advisor. Ann was a life-long volunteer. In the early years, she worked with the Pinawa Hospital Auxiliary and Canadian Figure Skating Association. At the age of 60, she ran her first marathon to raise money for the Arthritis Society. After retirement, Ann volunteered with the Pinawa Justice Committee and the Canadian Executive Service Organization (CESO). For CESO, she shared her professional skills with over 30 First Nations in Manitoba and Northern Ontario. She was awarded the Manitoba Premier's Volunteer Service Award and the International Year of the Volunteers Award by the Government of Canada.

A capacity crowd gathered to hear a proposal to sell the Pinawa Club on August 5, 1997.

The federal panel studying AECL's plan for storing nuclear waste issued their report on March 13, 1998.

Dr. Bud Opie was named "Doctor of the Year" by the Manitoba Medical Association on April 14, 1998.

The W.B. Lewis Business Centre has its Grand Opening in April 1998.

Blair Skinner and Leslie Strandlund win the Pinawa Curling Club Truck Raffle in May 1998.

Sean Greenfield (1983-2009)

Sean Greenfield (Member of 24 Field Squadron, 2 Combat Engineer Regiment, CFB Petawawa) was born in Pinawa. Sean's father, Keith, worked with Atomic Energy of Canada Ltd., in Pinawa, and then transferred to AECL's Chalk River Laboratories where they lived in Petawawa. Sean went to Fanshawe College in London after graduating from high school and became a graphic designer. Then, Greenfield signed up for the military. He was gifted both athletically and musically, trained as a military engineer and combat diver, and nursed dreams of joining Canada's special forces and becoming a member of the secretive Joint Task Force 2 commandos. A Manitoba hero, Sean died in January 2009 in Afghanistan.

Tony Sawatzky receives the distinguished Kroll Zirconium Medal in August 1998.

Pinawa hosts the Manitoba High School Golf Championship in September 1998.

Acsion Industries and Granite Internet each receive a loan from the Economic Development Authority of Whiteshell in November 1998.

The Lutheran Church had a mortgage burning celebration on December 13, 1998.

Peter Siemens resigns from the EDAW in December 1998.

John Westdal (1944 – 2009)

John Westdal was born in Winnipeg and grew up on Vancouver Island. His father's career as a bush pilot took John to The Pas, Swan River and Neepawa, with summers spent at Norway House. John graduated from Kelvin High School in Winnipeg in 1962. He graduated from the University of Manitoba in the Faculty of Engineering. It was during his studies that he met the love of his life, Heather Robertson as they carpooled together. John would take Heather on dates flying in a Piper Colt. John and Heather were married in 1967. John continued his studies at the University of Manitoba, completing his Master's degree in 1969. Schooling complete, John and his young bride decided on a new adventure and they travelled together to Tanzania, where he taught at a Technical College.

After the birth of their first child Tanis, John and Heather returned to Canada, settling in Pinawa. Their family continued to grow with the birth of two sons, David and Paul. John shared many gifts with his family, including his love of the outdoors, teaching his children how to sail, ski, canoe and camp. John loved life in Pinawa, where he formed life-long friendships cultivating his interests in bridge, ham radio, sailing, and bee-keeping. He was quick to volunteer in the community, particularly with the Trans-Canada Trail and radio-work at triathlons and cross-country skiing events. John and Heather shared many sailing adventures in the Florida Keys, including a crossing to the Bahamas on their boat Freyja. They shared dry land adventures as well, cycling the east coast of Canada, hiking Scotland and travelling to Mexico and Iceland. John loved learning through books, people and life-experience. While loathe to give advice, when asked, he would share his knowledge in his typical easy-going manner. John was a thoughtful, strong and wise man who loved deeply. His house was always open for a visit from friends and family. He loved spending time with his grandchildren. Plainly stated, John was an incredible man with an interest in everyone's story. John's friendship will be treasured by the many people he has met throughout his life.

Gordon Dale

Gordon Dale was born in Winnipeg, more or less by accident. His parents lived in Pinawa and, as a result of complications; his mother was transferred to a maternity ward in Winnipeg for his birth. His father, Bob Dale, was a school teacher, then principal, then superintendent. His mother had been a teacher also, but was forced to retire when she married. In rural Manitoba in those days, it wasn't considered appropriate for a married woman to continue teaching, and thereby occupy a job that could be held by a man.

Gordon described his childhood as magical, spent running wild in small towns, mostly in rural Manitoba. He spent two years in Malawi, in Central East Africa, after which he attended high school Pinawa. He spent most of his time either in the woods or on the water. At 17, Gordon moved to Winnipeg, where he took a Commerce degree from the University of Manitoba. He worked in Aerospace for several years after that, eventually becoming an independent consultant with clients in Hong Kong, Taiwan, and across Canada. He moved to California in 2005, where he completed an M.A. from San Francisco State University.

Gordon has lived in such disparate regions as the Sub-Arctic, the Canadian prairies and Central-East Africa, but presently makes his home in California. He began his writing career at age sixteen by winning second place, and ten dollars, in the annual poetry contest of a small-town newspaper. A copy of the text remains in the family archives, preserved for the edification of future generations. The ten dollars, alas, have been quite lost to history. Gordon has been a business executive, management consultant, and freelance writer of travel, adventure and humor articles for various North American magazines. Gordon's novel *Fool's Republic*, was published by North Atlantic Books in May 2011. He is currently at work on another, tentatively entitled *What We Remember*.

Janet Dugle (1934-2014)

Janet Dugle was born in Pierre, SD. Janet grew up and attended high school in Dupree, SD, then attended Carlton College MN, Yale University CT, and the University of Alberta, Edmonton, where she received her PhD in Botany. Jan worked at AECL in the Environmental Research Branch starting in 1967. She had a large research project in which she studied the effects of gamma irradiation on plants.

Jan was an avid photographer and was involved with the Pinawa Photography Club. She was also a member of the Trans Canada Trail committee providing her botanical and ecological expertise. She was instrumental in making the Ironwood Trail. She was also a member of the first Pinawa Art 211 group. Jan and Bill Murray started a framing and art business in town. Many a retirement gift or farewell gift was framed here.

Jan was part of the Pinawa Support Group who met on a weekly basis. There she found friends and travelling partners who were an important part of her life. An avid bridge player, teacher, and director at the Pinawa Club, Jan achieved her Bronze Life Masters. She enjoyed meeting people and travelling to tournaments.

She was pioneer survivor with an artificial heart valve for 33 years and then had another replacement in 2012.

2000s

Pinawa's new landfill opens in January 2000.

The Pinawa Secondary School graduated its 1000ᵗʰ student in the graduating class of 2000.

On April 11, 2000 the Province of Manitoba recognized the Land Development Group and its volunteers with the Premier's Volunteer Service Award in the Community Group Category.

Roger Smith is vested into the "Order of Manitoba" in May 2000.

ECOMatters and Channel Technologies each receive funding from the provincial and federal governments in June 2000.

The Pinnacle Triathlon/Duathlon Club was formed in 2001 to organize the Free Spirit Triathlon.

South Interlake Credit Union opens for business in July 2000.

Pinawa welcomes Dr. Richard Van Gend and his family to Pinawa in October 2000.

Premier Doer visits Acsion Industries in October 2000.

David Iftody, a former Member of Parliament for the region, died of injuries he received in a snowmobile accident in February 2001.

The Pinawa Sundial officially opens as a millennium Project in early 2001.

The Whiteshell Wolverines win the 2001 Midget C Female Hockey Provincial Championship in Pierson in March 2001.

Orville Acres received the Lieutenant Governor's Make a Difference Community Award on April 6, 2001.

Brian McKenzie, Heather Westdal, Hardy Velie, Helen Hayward and Moe Stepaniuk, with a combined 148 years of teaching experience, retired from the Pinawa Secondary School on June 28, 2001.

Ron Drabyk (1960 – 2012)

Ron was born and raised in Winnipeg. He graduated from the Computer Technology Program at Red River Community College and soon started work at AECL in Pinawa. Ron made many life-long friends through his work and in the community. Ron and his wife Anita jumped at the chance to transfer to China to work for AECL near Shanghai. While there, they were delighted to welcome Lian Zhou Jing to the family.

After returning to Canada, Ron and his family settled back into Pinawa and became very involved in all aspects of the community. Ron joined the staff of Whiteshell Technologies and NEHA. He continued to do what he does best – he kept the computers and local networks running for groups and businesses. Many a frustrated computer user knew they could call on Ron to 'save the day'. In October 2010, Ron took on a task that was dear to his heart – he was elected a councillor for the Local Government District of Pinawa. He thoroughly enjoyed learning more about Pinawa and helping to build a thriving community for generations to come. He spent many volunteer hours involved with the Curling Club, the Golf Course, and especially the Pinawa Minor Hockey Association.

Brian Gamley won $10,000 for a hole-in-one, sponsored by the Pinawa Chamber of Commerce, in July 2001.

The entire EDAW board resigns in frustration in September 2001.

Jerry Cousins and Clay McMurren become the new owners of the Pinawa Motor Inn on May 5, 2002.

Carl Sabanski wins the Manitoba Tourism Award in April 2002.

The Pinawa section of the Trans Canada Trail and the Bridge Pavilion officially opened August 11, 2002.

The Eastman Community Justice Committee Association received the Manitoba Community Justice Award in November 2002.

Co-Op replaces Esso at the local service station in May 2003.

The Arena was renamed in honour of Orville Acres in October 2003.

The Pinawa Panthers boys' basketball team wins their first Manitoba High School Basketball Championship in Glenboro in March 2004.

The Pinawa Panthers wins the Manitoba Midget C Hockey Championship in Riverton on March 14, 2004.

Ann Sisler is named Basketball Manitoba's "High School Coach of the Year" in April 2004.

Dr. Opie retires after 39 years in September 2004.

Pinawa hosted the 2004 Manitoba Men's Amateur Golf Championship, won by Jordan Krantz with a four-day total of 284.

Tragedy struck on July 26, 2005 when a 16 year old boy from Inwood drowned at the beach.

The Whiteshell Cycling Club was formed in 2006.

The Whiteshell Science Academy closed its doors in January 2007.

The hospital opens its new CancerCare unit in March 2007.

A fundraiser for Mike Reimer raised $11,000 in October 2007.

The first Mass was held in November 2007 at Pinawa's St. Francis of Assisi Roman Catholic Church.

Northeast Radio goes on the air in February 2008.

Solo Market comes to Pinawa in April 2008.

The RCMP Musical Ride performs in Pinawa on July 23, 2008.

Local author Andrew Davidson publishes *The Gargoyle* in August 2008.

Sapper Sean Greenfield died while serving with the Canadian Armed Forces in Afghanistan on January 31, 2009.

Peter Taylor

Peter Taylor was born in 1949 in Warkworth, England and grew up in Lesbury. He attended the University of Birmingham, graduating with a PhD in Chemistry in 1972. Peter then moved to Fredericton New Brunswick as a

post-doctoral fellow. His one-year adventure in Canada has expanded to 40 years, due in large part to meeting Sharon Barker from Branford, who was working at the New Brunswick Legislative Library. Peter and Sharon were married in 1973 and moved to Pinawa in 1975. Peter worked in Research Chemistry at AECL until his retirement 1998.

Peter and Sharon have had a number of adventures over the years, including two postings in France (1998 and 2003), where Peter did research on severe nuclear reactor accidents. They have also had visits to Kenya, India, Jordan, Central America and South America, often related to Peter's passion for bird watching.

Peter's interest in birds started as a child with his family. It blossomed when he came to Canada. He has become well known in Manitoba for his expertise and love of birding. He has spent the past 35 years involved with Pinawa's Christmas Bird Count, an annual event started in Pinawa in 1964 by Bruce Stewart. This count usually identifies 30 to 35 species of birds. Peter edited the "Birds of Manitoba" (www.naturemanitoba.ca/birdbook2/book-home.html), published in 2003, that highlighted over 350 species of birds. He is currently working on the "Manitoba Breeding Bird Atlas" (www.birdatlas.mb.ca) that will detail the bird distributions in the province. Asked to describe highlights of his birding tours, Peter described seeing the California Condor in the mid-1980s, truly a rare event. He is also excited to see rare birds in Manitoba, such as the Curve-Billed Thrasher, the White-Winged Dove and the Painted Bunting. Peter has shared his love of nature with his family, particularly his son George, who has moved on to nature photography.

Dr. Henry Beaumont, Pinawa's first doctor, passes away on April 23, 2009.

Jackie Sturton received the Prime Minister's Certificate of Excellence in October 2009.

The Pinawa Foundation was established in 2010 as a non-profit group focused on financially supporting groups and clubs in Pinawa.

2010s

The Pinawa Foundation presents Olympic mittens to all of the students of F.W. Gilbert School in February 2010.

A fire threatens Relax Ridge campground on April 10, 2010.

The Tim Hortons Camp was approved June 3, 2010.

On May 17, 2010, most of the Pinawa Motor Inn was destroyed by fire.

Fire at the Pinawa Motor Inn - May 17, 2010

The Ironwood Senior Housing Complex Grand opening was on July 18, 2010.

Pinawa hosted a special edition of TSN Sports Centre in August 2010. Pinawa also received a $25,000 Community Refresh Grant that went towards arena renovations.

Donna and Ray Warenko won $10,000 at the Arena Board fundraiser in January 2011.

Leslie Wilson was part of Cathy Overton-Clapham's winning team at the Manitoba Scotties curling championship in February 2011.

Nestle Canada presented $50,000 to the Pinawa Minor Hockey Association as winners of the WHL Delissio Hockey Challenge.

Don Daymond received the Premier's Volunteer Award

in April 27, 2011.

Ryan Bilinsky and Tyler George won the inaugural Pinawa Amazing Race in July 2011.

The Pinawa Cross Country Ski club opened the new Orange Trail cabin in February 2012.

In March 2012, Ben Dearing competed with the Manitoba team at the Canadian National Cross Country Ski Championships in Quebec City.

Fire threatened PTH 211 in May 2012.

On July 29, 2012, Pinawa experienced 47 seconds of havoc from strong shear winds.

The Pinawa Foundation signs up over 500 participants to the new Manitoba on-line organ donation program.

Happy **50ᵗʰ Birthday** Pinawa – July 2013.

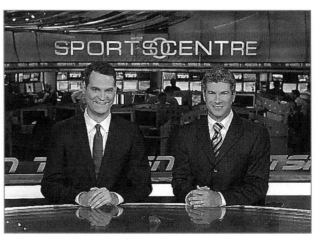

Jay Onrait and Dan O'Toole visited Pinawa on
August 23, 2010.

Happy 50th Birthday Pinawa
(Photograph courtesy of Stu Iverson)

Chapter 6
Celebrating Our Birthday

Pinawa has always had a special attachment to our annual birthday celebration, held in the middle of July to commemorate the anniversary of the LGD opening for service on July 15, 1963. Our first birthday saw all of the activities centred around the beach, including a community sing-song led by Don Thompson on the piano. There were canoe races and races to fill canoes. A 1920s Bathing Beauty contest was held and fishermen competed in a casting contest. The beach was full of people, all eager to share in the festivities. It ended with the first Pinawa fireworks display. The Lions Club did an impressive job in organizing the first event. And there was so much more to come over 50 years.

The July 17, 1965 Celebration saw a number of events added to the schedule. The Pinawa Christian Fellowship operated the snack bar. The Guides and Scouts supplied the drinks.

The following letter was published in the Whiteshell Gazette in August 1965:

1965 Birthday Events

Time	Event	In Charge
5:00 am	Fishing Derby	Ev Dobbin
9:00 am	Fastball Tournament #1	Chuck Tomlinson
9:00 am	Fastball Tournament #2	A.K. McIntrye & Don Thompson
9:30 am	Bicycle Rodeo	Chuck Tomlinson
11:00 am	Children's Carousel	Bob Randell
12:00 pm	Channel Canoe Race	Howie Gilmour
12:30 pm	Swimming Races	Alex Mayman
1:30 pm	Sand Castle Contest	Alex Mayman
2:30 pm	Mayor's Canoe Race	Howie Gilmour
3:00 pm	Bathing Costume Contest	Byfi Walterson
3:30 pm	Canoe Races	Alex Mayman
4:00 pm	Lions Canoe Race	Alex Mayman
5:00 pm	Fishing Derby Closed	
6:00 pm	Log Rolling	Alex Mayman
7:00 pm	Casting Tournament	Ev Dobbin
8:30 pm	Awards and Draws	Barrie Banks
9:00 pm	Hootenanny & Bonfire	Don Thompson
10:30 pm	Fireworks	

Dear Sirs,

We, the Lions Club of Pinawa, wish to thank the various groups and individuals that assisted us in our recent Pinawa Birthday Celebrations. We would in particular like to thank the many enthusiastic participants, especially the youngsters, without whom the day would not have been complete.

Although this is our first attempt at this type of venture, it is felt that the enthusiasm of the Pinawa Residents and visitors over-rode any errors that we may have made.

It is our hope to continue the Birthday Celebrations each year, and also to maintain a non-commercial, "family day" atmosphere. We would certainly be remiss if we did not thank the local and area businessmen for their many fine donations of prizes. Without their support the day would not have been economically feasible.

As can be realized, even with all the planning and organization needed for an affair of this scope, some ideas pass us by. We would therefore certainly appreciate any suggestions that the residents may have for inclusion of new events, change of present events, etc. that will assist us in next year's programme.

Once again we thank you for the support given our Lions Club in our many endeavours.

Yours sincerely
D. Graham P.R.O.

Birthday Highlights

Over the years certain events have become synonymous with the birthday celebration weekend: the Lions Club dances, the parade, the beach activities and the fireworks. This section highlights just some of these special memories over the past 50 years.

1960s and 70s

The first birthday celebration was in 1965, all centred around the Pinawa beach.

The Birthday Raffle in 1966 was for an aluminum boat, 6 HP motor and trailer.

The Women's Auxiliary Fire Competition was held for the first time in 1966.

The first Pinawa Birthday Dance was July 15, 1966 in the shopping centre parking lot.

Prizes for the first "1920s Bathing Costume Contest" were a wrought iron candle spray for the ladies and a teakwood table lighter for the gentlemen.

The 1967 Birthday weekend theme was "Canada's Centennial Celebration". The big event for the weekend was the visit of the Canadian Centennial Voyageurs.

Water jousting made its birthday weekend debut in 1967.

The Birthday Dance moved to Kelsey House in 1968 with two bands; one for the younger folks and one for the older folks! The bar was in the in the courtyard, rain or shine.

The 1974 parade theme was "The Way We Were".

In 1974 the Birthday Dance was July 12, with music supplied by Flying Tiger and Mosaic. Tickets were $2.50.

1975 saw the dance ticket prices increase to $3.00; music was supplied by Crawford and The Matched Set.

The Great Bathtub Race and the Egg Toss made their debut at the beach activities in 1976.

The Birthday Celebration and the Eastman Summer Games were both in town on the weekend of July 10, 1976.

1980s and 90s

There was severe rain and wind during the birthday dance late Friday evening in 1982.

The "Dancing Cow" stole the show at the 1982 parade.

The 1982 beach activities were moved to Sunday because of rain.

The Cubs raised $700 with their door-to-door campaign for the fireworks in 1982.

Bicycle Rodeo - 1965

Always a fan favourite – log rolling

1967 Parade

Pinawa Birthday Dance - 1967

Pinawa Parade - 1967

Beauty Contestants

This is fun

Get your hamburger and drink

Where does the parade start?

Can this go faster?

True Beauties

Happy Birthday Pinawa!

Did you have fun?

Robin Andrews

The Pinawa Goldeyes beat the Beausejour Ladywood Chiefs 7 to 3 to win the Birthday Softball Tournament in 1982.

Helen Ritchie was the first Pinawa lady to finish the 5 km road race in 1983, placing 18th. David Mancey was the first Pinawa runner to finish the Pinawa 15 km race, placing 5th.

The 20th Birthday Celebration was held in 1983.

Justice and Hard Times played at the Birthday Dance on July 15, 1983. Tickets were $10.

Forty–seven entries were registered for the parade.

The dunk tank was a big hit at the beach activities, particularly when WNRE Site Head Ralph Green took his turn.

The beach activities in 1983, moved to Sunday because of rain, included the popular jello eating contest.

The 20th Anniversary saw many former residents come home, among them were Mary and Stewart McIntyre, Burt and Mary Jane Meeker, Sue and Rick Cronin, Brian and Nelda Turner, Bob and Nikki Seabloom, Bill and Edna Allwright, Cy and Audrey Luxton, Robin Lamb and Roy Barnsdale Jr.

The 1984 parade was televised, thanks to Mac Pellow, Ray Bird, Dale Johnson, and the staff at both Gilbert and Lewis Schools.

The Art and Craft Sale drew a big crowd in 1984.

A Sailing Regatta and a demonstration of the Jaws of Life by the Lac du Bonnet Fire Department were part of the 1984 celebration.

The 1985 parade included four bands (Pinawa Junior Band; Generics Band; Ladies Kitchen Band; Selkirk Pipe Band), along with Ollie the Owl and Buzz and Boomer from the Winnipeg Blue Bombers.

Queen Elizabeth, Prince Phillips and their Honor Guard (thanks to the Pinawa Players) were part of the 1985 parade.

The Foul Balls won the 1985 Birthday Softball Tournament, beating Elma 11 to 6 in the final.

A cricket match was part of the 1985 festivities.

MP Jake Epp and Premier Gary Filmon visited Pinawa for the 1986 Birthday.

1987 saw the Lioness Club sponsor a folk music coffee house on Saturday evening. Local singers, along with the comedy trio of "Peter Paul and Dave" performed at the coffee house.

The fireworks were cancelled in 1987 because of high winds; they were rescheduled for a week later.

MLA Darren Praznik, Mayor Marvin Ryz, and AECL General Manager Mike Wright unveiled a plaque to commemorate Pinawa's 25th Anniversary.

The Transcona Pipe Band and the Pinawa Pioneers Float were part of the 1988 parade.

On the Saturday of the 1987 Birthday, a community barbeque was held on the Kelsey House lawn, with the band "Double Eagle" performing.

Thirty nine of the first 83 families to move to Pinawa still made their home here in 1988.

RCMP Constable Joe Laughlin made an appearance at the dunk tank in 1989.

1991 saw hot weather and the Pioneer Square Dancers in the parade.

The Kelly-Miller Circus and rides from Rotorway Helicopter Inc. were part of the 1992 Birthday Celebration.

The Birthday Dance in 1992 included Pinawa's own Dan Frechette.

The 30th Anniversary Celebration in 1993 was blessed with beautiful weather, resulting in the largest crowd ever at the beach activities, according to Lion Jerry Farr.

The 1994 Birthday included the always popular Texas Scramble Golf Tournament.

The Health Auxiliary was "Odoriferous Paraders" in 1994, dressed as skunks.

The Raivo Tamm Memorial Triathlon was held in 1995.

1996 saw Ron Wiggins in the parade as a proud WWII veteran, dressed in his best formal kilt.

The first celebrity in the 1996 dunk tank was teacher Lorne Schram. He raised a lot of money.

1997 saw threatening skies, with many events squeezed between showers, including the annual two-ball golf tournament, and the Kids of Steel bike races.

Carol Findlay was the 1997 "Tomato Queen" of the parade.

AECL missed the parade for the first time in 1997.

Welcome to the sixties

The beach activities in 1998 included a superbounce.

A full slate of Sunday activities in 1998 included a kid's dance and the street market.

Events in 1999 began on Wednesday, July 14 with a hole-in-one contest sponsored by the Chamber of Commerce. The finals for the event were on Sunday, July 18.

The 1999 Birthday Dances (both Friday and Saturday evenings) were held in conjunction with the Pinawa Motor Inn.

The Scouts and Lions raised $7,000 for the fireworks in 1999.

The 1999 Celebrations included a talent show, the RE/MAX craft tent for children and a kids' dance at the Pinawa Motor Inn.

2000s

The 50+ Club won the Best Community Group in the 2000 parade. The Health Auxiliary won the Most Humorous Award for their Raggedy Anns.

Don Daymond had a hole-in-one on the thirteenth hole in the annual Birthday Golf Tournament.

The Birthday Dances were held Friday and Saturday evening under the Big Top Tent.

A petting zoo was popular in 2000, including a big black pig.

There were 47 entries in the 2001 parade, including the Army, Navy, and Airforce Veterans Pipe Band.

The 2002 parade was judged by Tyler Thomas and Brian Gamley. The 50+ Club won an award for the loudest float.

You are never safe at the Pinawa parade with David Kryschuk and Alyse George

Founders Gala

High School Memory Lane

Graduation Wall at Pinawa Secondary School

The 40th Birthday Celebration in 2003 included two dances under the Big Tent, Mayor Simpson cutting the special birthday cake, a pancake breakfast, a community supper and a community worship service.

A Raft Challenge Race was part of the 2004 Celebration. All boats had to be made from recycled materials. Deanna Kazina and Scott Reid took home the first place prize.

HAPPY 50TH BIRTHDAY PINAWA
July, 2013
Pinawa Birthday Founder's Gala - July 12; Invitation only.
Pinawa Amazing Race - July 13 starts 9:00 am.
Adult Junior Golf Tournament - July 14
Pinawa Birthday Alumni Walk - July 15; Pinawa Secondary School.
Pinawa Teen Dance - July 17; Ages 11 to 17.

July 18th Events
Men's Senior Golf Tournament
Technical Achievements of the Whiteshell Laboratories - 10:00 am; The Ironwood
Community Picnic - 4 pm, Community Centre

July 19th Events
Technical Achievements of the Whiteshell Laboratories - 10:00 am; The Ironwood
Pinawa Art Extravaganza & Sale Noon - 8:00 pm; F.W. Gilbert School Lund Mania Boat parade - 4:30 pm; Start at the Marina
Fender Benders Reunion Social - 8:00 pm - 2:00 am; Community Centre
Lions Social - 9:00 pm - 2:00 am; Sundial Park; Music by Grant and His Band

July 20th Events
LUND Mania fishing derby - 8:00 am - 3:00 pm
LUND Mania Awards Ceremony - 3:00 pm; Sundial Park
Pinawa Art Extravaganza & Sale -10:00 am - 4:00 pm; F.W. Gilbert School
Pinawa Birthday Parade -11:00 am
Winnipeg River Car Club Show & Shine - noon - 4:00 pm; Marina
Beach Activities - 12:30 pm - 3:30 pm, Pinawa Health Auxiliary Burger Shack open from 11:00 am to 5:00pm
Birthday Golf Scramble - 5:00 pm
Pinawa Stage Band - 9:00 pm - 10:30 pm; Sundial Park
Lions Social - 9:00 pm - 2:00 am; Sundial Park; Music by Dog Pound
Fireworks at Dusk -Marina

July 21st Events
Mass - 9 am; St. Francis of Assisi Roman Catholic Church.
Pinawa Foundation Pancake Breakfast - 9:00 am -11:00 am; Sundial Park
Open Worship Service – 10 am; F.W. Gilbert School.
Pinawa Town Market - 11:00 am - 3:00 pm; Community Centre
Legacy Park Dedication - 1:00 pm; Community Centre
Concert Community Band Concert - 1:30 pm - 3:00 pm; Legacy Park
Ironwood Open House - Noon - 3:00pm; The Ironwood
Additional Events: Pinawa Lions Club Amazing Duck Race (August 18), the Pinawa Kids of Steel Triathlon (August 24), the Free Spirit Triathlon (August 25), and the Northwest Run for Diabetes (September 1)

Los Grande Ninos played the 2005 Birthday Dance.

2006 saw Manitoba Conservation lift a fire ban just in time for the Saturday fireworks.

The 2007 parade included the Manitoba Sea Cadets and the Shriners.

Blair the Mayor, dressed in his favorite Maple Leafs jersey, was a popular target at the 2008 dunk tank.

Fifteen teams took part in the 2009 Texas Scramble golf tournament.

The Art Show and Sale was again a big hit in 2009.

The 2010 Birthday Weekend included the Art Extravaganza, "Yours Truly" playing at the dance, a scavenger hunt, and the official opening of the Ironwood.

The Health Auxiliary Raffle in 2011 was won by Mayor Blair Skinner, who immediately donated half of the proceeds back the Auxiliary.

When did you come to Pinawa?

Local author and high school student Shannon Gibson was selling her first novel entitled "Made to be Broken" at the Birthday market in 2012.

Marnie and Norm Sagert at the community picnic

Fred Penner entertained everyone at the picnic

The Ewing family spending time together

Community breakfast hosted by the Pinawa Foundation

Eleanor and Kim Reimer

The Reid family enjoying the sun

Happy 50th Anniversary - July 2013
By Louise Daymond

A year's worth of planning culminated in a week of celebrations that will be remembered for years to come as one of Pinawa's best birthdays ever.

As visitors came to town, they saw many of the homes decorated with signs stating the year that each resident came to town. It was a wonderful first impression; a chance to stop in your old neighbourhood, knock on a door, see old friends, or make new ones.

A Founders Gala, sponsored by AECL and the LGD, kicked off the celebrations Friday, July 12. The Gala was a tribute to Pinawa's Pioneers and AECL. The evening's emcee, Louise Daymond, introduced a series of guest speakers including Pinawa Mayor Blair Skinner, the Honourable Flor Marcelino (Minister of Culture, Heritage and Tourism), Lac du Bonnet's MLA, Wayne Ewasko, Hudson Bay Manager Desiree Blackmore and WL's General Manager, Russ Mellor, who brought greetings on behalf of AECL and Whiteshell Laboratories.

It was estimated that 400 people went through the High School Memory Lane! What a joy to watch former classmates recognize and see each other after many years, and to see their expressions when they walked down the halls. This was put together by a small committee of Lori Graham, Holly Parcey, Wendy and Mike Berry, and Lorne Schram. Special mention to Lorraine Nelson and the Pinawa Foundation, who managed to get the Graduation Wall finished in the nick of time.

An open air teen dance filled the air with music July 17. The dance was held at the tennis courts. It sounded like the kids had a great time.

The highly anticipated community picnic was held Friday afternoon. The crowd was large, families mingled, local entertainers performed throughout the afternoon, and the headliner Fred Penner was a huge success. The family theme continued Sunday morning with a pancake breakfast hosted by the Pinawa Foundation.

Lund Mania – An early morning start

The first ever Canadian Lund Mania Fishing Tournament was a tremendous success. Wilderness Edge Retreat and Conference Centre with host Kevin Penner was a partner for this community event. Lund Mania created many memories, not only for Pinawa, but for all of the participants as well. The boat parade had people lined all along the route to see some pretty impressive boats. The people who came to see the boats launch in the morning were treated to the very cool site of all the fishers standing at attention in their boats for the national anthems. And then off they went. The boats returned by 3 pm to find the marina lined with people watching the boats come in. Around 4 pm in the afternoon, about 500 people packed the beer garden tent and were treated to an hour long "warm up" set by Dog Pound and then Jason Gauthier took over for

the awards ceremony. Jason thoroughly entertained the crowd and invited many individuals to speak. Just to add to the excitement, Bobby Hull fished in the tournament and spent a couple of days right here in Pinawa on our 50th Birthday. He was very accommodating with autographs and even got his haircut by Clay the Clipper while he was here. But the icing on the cake was having the first ever tournament won by the Pinawa team of Dean Randell and Wayne Haner. The roar from the crowd when their weight of 24.2 lbs. was announced was deafening. The first Lund Mania could not have been scripted any better.

Acsion Industries hosted the Symposium entitled "Whiteshell Laboratories – A Science and Engineering Legacy for Canada" on July 18 and 19. The symposium covered a wide range of topics from Reactor Safety Research (presented by Len Simpson), to the Nuclear Waste Management Program (presented by Colin Allan), to the accomplishments in Life Sciences and Environmental Research (presented by Stu Iverson). On Day 2, there was a presentation by Grant Unsworth (WR-1's longest serving Reactor Superintendent – 1967-77) on the history of WR-1 Reactor and a talk by Grant Koroll on the Decommissioning of Whiteshell Laboratories. Over 175 guests participated in the symposium over the two days. The day concluded with tours of WL for the general public. For those who were unable to visit the site, a collection of AECL memorabilia was displayed in the old fire hall in Pinawa thanks to the efforts of former employees Jane Sargent and Christine Nuttall.

As part of the birthday celebrations, Acsion also produced series of reports entitled "History of Whiteshell Laboratories in the Media." This was a compilation of all of the news articles about Whiteshell Laboratories from 1959 to 2013. The reports were displayed at the AECL Exhibit during the birthday weekend and they have also been added to the webpage www.pinawa.com.

There were three adult dances over the weekend – two on Friday and another on Saturday, plus a band and beer gardens on Saturday. Just remember that our population is only around 1500, but somehow we got 400 people to each dance on the Friday night and 500 on Saturday.

Len Simpson, Colin Allan and Stu Iverson

Jane Sargent explaining a display at the AECL museum

The Fender Benders Reunion Social on Friday was pure joy, plain and simple. The Pinawa Foundation sponsored the event and volunteers from Survivor's Hope set up, served and cleaned up the lunch. Many volunteers made this event special.

In the 60s the Fender Benders formed in Pinawa; boys who loved music. The Benders dispersed in 1969, all leaving Pinawa. It was this love of music and the approaching birthday milestone that spurred a plan; playing at the 50th Birthday.

The Pinawa Parade for the 50th Birthday was large, exciting and brought out groups and individuals from far and wide. The parade included Ruth Dobbin as the Grand Marshall, the Pinawa Pioneers, and floats and displays from clubs like EMCA,

Sandy Wood, Peggy Mooradian and Doreene Gordon enjoy the Fender Benders Reunion Social

Pinawa Players, the Pinawa Foundation, the Health Auxiliary, AECL, and various high school classes holding their own special reunions.

Enjoying the thousands of pictures at the AECL museum

Pinawa's Royal Couple – Helen and Mike Tomlinson
(Photograph courtesy of Larry Friesen)

Ruth Dobbin as Grand Marshall of the parade

Pinawa Health Auxiliary's Mary Spitz - please note my tail

Pinawa's Pioneers

Rich Hamon - Pinawa's Bubble Man

John Tait and the Pinawa Players

Ralph Moyer – Going drag racing

What is so interesting?

Holly Kerr displays her face painting from the beach

Ray Warenko hard work

Class of 1986

Oliveiras celebrating Pinawa's 50th at the
birthday golf scramble

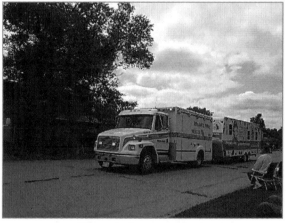

Where is the emergency?

The community owes a debt of gratitude to the Pinawa Lions Club for their contribution to our Birthday celebration every year, but especially for the 50ᵗʰ Birthday. This small number of extremely dedicated volunteers outdid themselves. They ran socials on Friday and Saturday night, the beach activities, the Saturday afternoon beer garden in support of the Lund Mania tournament, the fireworks, and arranged for the STARS helicopter to visit Pinawa. All of these events had more people than "normal" so were extra challenging. People are still talking about the fireworks. All of the proceeds from these activities go right back into our community. So thank you to all of the Lions for a job well done.

Cool vehicles at the Show and Shine

Heather Westdal Singing at the Fireworks
(Photograph courtesy of Stu Iverson)

Brass Ladies
(Photograph courtesy of Stu Iverson)

Pulling a water skier before Pinawa's birthday
fireworks

Birthday events all year long.

Brenda McKenzie at the town market

Mrs. Inez Streimer, Grade 1 teacher 1964, with one of her students, Louise Daymond (nee Plunkett) in 2013

Fender Benders' Reunion Social - Pinawa's 50th Anniversary – July 2013
By John Hammond Fender Bender and Past Resident Of Pinawa

"... The last time the Fender Benders played on stage before a live audience was 1969 right here. Now, where were we?!"

And so began the Fender Bender Reunion Concert on the stage of Pinawa Secondary School Friday July 19, 2013. The Pinawa 50th Birthday Facebook page had generated a buzz in the months before the 50th year celebration but until the moment we launched into G-L-O-R-I-A, we didn't know how exciting the Bender Reunion Concert would be! We couldn't have scripted it any better.

A little history here – 50 years ago, Pinawa's first group of teenagers hit the scene in the newly developed A.E.C.L. town, 75 miles northeast of Winnipeg, near the Whiteshell. Some of us were from Deep River, others from Winnipeg, Manitoba and beyond. As kids, we were transplanted to the new community and, we made the best of our new lives, exploring all that Pinawa had to offer. We were all pioneers. It was in the 1960s that the Fender Benders formed; boys who loved music and practiced in various basements or living rooms of parents who

Fender Benders

put up with the loud music and blown fuses. The Benders dispersed in 1969, all leaving Pinawa, to live our lives taking with us those formative years of bonding friendships, love of music, and solid values of community.

Through what some would call fate, some would call a "bucket list", the Benders reunited in 2010, which began the journey back to Pinawa for the 50th Birthday in 2013. The group had some communication over the years but mostly education, careers, and families had been the focus which took us all too different places. It was the combination of good memories and love of music and the approaching 50th Birthday that spurred a series of phone calls and emails resulting in the Fender Benders renting equipment and jamming for four days in Kenora, September 2010; Del Dunford, Tom Dunlop and Gary Griffith from Winnipeg, John Putnam from Seattle, Gerry Reimer from Vancouver, and John Hammond from London Ontario. Despite the challenge and logistics, there was never any doubt about the commitment and the goal of the 50th Pinawa Birthday. Some pals meet every year to fish, hunt or golf but for the next three years the band met four times to practice and reconnect through our music.

The Fender Benders would like to thank the Pinawa Birthday Committee, the LGD and especially Louise Daymond (Plunkett) for making the Bender Reunion Concert happen. We had met with Louise and committee a year or so ago, and knew that Louise was 500% committed to the success of the Birthday Celebrations and the Fender Benders. Thank you so much Louise. XOXOXO

The Benders will always think of Louise when we play "Down by the River". The songs that we played for the 50th Birthday were all the favourites as we best can remember them – and that night we played our hearts out in a gym decorated just the way it was for the 60s dances… One thing that was different about this concert was that now our teachers were dancing with us!! How awesome was that?

The kids of the 1960s, those first teenagers in Pinawa, have lived lives rich and full of the experiences that 50 years can bring. But there was something special about our time living in Pinawa and the Pinawa 50th Birthday weekend was proof of that. It was a time to share our experiences, renew friendships and make plans for the next 50 years. We had the time of our lives!!!

On behalf of the Fender Benders, thank you to everyone, organizers, volunteers, etc. who through this entire community effort, made the Birthday Celebrations such a success. Your welcoming smiles and friendly greetings were certainly a tribute to your wonderful community.

Reunion social poster designed by PSS Alumni Keith Gauthier

Extraordinary hospitality welcomed the Benders and their families at the homes of Lori and Don Robb and Lynn and Don Patterson. The endless stream of visitors throughout the weekend enjoyed a place to reminisce, refresh and refuel. It felt like we were at home. We all will be back!!!

Thank you also to Kevin Penner at Wilderness Edge, who was able to provide the Benders with great accommodation despite the tremendous challenge of being one of the busiest weekends ever!!

Thank you also to everyone who journeyed back to Pinawa to make this occasion so memorable. We hope you enjoyed the Birthday Celebrations as much as we did; Safe travels. We'll meet again some sunny day.

Pinawa is still a beautiful place to be. Happy Birthday!! Rock On Pinawa, Rock On!!!!

Chapter 7
Life in Pinawa

The Pinawa story cannot only be told through a list of events or a series of facts. You also have to look at the residents and their stories. Pinawa has been the working home of thousands of AECL scientists, engineers, technicians, trades peoples, and support staff. Pinawa residents travelled from around the world to be part of the Whiteshell team. Some were here for only a few years. Many chose to have a career and make Pinawa their home. Second and even third generations are now working and living in the community.

This final chapter tries to capture what it felt like to live in Pinawa through pictures. From the earliest days building the town, to completing the many buildings, to living through the current efforts by AECL to decommission the research site and depart Manitoba.

Look at the pictures. Remember your friends and colleagues. Follow the newspaper headlines. We hope you get a feel for what it was like to be part of the Pinawa Family.

A Town is Born - Meet Pinawa; Population 3
'Brains' of Nuclear Project to Live in Whiteshell
By John Dafoe *[Winnipeg Free Press, Saturday, July 20, 1963]*

PINAWA (Staff) – a town was born in Manitoba this week. Its name is Pinawa and its population – at the moment – is three. Within the next 10 years, however, it will swell to a model community of 5,000 with probably Manitoba's highest concentration of brains.

Pinawa is town site for Atomic Energy of Canada Limited's new Whiteshell Nuclear Research Establishment. It will be the home of the nuclear physicists, chemists and engineers who will carry out advanced research into the production of nuclear power.

Moved in This Week

The town's first three citizens moved in this week from Atomic Energy's first nuclear research station at Chalk River, Ont. They are: security chief Ben Banham, his wife and his son Donald. They set up a temporary home in a four-unit row-housing project until their fully-detached two-storey house is completed.

Another of the units was adapted this week as the town office and post office and a third is ready to take another family as soon as their belongings arrive from Chalk River.

Construction is nearing completion on the rest of the 160 housing units being built in the town by three Winnipeg contractors and, by the end of next month, 50 to 60 families will have moved in. The growth of the town will parallel that of the research centre nine miles away.

Use of Organic Liquids

Research will be centered on a nuclear reactor, scheduled for completion in 1965. The chief subject of the initial research will be the use of organic liquids – carbon and hydrogen atoms linked in unique ways – to remove heat from the reactor core.

Much research will be launched even before the reactor goes into operation. Scientists of the environmental research branch are already at work taking radiation counts in the area to use a check against which the radiation produced by the reactor can be measured.

Laboratories are almost ready for use in the centre's medical building, which is also being used temporarily as the administration building for the project, and work will be started by the time official opening ceremonies are held August 31.

The town will have one of the most beautiful settings of any in Manitoba, on the shore of Sylvia Lake, bordering the Whiteshell forest reserve. It will be a completely self-contained community. Tenders closed Friday for construction of a shopping centre, a hospital, a town office and a fire hall.

School Opens in Fall

An elementary school is scheduled to open in the fall.

The shopping centre will be built adjacent to a marina which will permit summer campers from the Whiteshell to do their shopping in Pinawa by boat.

Three thousand tons of sand was brought in during the winter to create a sandy bathing beach on an inlet in the lake on the edge of town.

The Banham home, at the moment, is an island of domesticity in the midst of a turmoil of muskeg, mud roads and construction equipment.

It boasts a tiny patch of lawn and a hand-made street sign.

The town is being developed by Central Mortgage and Housing Corporation and administered by the provincial government as a local government district.

Fills Many Roles

Town administrator Ed Lundman, a provincial employee, fills the roles of mayor, town council, school board and postmaster.

Most of the town's residents will rent their houses initially but arrangements may be made later for them to buy them.

Mr. Lundman has purchased a lot and is building his own house and several Chalk River people have obtained lots with plans to build when they are moved to Manitoba.

Growth of the town and the research centre will be gradual. It is expected that the centre will add 100 employees each year until it levels off at more than 1,000 in 1972. By that time population of the town will be about 5,000 and future growth will depend on the progress of the research.

Pinawa on a foggy morning
(Photograph courtesy of Sean Roberts)

Building along Athlone Crescent

The new Hudson's Bay Company Store

Installing the first sewers along Burrows Road –
February, 1963

Burrows Road and Alexander Avenue

Pinawa Militia – 1975
(Photograph courtesy of Larry Gauthier)

Pinawa – Its Past and its Future
By Roger Smith – Grand Opening of Pinawa Motor Inn, November, 1968

While I am not the first, I must add my congratulations to the management of the Pinawa Motor Inn for the design, decoration and furnishings of this fine motel. It is very evident to us all that this inn will make Pinawa a more enjoyable place in which to live.

Roger Smith

Those of you who work at the Whiteshell Nuclear Research Establishment, or have visited our plant, know that it has been built as a result of the ingenuity and experience of scientists and engineers across Canada. Its buildings and services have been designed by Manitoba architects and it has been built by Manitoba construction firms. As a result, we have one of the most modern, well equipped nuclear centres in the world. While this growth at WNRE was underway, the town businessmen, the municipal and school district personnel, and AECL Pinawa staff were striving to build a modern town. They also called upon their own experience and talents of many Manitoba professions to build what you see in Pinawa today. I think that these town personnel can all be very proud of the results of their work.

At our research establishment we have a reactor which is the only facility of its type in the world. We have enormous remote control caves for examining highly radioactive material, we have modern equipment of all types, but the most important item at WNRE is our professional and non-professional staff. While an automobile plant produces cars and trucks, and other manufacturing firms produce chemicals, radios or working machines, at WNRE we do not have any tangible commodity as an output. A research establishment such as WNRE produces only technical information which can be used by others to produce better materials, reactors, or equipment. This technical information is produced, not by the complex research facilities and equipment at WNRE, but by our scientists, engineers, technologists and tradesmen. These people cannot do their tasks properly unless they are backed up by staff in the workshops, the design officers and the medical and administrative groups. People are the most vital and valuable commodity at WNRE. As WNRE grows it is essential that we find and retain the best people to perform the tasks that have been assigned to our research establishment.

All of us are very much aware of the high cost of living but there is another factor which is also of great concern to the supervision of industry and research establishments. This is the high cost of staffing. If one of our employees leaves, he takes with him the skill and knowledge in a specific field that is necessary for the operation of the research establishment. AECL may have spent many thousands of dollars in training this man for his work. If he leaves, we must undertake the costly and lengthy job of finding and hiring a replacement. This requires much costly advertising and interviewing before a suitable man or woman may be found and relocated in Pinawa. He must then be trained in the job that he is to undertake. The cost of hiring a new employee can be up to $2,000 for an average employee and for scientific and engineering staff these costs can be over $5,000. This is only the initial expense; we must then train the person so that he can perform the work that needs to be done and this can take up to two years.

I hope that those of you who are visitors today have had a chance to look around Pinawa. We are proud of it as a fine, modern, well equipped village. AECL has been preparing to employ both money and staff to make Pinawa what it is today. This is just sound economics as it is cheaper to spend money on a town that will help retain plant personnel and keep them happy than to spend money in recruiting new staff.

Pinawa of the Past

The man who talks of the early days of a community is usually old, white haired and is inclined to ramble. As the history of Pinawa is only eight years' old, I can at least claim that I am not ready for a wheelchair and am not all that grey. However, let me claim the third prerogative of the almost oldest inhabitant and ramble about the old days way back five years ago.

After we had selected the site for WNRE we knew that we must find and build a place for our employees to live. None of the neighbouring towns were large enough to absorb more than a fraction of our staff, so we recognized from the outset that we would have to build a new town site. With the help of Central Mortgage and Housing, four possible sites for the town site were considered. We surveyed the merits of each of these alternatives and finally chose the present location of Pinawa. I must speak highly of CMHC's work at that time. Pinawa then had no roads and there were not even any clearings – it was a tangled mess of trees, swamps and mud that could be reached only by boat. We tried to look impressed as the CMHC town planners described the streets, houses and marina, and even the motel that they had included on the plans of this wilderness. I looked back over of these CHMC dream plans the other day and was surprised to note that in the dirty bay where they had predicted we would moor the pleasure boats for the town there is now our marina, and in the area where they showed a motel now stands this fine building – the Pinawa Motor Inn.

Back at Chalk River there was always considerable confusion because the town site was called Deep River. Some people never quite get straight which is the research establishment and who lives where. In all our innocence, the Whiteshell staff planned to avoid these complications by naming the town site Whiteshell. This sounded very simple and logical until a friend of mine in the Winnipeg Post Office got in touch with us and dispelled any ideas we had for this name. Our trusted postman who delivered the mail despite rain, snow, sleet and floods (strikes, of course were accepted) have some very fixed ideas about what you can name one of their post offices. It appears that stuck away on a remote Manitoba lake there was then a post office named Whiteshell. It was only open a few months a year. Our post office friend informed us that any mail addressed to Whiteshell was going to be delivered to that remote lake, despite whatever mystic atomic symbols or radioactivity we might put upon the envelope. While there might be some advantages to not getting some of our letters, we did not think that we could operate quite satisfactorily with our mail being sent to another part of Manitoba. Fortunately, close by to our new town site, were the remains of the first hydroelectric station in western Canada. This power dam and its town site had been called "Pinawa" back about 1900. Now the concrete for the old dam is still there but the generators have been removed and the houses for the town site are decidedly empty and moldy. The Manitoba Hydro kindly let us take over the name of Pinawa. I think that they had also hoped that we would take over the houses, too, and so our town was christened!

Incidentally, Pinawa in Ojibway, means "gentle water". We thought this sounded quiet and restful for the nuclear scientists resting after the cares of work at the research establishment. One of our staff consider it would be much more appropriate to call the town not "Gentle Water" but "Heavy Water". Perhaps, fortunately, the Ojibway tongue had never developed such scientific terms so we were spared such rank commercialism.

About that time, a reporter from a Winnipeg newspaper became interested in our activities and came out to look over the happy little wilderness that we had christened Pinawa. He apparently was not impressed with our own or CMHC's dreams for the town site, and when his article was published about our fair future city, it was headed "Pinawa – a name without a town."

Meanwhile, back at the ranch or, shall I say at the research establishment, our engineers were also encountering difficulties or, shall I say "a difficulty" in the shape of a rugged individualist who was not selling his farm to any group of people whom he considered was scaring his horse with our flying saucers. Our old farmer was a little difficult to argue with and he also carried a wicked shotgun that he used to emphasize his arguments. However, one day he and his faithful old horse were in a pleasant mood and he offered to sell out to us. We hastily telegraphed the money down to our engineer in the area but our old farmer was not going to accept any little cheque for his farm. So we went to the bank and obtained paper money for him, but the pile of money did not impress him. We returned to the bank and came back with 4,000 $1 bills. These, when heaped on his table, convinced him that he should do his patriotic duty for the country. So we moved old Peter Manistov's farm house out to the edge of the property on some land that the Manitoba provincial government had given us for him, and he now lives happily – convinced that he had been swindled by big business. Just the other day he wanted to know when he was going to get the royalties for the oil that we were taking off the farm. However, I have never been convinced that our old farmer was as eccentric as he made out. On looking back, we find that got more per acre for his land than anybody has ever been paid in these parts for farmland.

The research establishment was scheduled to start operation in 1963, so back in 1961 our contractors were hard at work digging sewers and water lines. This was not a very profitable activity to some of them as a rock ridge appeared in almost every location that was where they had to dig. So, for a long time, Pinawa experienced the sounds of dynamiting. The tops of all the temporary shacks were covered with bales of straw to protect them from the rocks that came flying out of space and landed on the buildings or any person who happened to be living or working at the town site.

During the first summer the weather was hot and dry and there were fires everywhere. Pinawa was not unique and one blaze started that could have easily burned out the town and left us without any trees. Fortunately, a resourceful engineer who happened to be near the site of the fire stole a big tractor that one of the contractors had left parked in the village and used it to cut a fire break which saved the town.

The next year Nature tried to compensate for the previous year's drought and it rained and rained. The streets that had then been built in Pinawa became stretches of mud, deep mud, which even a four wheel drive truck could not traverse. So in this modern age of thousands of horse power and atomic energy, the construction work around Pinawa was accomplished by wagons drawn by horses that could wade through the mud.

Some of you may have heard of a device known as a mechanic's lien, whereby a workman can claim temporary ownership of a building or piece of equipment upon which he has worked and for which he is being paid. It appears that one of the sub-contractors for the underground services at the town site had not been paid all to that he thought he was entitled, and decided to place a mechanic's lien in order to enforce payment. No building had been put up in Pinawa, so we decided to be thorough and placed a mechanic's lien against the whole town site. So, for several months the town of Pinawa was in the hands of the Bailiff, while the legal authorities studied the interesting problem as to how we could get our town back and go ahead with our work.

Despite all the difficulties, the research establishment was ready for operation in the summer of 1963 and people arrived who had to be accommodated. This brought about the era of the row houses. Let me explain …

While I have boundless admiration for CMHC town planning and some of their building design, I still have not forgiven them for the row houses that you see on some of the streets in Pinawa. Back in 1961 the CMHC house planners vehemently insisted that all housing of the future was going to be in the form of row houses, and that it was just inconceivable that a modern town site such as Pinawa would not have a large number of this type of structure. Despite our better judgement, we agreed to build a few of them at the town site. We have not built any more, as people generally agree with us and move to normal housing as soon as they have the chance. Fortunately, the contractor who was awarded the job of building the 34 row houses was much faster than the other house contractors and when Pinawa opened almost all we had for accommodation were these row houses. These row houses saved our skin. We used them for everything and everybody stayed in them for a time. The first municipal office was one of these row houses with the police station upstairs, municipal businesses being conducted in the living room and the kitchen serving as a town post office. Behind the house there was a big tank of gasoline and our Secretary-Treasurer was on duty every morning selling gasoline to anybody who needed to go into work. The first books that were bought for the Pinawa library were from the profits of the gasoline sales.

The Staff Hotel was still under construction so we took some of the row houses and turned them into single person accommodation with four girls or men in each house. Some of the staff suggested that we be broad minded and mix them up a bit, but we insisted on being rigidly Victorian. The single people cooked their meals in these houses as there was no fine motel like this or coffee shop to provide food. This did not seem to cause any particular trouble, as when I inquired from one eligible male how he was getting on with his own cooking he looked surprised that we should be worried. It appeared that he had been dined, and perhaps wined, at a different one of the girl's row houses every evening for the past month.

All of our inhabitants were not people, as the first summer brought almost as many bears as humans to Pinawa to dine on our succulent garbage. They had quite a few skunks along with them for company. Every morning at work there were new stories of householders being somewhat embarrassed by having bears make themselves at home on their front door step and sometimes on their back door step at the same time. Our only phones were on posts scattered around the town site. I don't believe that the Manitoba Telephone System ever believed the true story of one housewife who quickly terminated a long distance telephone conversation from one of these outside phones, on the grounds that there was a bear coming up behind her and she thought she would let the bear have the phone.

For the first year the only store was operated by the Bay in a garage beside one of the houses. One enterprising individual at Beausejour persuaded the merchant of that town to operate a bus service each week between Pinawa and Beausejour, so everybody went in on this special bus for their weekly shopping. We were very pleased to have Eyfe Walterson, the same enterprising Beausejour businessman and pharmacist who organized the bus service, come to Pinawa to start up and operate the Pinawa Pharmacy. Since that time, I understand he has ceased advocating a shopping bus service between Pinawa and Beausejour.

A great deal has been said about the benefits and efficiency of private enterprises and private capital. Full of these platitudes, we had presumed that the town shopping facilities could be built and operated by private individuals. It seemed logical and would comply with the oft-made statement that the government should not take on that which could best be done by private companies. However, it appears that the Canadian investor had not heard or did not agree with these sentiments as we could not find anybody who was prepared to build a shopping centre for Pinawa. As there had to be some place for our wives to go to spend our salaries, and incidentally buy food for our meals, AECL proceeded to build a shopping centre we were very fortunate in finding companies and individuals who were prepared to lease space and operate the stores and businesses that are necessary in a modern community.

After our disappointment in attracting private capital to build shopping centres, it was a very pleasant surprise for us to find someone such as Bill Chyzzy who is prepared to take the normal business risks to construct and operate a Pinawa commercial venture. We believe that this is the way business should be done in Pinawa, and we hope that other business men in the future will follow his excellent lead.

Pinawa of the Future

It is always easy to make pessimistic or very rosy predictions of the distant future if you are fairly certain that you will be either dead or will have left the area by the time you can be proven wrong. Within ten years I may still be around, and I hope not dead, as I should avoid predictions. However I will be rash and try to forecast what is going to happen to Pinawa in the future.

At the present time, our population is about 1,900 – men, women and children. We have firm plans for the expansion of the research establishment which will mean a corresponding increase in the number of people living in the village. Based on the predicted growth of WNRE, it is fairly evident that in the near future, that is not more than ten years, the population of the town will be about 3,500 people. In order to provide for this population, we will have a total of about 750 homes in the village. We will have extended the W.B. Lewis School and will have built a third elementary school. The high school will be extended and will have a gymnasium and additional recreation facilities. The Town Recreation Planning Board now proposes an ice arena, additional club rooms and a swimming pool to be added to the present community centre. Speaking as a householder, I believe that these recreation facilities will be built as a town project with funds provided by our townspeople.

At the present time our housing extends about ½ mile east of this motel. The town of the future will stretch out for another ½ mile and will probably have another swimming beach on the West side of town. We already have preliminary plans prepared for the extension to the shopping centre so as to include at least one supermarket, specialty stores, and business offices. This shopping centre will probably extend to the edge of the Pinawa Motor Inn. I think it would be a little unfair to make predictions as to what Mr. Chyzzy is going to do with his own motel in the next ten years, but I suspect that in that time he will have built some cottages on the rocky hill in the south overlooking the river.

Conclusion

All research and development does not only comprise mazes of glittering glassware, crates of stainless steel or rooms of electric currents. Development work also comprises buildings, facilities, roads and motels. Tonight we are here to thank Mr. Chyzzy and his staff who have developed this fine facility for our village. On behalf of the townspeople and AECL, I would like Mr. Chyzzy to know we appreciate the high standard of his result.

Joyce Brown, Lorna Lubitz and friends helping the fire fighters

Playing on Alexander Avenue

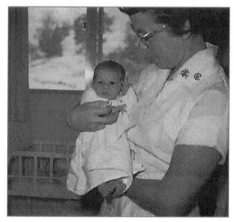

Three day old Marcia Banks – born at the Pinawa Hospital on McDiarmid in 1964

Cafeteria at Kelsey House staffed by Dominion Catering

Pinawa in 1964

Pinawa in 1964

Pinawa Construction in 1964

Pinawa Club Building Committee in 1964 – Ray
Sochaski, Bill McKeown and Bob Jones

Short History of Pinawa
By Ed Lundman, May 7, 1970

Local government in the District of Pinawa came into being in January 1962 and I became Resident Administrator and Official Trustee on October 15, 1962 after the resignation of Lieutenant Colonel Kirby.

My recollections will deal with incidents which came from my first knowledge of Pinawa back in 1961 in the contracting and will go forward from that point. Most of these will be recollections of personalities and incidents rather than any attempt to provide a chronological history of Pinawa.

My first contact with Pinawa was when we bid the contract for the sewage lift station, the lagoon and the pipeline. I remember crossing the dam at Seven Sisters, going along the partially built road and then along a trail leading to the lagoon site, the force main and finally to the sewage lift station. This trail had been an old logging trail in the fall of 1961 and was extremely dry and we hauled all the gravel along this trail. The next summer, that same trail, in some places, was under 3 feet of water and the whole thing was a quagmire from one end to the other.

A crew of men lived in trailers there and the foreman's wife, a young bride of 18, cooked for the crew. An incident that I remember from here is when Naayken's Transfer came down with a semi-trailer truck which had been to the plant and then came with two kegs of nails for the project. I stopped at the trailer and asked Gordon's wife where the crew was, and she said down the road at the sewage lift. He headed through the bush on this trail with the large semi-trailer truck. He delivered two kegs of nails, turned his semi-trailer around in the middle of the bush and headed out. That is what we call service!

In the spring of 1963 just before the opening of the town's site, I took my Sunday school class out to Pinawa to see the site. These were boys ten to twelve years of age. I had a station wagon with ten of these youngsters in it. It had rained, as per usual, and we borrowed rubber boots from the men.

As we were leaving, three of the boys were missing and we went to look for them. We met two of them who said that the other one was stuck in the mud. Don Green and another man went down with a shovel and literally dug the young fellow out of the mud which was up to his hips. He was one of the trouble-makers in the class and his companions would have been quite happy to have left him in the mud.

The actual opening of the town on July 15, 1963 will be remembered for a number of reasons. The water began to flow in the pipes with very incomplete water treatment, sewage was handled, garbage collection started and the post office went into operation. It was one of my many jobs at that time to be the Resident Administrator, the Official School Trustee, the Post Master and the Responsible Authority under the town planning scheme, etc.

Jim Spencer came out directly from high school as Recreation Director and this meant any job that vaguely resembled recreation became his responsibility. The area now occupied by the beach was a deep creek mouth and this had been filled with rock fill on the ice the winter before. In June and July of that first year, we went down and you could see rocks sticking out in piles in a real ragged mess. A drag line was moved on to the site and Jim was taken down and told to make a beach out of this area. He spent days dressed in a pair of swim trunks and my knee boots to keep from cutting his feet on the rock while helping to direct the drag line in leveling out the bottom on a regular basis and then spreading the necessary sand. This was the case many times. Here was a job to be done, get it done, not how. Jim did not disappoint us.

The move-in at the end of July into the new house was also a close timing item. When the truck arrived with Don Graham's and my furniture on it, we had to haul it in with a cat through mud. The housing unit that I was to occupy was not ready. They were still laying floor tile. Therefore, I moved into the other unit and by the time my furniture was unloaded, the floor tile was laid in the other unit and Don moved in there. As we were moving our furniture, in a painter comes to varnish the stairs and he varnished the stairs, move or no move. We took the brush and paint away from him and he went and got more. He spoke not a word of English.

One night, Pete Kingston had a house party and invited the entire town. We had rigged up in the basement of an unfinished house, lights and power and we had a dance at the corner of Athlone.

If you danced too strenuously and went too close to the edge, you would fall off into the excavation. Fortunately, that did not happen. Those first days of knowing all created a comradeship which helped us through many rough situations and also made it difficult for the future people to be absorbed.

In the spring of 1964, many boats required docking. With a little bit of material borrowed, bought and stolen, the citizens built a dock. Harry Smith was the moving force behind it. Saturday and Sunday you would find the men standing up to their waists in water driving posts with a post maul, and then putting the deck on it. Though we spent our recreation hours there, Harry was there every day.

Then, there was the day when Peter Thiessen, the school principal, decided to change Hallowe'en. I don't remember the reason now but for some strange reason he felt that Hallowe'en that year would be better celebrated on October 30th. We might have all agreed with his reasoning but people felt that the school was going a little too far when it sent out a letter stating that Hallowe'en would be held on October 30. It was a fine line to tread between assistance and good ideas and officious officials.

We go back to the days when the first people moved in and everyone watched to see the boat trailers hauling in the temporary possessions of people who had lived at the lake while their house was being prepared for them.

After we opened the high school, the first marks were forthcoming. Standards had been set high and the low results infuriated parents. I went down on Parent's Night and for a while it seemed to be a difficult situation but fortunately reason did prevail.

With the town only six years old, it was apparent that it would be easy to write and history and yet what is history? I remember the delays, the frustrations, the heartaches; they are all in the past. They have no relevance to the other people of today and rightly so.

We can thank people such as Fred Gilbert who did so much work and gave his life to make Whiteshell. The unpleasantries and confrontations have no meaning now in that they were only a means to an end. I remember the people, the persons who contributed to making Pinawa what it is today. They took those unpleasant steps; they underwent inconveniences as they saw building for the future.

You will note that most of my recollections are of people and not of facts. The fact is actually; what is Pinawa today and what is its future tomorrow? I would hope that some of your history for your centennial project would deal more with the goals, aspirations from here on. History would show only that people took actions for a better tomorrow not knowing necessarily what it would be.

Tent over school construction – 1963

Pinawa's young residents

Pictures from W.B. Lewis School

Pictures from W.B. Lewis School

Pictures from F.W. Gilbert School

Annual F.W. Gilbert school picture

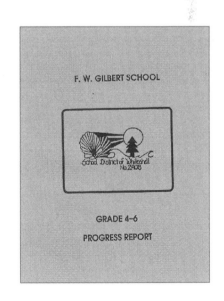

Teachers who graduated from Pinawa Secondary School and then taught in
Pinawa Schools: With Principal Darcia Light second from left: Devon Turner,
Christine Reimer, Suzanne Rueckert, Jennifer Donnelly, Lisa Krupka
(Photograph courtesy of Louise Daymond)

Pinawa at 50 – The History of a Town Built for the Future
By Louise Daymond, - The Paper, April 8, 2013

The first anyone heard of AECL's plans to site a new research facility in Manitoba was through a story in the Winnipeg Free Press in 1959. It was the lead article on the front page, October 1, headlined: **"Huge Atomic Research Plant Set for Manitoba; Second Chalk River in Size and Cost"**. Residents of Lac du Bonnet, Beausejour and throughout the region then looked to the Springfield Leader, Beausejour Beaver or the Steinbach Carillon for updates on the story, which was very exciting news for the province.

In Ontario, the news was broadcast through internal sources at AECL's Chalk River facility (CRNL), and as plans began to take shape, and employees started to make plans to relocate (willingly or otherwise) to Manitoba, a need arose to begin publishing a newsletter dedicated to updates on Pinawa and the Whiteshell Nuclear Research Establishment (WNRE). And so was born the Whiteshell Gazette. Interestingly enough, the first editor of the Gazette, Mr. John Leng, never did make the journey from Ontario to Manitoba.

The first editions of the monthly Gazette were published in Deep River, Ontario, mimeographed copies typed on legal sized paper. They were an invaluable resource to the young men and women who were embarking on an adventure even they weren't fully aware of at the time. The Gazette continued to publish monthly editions under a variety of editors, until 1967.

In 1968, the first edition of The Forum was introduced to the community. The Forum was a booklet for, printed on 8.5" by 11" paper, owned and operated by Mr. John Barber. It had paid advertising and photographs, which was not possible with the LGD's copying equipment.

The Springfield Leader had a regular weekly column for Pinawa news, in addition to all the communities within the region. Regular contributions were also made to the Beausejour Beaver by Pinawa residents, most notably Mrs. Jo Hillier.

The LGD also began publishing a newsletter in 1963, which provided much needed information on services for the influx of residents in the aforementioned migration from Ontario and points elsewhere.

Pinawa's first bone fide weekly newspaper was owned and operated by Mrs. Pat Roy, whose husband was the RCMP Corporal in the Pinawa detachment. Pat had apprenticed with the editor of the paper in

Whiteshell Here We Come!
J. Leng, Editor – The Whiteshell Gazette, Vol. 1, No. 1, January 1963

After months for some and years for others, what appeared to be a vague and distant future, the year 1963 has finally arrived. In six short months the trek to what many an Ottawa Valley joker refer to as the "Wild West" will begin.

Many forget that a similar migration took place from Montreal and other points to Chalk River some 18 years ago. Things were not quite so comfortable in Deep River at the time, "war-time fours" and "sixes" and some P.O.W. buildings carried the major housing, hotel and shop load for some while. The new migrants to Pinawa, however, can look forward to what will shortly be a modern new town complete with all services and brand new housing, advanced and attractive laboratories to work in, a well-developed recreation area in adjacent Whiteshell Park, and a bustling city just 90 minutes away. This you will agree is quite an advance over Chalk River's starting point.

The most important asset to a community however is its people; if they do not "tick" then nothing does. Pinawa is fortunate in this regard in attracting a talented, ambitious and spirited group. We are not even there yet and already the first reports have been published, the first party held, the first community organization formed, and now in order to keep you up with all these goings on, here is your first newspaper.

Louise Daymond with copies of the Paper

Thompson, and set up shop in the garage of their home. The Pinawa Press had a small press for business cards and other small print jobs, but the camera ready negatives of the Pinawa Press were printed weekly at the Leader in Lac du Bonnet. The final edition of the Pinawa Press was published in 1988, whereupon it was sold to Dale Brown under a new name, the Pinawa Channel (1988-1995). The Paper has been publishing continuously since Nov. 28, 1995.

Chris Saunders at Philanthropy
Day for the Pinawa Foundation

TSN Sports Centre in Pinawa

Pinawa Panthers

Pinawa Panthers High School Basketball 2013 – Back row – Abi Voth, Tessa Trueman, Madison Chapel, Hannah Voth; Front row – Beth Nelson, Avery Goodwin-Stam, Lorraine Nelson (coach), Jill Lauze, Emily Shewchuk

Blair Skinner and Ron Drabyk accepting donation for arena from Delissio

Curling with Ernie Bialas, Pat Sullivan, Randy Herman and Shirley Boyle

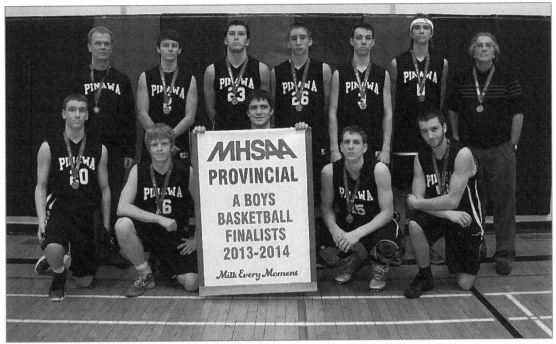

Pinawa Panther's High School Basketball Team – 2013: Back row – Jeff Hayter (coach) Dylan Daymond, Nic Pinel, Bob Nelson, Tyler Flood, Grant Trueman, John Fagan (coach); Front row – Josh Hayter, Steven Simpson, Adam Wyryha, Jon Hayter, Jordan Daymond

Pinawa Panther's High School Soccer Champions 1984: Back Row –Bob Dixon (coach), Martin Rochon, Andrew Simpson, Kevin Ticknor, Michael Bratty, Cam Buchanan, Paul Amos, Todd Hawton, Kevin Daymond, Paul Ingham (coach); Front row – Paul Hayward, Kevin Henschell, Steve Biddiscombe, Scot Halley, Mike Kerr, Jim McDowall, Marcello Chuaqui, Paul Nuttall

My Move to Pinawa
By Lloyd Rattai

In 1964 Susan and I lived in Winnipeg. Susan was employed as a Teacher in Elmwood and I was employed as a process operator at the Imperial Oil refinery. I had just hired on at the refinery in 1960 after going through a period of layoffs at Canadian National Railways as an Engineer/Fireman. News of an impending move by Imperial Oil moving to Edmonton was not an option for us. I had the option of returning to the CNR with full seniority.

I had heard of AECL building a research centre near Lac du Bonnet. Since both Susan and I came from the Beausejour area we decided that we would explore the possibility of employment in the area. In July of 1964 I had a promising interview at the Whiteshell site. After the interview I took a ride down the road to the new town of Pinawa. It was a sea of mud. I decided if I got the job I would commute from Winnipeg or Beausejour for the first while. Susan had her employment obligation in Winnipeg.

When Susan and I went to see Pinawa together, we decided we would move to Pinawa if she would get employment at the Whiteshell School District and we were assigned one of the new

Susan and Lloyd Rattai

homes being built. We got a very nice new home at 20 Devonshire with no finished lawn. In 1966 we purchased property on Grey Crescent with the intention of building one of only six private homes in Pinawa at that time. We raised our children Melony and April in the safe and natural environment Pinawa has to offer. We were pioneers in a new town and grew to love it.

Old Pinawa at dawn

An Early Memory
By Bruce and Murray Smith

The original Pinawa rifle range was under the Gilbert School. The facility was largely built with volunteer labour. Even high school students were involved in laying the bricks. I can remember putting in pop bottle caps to establish the correct distance between bricks and therefore the correct amount or mortar.

One funny incident that we remember from the early years of Pinawa was when the military invaded AECL WNRE site in the mid-sixties. The plan had been to conduct a takeover of the site, but somehow the site was miscommunicated as new Pinawa rather than Old Pinawa. The exercise was carried out with military precision on a weekend with guns but using blanks. We remember our father, Roger Smith, madly searching through his war chest for a uniform that he had not worn for a good 15-20 years. He was still part of the Army reserve at the time and held the rank of Major, which they no doubt hoped would make him a higher ranking officer than those conducting the exercise, but with a uniform that bore no resemblance to anything used in the sixties. Tom Lamb, the head of security at the time, careened out to the plant with our father trying to persuade his uniform to stretch to unattainable lengths. We believe they managed to confuse the officer in charge of the

Pinawa Beach in the 1960s

operation with our father outranking him but the officer not really sure what military organization that he belonged to. Somehow Tom Lamb was shot at while going through a road block but it was with blank bullets fortunately. No permanent damage was done but we would hazard a guess that the military people involved in this exercise were given a lesson on radioactive workplace security risks.

Near the Marina

2012 Manitoba Loppet
(Photograph courtesy of Stu Iverson)

Build a Town in a Bush
By Ray Henschell

What! You really think they will build a town in wilderness with all the bears, wolves, deer, rocks, bush and no roads. An engineering consultant, W.L. Wardrop and Associates was hired to investigate an appropriate site that was near the AECL plant. The Pinawa channel area was selected and work on it began.

When I came into the picture, I had heard they decided to build a town somewhere close but not in Lac du Bonnet. My father, Alex Henschell, said they chose a site by the Pinawa control dam and had already started surveying and cutting lines to run elevations. At that time, there were no roads leading to the site, only a winter trail where they took out logs with horse and sleigh and one from Lac Du Bonnet. My father had rented a boat at Otter Falls and was bringing in the surveyors and men to do the labour. I got a job there with a starting salary of $1.25/h, with an extra $0.25/h for my chainsaw. I took over my father's job of driving the boat.

Our survey crew consisted of Gerald Benoit, Gerry Pluchinski, Bruce Tittlemier and me. Sometimes we had up to 21 men working at the site clearing the bush so we had to make sure they made the lines straight. Many times I had to make two trips with the boat in and two more to take them back out.

One day, I brought in Mr. W.L Wardrop who to investigate the site. We docked at the marina and we all gathered around to hear him say "Ok boys, if we are going to make any money we have to make this place look good". So off we went to work, rain or shine.

Take a trip with me to see what a typical day was like to get to this new town site! First, we had to drive to Otter Falls from Seven Sisters on a muddy, gravel road, barely passable at Big Creek (now the Park entrance). We would rent a boat from Riverview Cabins (16 ft. wooden Peterbourgh with a 17 HP motor). It was a 3 mile boat ride on the Winnipeg River, through Sharky's Channel, making sure we went around the part that was blasted out with the rocks in the middle.

Ray Henschell

When we arrived at the Pinawa control dam we saw a small control building on the left side and the remains of a Model T Ford just next to the dam. When the weather was hot, we saw many snakes sunning themselves on these rocks.

We established docking areas at the first bay just west of Aberdeen road on the base line. The second landing at the marina, but back then it was just a creek with lots of stumps. Now that we had arrived, we had to walk through the forest and over the rocks to set up our instruments from where we left off the previous day, on the baseline going north for a half a mile. From this baseline, we ran lines every 200 feet west towards Seven Sisters for about a mile. We needed these lines to be cleared so we could take elevations every 200 feet and record it in the field book. We also hired some men to drill test holes with a 2" hand auger every 200 feet so we could take soil samples and plan where to put the sewer lines. Soil samples were bagged and taken to Winnipeg for analysis.

We had lots of problems daily with the mosquitoes, black flies, horse flies and hornets. One time, I went down the trail to check on one of the workers and he came running like crazy. As he passed me, I could see hornets following him, I backed up into the bush and they missed me, but he got stung and we had to take him home.

In order to have the correct elevations at the site, we had to run levels from the Seven Sisters dam and back. That meant using a 200 ft. tape and driving stakes along the path, all without an error of more than 2 inches. We placed a permanent benchmark on a high rock by the high school.

For water quality, we were asked to take 3 gallon jugs halfway to Pinawa from the Seven Sisters dam. When the snow was too deep, we took our snowshoes, a toboggan and an axe. The weather was cold so we bundled up. When we got out there, we started chopping a hole. The ice was about 2 ft. thick but we got our samples. On the way back, the water froze and the bottles broke. Not performance.

When winter approached we had to put the boat away and walk in from Seven Sisters along the winter road. When things were frozen we drove in with a small camper trailer for shelter and a camp stove to make coffee. One day in spring we walked to the trailer and found the door open, muddy bear footprints on our bed and all the cooking tools crushed.

One day, I had to bring some managers from Chalk River to see how things were progressing. We were docking at the Pinawa control dam and the boat came to a halt just before we touched the shore. We were aground on a rock and water coming up through the bottom. I reversed the engine and pulled it off the rock with water gushing into the wooden boat. I quickly pulled a plastic bag from my lunch and plugged the hole and away we went.

Well, this was not all work and no play. During duck and deer hunting seasons we would bring along our guns; there was plenty of wildlife in that area. Oh yes, what about the bears? One sunny day while we were eating our lunch we heard a crack behind us and turned to see a mother bear and her two cubs. I guess they smelled our garlic sausage sandwiches. We stood up and hollered "Are you leaving or are we leaving?" We left.

During the winter we came across a tree that had fallen over and that had a large stump at the bottom. I noticed that there was some frost at the top. I asked who wanted to see it there was a bear in there. There were no volunteers, so I took a stick and poked a hole in the top and looked in. I saw black fur and it was breathing. We took off like a shot! The next day we brought our guns along and I had the pleasure of waking him up. This time, I poked down real hard and ran like crazy. Again nothing! The third time, I really gave it my all and ran. Well, now he woke up and out he came. The boys were ready with their guns and we now had a nice bear rug. The bear had to be removed as it was right on the baseline and we did not want any surprises.

Now you have gotten a glimpse of the early start of your town of Pinawa. As I look at your beautiful town, I never could have imagined that anything like this would be possible.

Anecdotes of the Early Years
By Len Horn

I was fortunate to be the first tradesman hired by AECL. The thought of moving to a brand new house in a brand new town was more than our family had ever dreamt of. But sure enough, 16 McDiarmid would be simply the best. Pinawa was a town being built to perfection and to live there when everything was new, was a once in a lifetime experience. There were lots of animals around the town site; there were deer, skunks, the odd fox and more than enough bears.

Prior to telephone hookup we used to use an MTS phone booth. I recall one late evening a woman making a call noticed a large black bear coming towards the phone booth. It started sniffing around and then stood up on the booth and gave it a good shake. Lucky for her he stood down and wandered off, back into the woods. The screams must have gotten to him. Without concrete roads, a team of horses with driver was hired to pull wagonloads of building material through the muddy streets to the houses being built. After working for several long days in the mud, the horses came down with hoof rot and had to be put on the sick list for a couple of weeks.

In the winter, we would take our tape recorder over to the skating rink and people would skate all afternoon to music. School classrooms were used for church meetings as well as evening entertainment, such as productions by the newly-formed Pinawa Players. There was also room for the Cubs, Scouts and

Girl Guides. There were fun parties, be it Hallowe'en, Christmas or square dancing. With hockey and broomball in the winter, and baseball and camping in the summer, you got to enjoy the companionship of other young people and their young families.

It wasn't long until Thomas Baxter Lamb formed up the first Volunteer Fire Department. I worked with Tom and put together the first fire truck on the plant site. It had a Wajax pump, lots of hoses and fire fighters' gear for twelve to fourteen fire fighters.

Pinawa is a wonderful town and it was good to us throughout our seventeen years.

Memories of Pinawa
By Florence (Sis) Smith

Arriving in Pinawa in 1963 was an introduction to roughing it, much like the Klondike was in the beginning. No roads, no store, construction everywhere and lots of mud when it rained. A little line of rubber boots down Burrows where mothers had pulled their charges out of the mud, leaving their boots behind. In cities, noon-hours saw a congestion of traffic. In Pinawa noon-hour saw mothers running toward the school to gather the kids. Traffic was a mother bear and cubs heading down Burrows. Bears were a common sight in daylight, as well as at night, rummaging through the garbage (which we later learned not to put out). It gave us great delight to tell visitors we had a drive-in theatre! We knew, of course, we meant a garbage dump where visitors were taken to watch bear antics.

Sis Smith

Roughing it was exciting because all news of progress was welcomed. Such was the announcement the Hudson's Bay would be opening a "store" in the garage of the Bay house on Athlone. A group of we Pinawa gals got all dressed up (high heels included) to buy flour, etc. Wow!!

Progress did go in leaps and bounds and did expand to a mini-mall with a Hudson's Bay store, drug store, bank and post office.

My introduction to nursing in the community was to be hired to work in the house/hospital. The house was located on McDiarmid Road and converted to a hospital. Bedrooms were "wards" shared by both adults and children. The nursery was the size of a closet, but the busiest was the room converted into a delivery room. Babies and more babies! At night the doors were locked, as you worked alone; the doctor a few doors down, on call. This was a new chapter in nursing experience after working in a big city hospital.

We moved into the new "real" hospital in 1965. Awesome! We had lots of space, a real nursery and delivery room and more and more babies!

One thing did not change: the doors were locked at night. A new physician arrived and we forgot to mention that when he was called, he must 'buzz' for us to let him in. One night on arrival, finding the door locked, he broke it down – oops!

We were very fortunate to have a staff (and some spouses) with very creative minds. This creativity resulted in some very amusing and sometimes very risqué (as one friend put it) "theatrical productions", which will long be remembered.

I lived in Pinawa from 1963 to 1997, watched the town grow, enjoyed good friends, much fun, beautiful landscape, and it was a great place to raise your family.

During those years I worked with many wonderful people in my nursing career. In 1992 my retirement party was a fantastic "theatrical production".

The Beginning of a Dynasty?
By David Ledoux, March 6, 1985

Being the backup goaltender and the only member of the Midget Panthers who can read and write, I felt obliged to write this on behalf of the team. The Midget Panthers entered the Provincial 'B' Championship Tournament in Souris on March 1 ranked fifth, and emerged victorious, ending a twenty-one year drought in Pinawa.

The team has not had great success in opening games in tournaments, so the majority of the team went down on Thursday night and stayed in a hotel in order to get a decent rest. The Panthers started the tourney Friday afternoon against Carman, a good team but one that Pinawa has had success with in the past. In the usual fashion the team's start was less than spectacular. Carman opened the scoring at 9:26, a 40 foot cannon that evaded the grasp of net minder Kevin Daymond.

Pinawa's pace picked up after that, with the resulting goal by Andrew Davidson at 3:28. This was the beginning of a spectacular tournament by the line of Andrew Davidson, Jim McDowall and Todd Hawton, who combined for almost fifty points in the tournament. Davidson's goal was set up by Cam (Ska) Buchanan and McDowall. The only goal in the second period was scored on a blast from the blue line by star defenseman Bill Fenton, on a pass from Wayne Early. The third period was not a good one for the team. Carman tied the race, scoring at 13:35, and then went into the lead at 1:18. Wonder Coach Chris Saunders pulled the goalie for an extra attacker, which turned out to be a wise choice when Dan Zerbin stuffed a bouncing puck to pull Pinawa back to a tie at three. But the game was not over. Right off the face-off, McDowall charged forward with the puck. He deked both defencemen out of their socks, falling to his knees in the process. Using Hawton as a decoy, he trickled the winner in from the prone position at 0:10 seconds to give Pinawa the 4-3 win.

Pinawa's second opponent was the powerful Killarney team. The Panthers knew the task at hand and came loaded for bear. Jim McDowall opened the scoring at 14:17, converting a pass from Andrew Davidson. Pinawa struck twice more on goals by Bill Fenton and Marcello (Whatever) Chuaqui before Killarney replied at 4:11, squashing any hopes Daymond had of a shut-out. Pinawa stayed high though and scored twice more before the end of the period. Hawton and McDowall scored within 14 seconds of each other to give Pinawa a 5-1 lead at intermission. The domination continued over 2nd ranked Killarney in the second, with Like Sprungmann and McDowall again scoring. Killarney replied with one goal. Effort in the third relaxed slightly, with Killarney scoring four goals with Pinawa's three to make it respectable. Todd Hawton, John Amos and Wayne Early found the net to finish the game at 10-6.

The Panthers finished the round robin against little-liked Roblin. The last meeting was a 12-3 blowout in Pinawa's favour and this game left the watchers with a feeling of déjà vu. John Amos opened the scoring at 6:56 of the first period. Roblin replied with one just 50 seconds later, a 30 foot blast past net minder Daymond. Todd Hawton got it back at 5:06 to round out the scoring for the period. The rest of the game was all Pinawa which scored four unanswered goals in the second period. Sharpshooters for the Panthers were Andrew Davidson, Dan Zerbin, and captain Bill (Cap'n Crunch) Fenton with two. Roblin notched one in the third, which wasn't noticed against another four Pinawa goals. John Amos, Todd Hawton, and Dan Zerbin, all with their second of the game, and Wayne Early scored to help give the Panthers the 10-2 victory and first place after the round robin.

In the semi-final Pinawa came up against the home team Souris. The Panthers scored two unanswered goals in the first period, 15 seconds apart by Todd Hawton, set up by Davidson and McDowall. Jim McDowall scored first at 9:23, followed by John Amos at 8:35 of the second period, to give Pinawa a 4-0 lead. Souris came storming back, notching one at 8:07 to spoil Daymond's shut-out. Scoring in the second was rounded out by John Palson on a blast from 15 feet with his patented bacon-slicer shot. Souris came out steaming in the third, scoring two goals. The home team had momentum and was applying great pressure, causing a lot of scrambling defensive play. Luke Sprungmann's goal at 1:31 relieved the pressure and topped the 6-3 victory, paving the route to the final.

The final was a rematch versus Killarney who edged Minnedosa 7-5 in overtime. The team had the mental edge and was well rested after the semi-final. The mood in the dressing room before the game was one of excitement. Pinawa exploded right off the draw. Jim McDowall won the draw, and raced forward splitting the defence. A cannon-like slap shot followed, finding the top corner just six seconds into the game. A tough defensive battle followed over the next period and a half. Pinawa's second goal was scored at 4:50 of the second period on another slap shot by Jim McDowall. The Panthers went to the dressing room after two periods knowing the hardest was still ahead. Killarney opened the scoring at 15:32. A much-needed goal by John Amos followed at 13:53, relieving some of the pressure. But a resilient Killarney scored just 50 seconds later on a defensive miscue. The score stood at 3-2, with still half the period remaining. Andrew Davidson added some padding to the lead at 6:35 on a pass from Jim McDowall. McDowall's third and fourth goal of the game followed to give the 6-2 victory and the championship to Pinawa.

A short awards ceremony followed and a photograph session, then the team paraded to the dressing room, followed by the jubilant parents. Two chilled bottles of Champagne were opened and coaches Chris Saunders and Dave Shoesmith got a bath in the bubbly. Everyone got to sample the winnings. And the taste of victory? Satisfying!

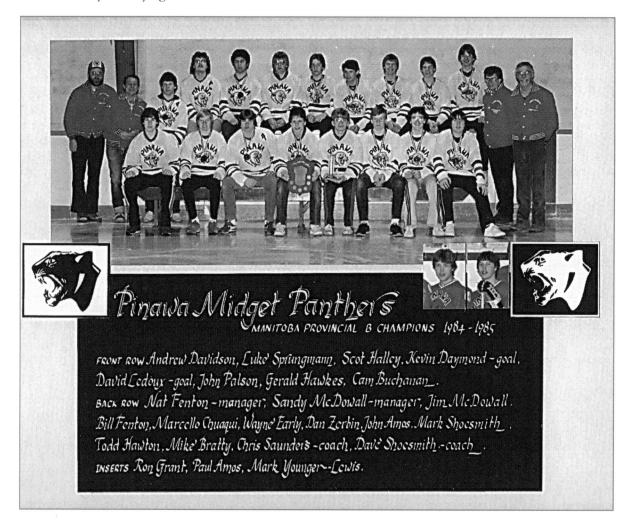

Pinawa Midget Panthers
MANITOBA PROVINCIAL B CHAMPIONS 1984 - 1985

FRONT ROW Andrew Davidson, Luke Sprungmann, Scot Halley, Kevin Daymond - goal, David Ledoux - goal, John Palson, Gerald Hawkes, Cam Buchanan.
BACK ROW Nat Fenton - manager, Sandy McDowall - manager, Jim McDowall, Bill Fenton, Marcello Chuaqui, Wayne Early, Dan Zerbin, John Amos, Mark Shoesmith, Todd Hawton, Mike Bratty, Chris Saunders - coach, Dave Shoesmith - coach.
INSERTS Ron Grant, Paul Amos, Mark Younger - Lewis.

1978-79 Pee Wee Team – Back Row: Ken Meek (Coach), Sean Daymond, John Truss, David Johnson, Mike Velie, Vaughn Thibault, Jeff Bender, Garry Buchanan (Coach); Middle Row: Brian Stefaniuk, Dean Gillert, David Remington, Todd Meek, John Borsa, Kelly Buchanan, Ron Frechette; Front Row: Dean Jarvis, Derek Acres, Ian Pollock, Kevin Henschell, Grant Bailey, Ian Dixon

1964-65 Pinawa Bantams, coached by Orville Acres; back row: Danny Barnsdale, Del Dunford, David Pummett, Murray Smith, David Robertson, Jim Lawson; front row: Glenn Hawley, Allan Green, Brian Reid, John Putnam, John Hammond (goalie), Doug Reid, Bruce Rankin

1967 Pinawa Collegiate Hockey Back row – Allan Green, Rick Plunkett, Orville Acres (coach), Kent McKellar, Dan McGinnis; Front row – Dan Barnsdale, Bruce Rankin, Murray Smith, Don Hart

More Pinawa Stars

Pinawa Skating Rinks
By Len Horn

Rink #1 was built behind the Gilbert School on Massey. It was a temporary job comprised of posts, rails and sheets of plywood. The following year the Gilbert School was to be extended and the rink was taken down and rebuilt further back, parallel to Burrows Road, hence Rink #2 was born.

After the third winter, Rink #2 was torn down in order to complete the landscaping around the school. An arena was too far off in the future to be seen, and in order to continue the skating programs, Rink #3 was built behind the high school and near the track. This time it would be much more substantial, and it included a fairly large trailer. There were dressing rooms built at each end, leaving a good-sized common room in the middle. With help from the LGD and volunteers, the ground was leveled, the posts and rails were in and the endless number of 2x6's were cut to length, painted and nailed in place. "Keep using that level, boys; we don't want those boards to lean." The rink was completed with electric heat and a toilet. A time clock, electric buzzer and red light were installed to end the periods. After the games there was hot chocolate and cookies for the players.

Rink #3 was dismantled and relocated alongside the new arena. It was used for pleasure skating, broomball and shinny hockey games.

Len Horn with son Larry celebrating Northeastern Midget League Championship, 1971-72

1978/79 Pinawa Panthers - Back Row L/R Alan Abraham (asst. manager), Eric Ayres, Mike Borgford, Dean Randell, Nigel Boulton, Doug Hollies, Brent Donnelly, John Bird, Brian Friese, Wendel Schatkowski, Jeff Allan, Mike Barnsdale, Bill Ayres (manager), Marty Stanley, Len Williams (coach). Front Row L/R Doug Grant, Harold Levesque, Tom Harding, Jeff Seifried, Gord Sochaski, Bruce Donnelly

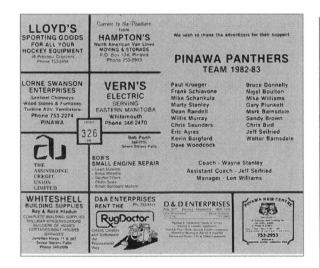

1972 North Eastern Manitoba Champions – Pinawa Lions
(Photograph courtesy of Len Horn)

PINAWA PANTHERS NOVICE - 1998-99

First Row: Gordon MacDonald, Marshall Spinney, Jason Bilinsky, Kirk Vilks, Michael Nelson, Jordan Legall, Brandon Betteridge
Mid Row: Stuart Mayoh, Calvin Bueckert, Matthew Reimer, Tyler George, Andrew Hampshire, Kevin Krampetz
Back Row: Chris Saunders (Coach), Dennis Bilinsky (Coach), Jim Betteridge (Coach), Ian George (Manager)

Pinawa Panthers – Team Photographs

1998-99 Female Pee Wee Team – Back Row: Peter Symchuk (Coach), Lisa Goodman (Coach), Gary Hanna (Manager), Martha Laverock (Coach), David Light (Coach); Middle Row: Diane Berry, Ashley Augustine, Sarah Gibson, Toiny Farr, Jessica Pedruchny, Amy Attas, Jennifer Bilinsky, Lisa Stepanik; Front Row: Amanda Symchuk, Kelly Hanna, Jillian Light, Dawn Lamoureaux, Adriana Luke, Carly Krampetz, Nicole Bilinsky, Desiree Lamoureaux, Randi Augustine

Pinawa – First Impressions
By Kay Harvey

At the end of April 1979 Keith and I set out from Fredericton, New Brunswick, in our station wagon filled with our three kids, Cheryl, Neil, and Mark and enough supplies to last four or five days for our drive to Pinawa. At the time Cheryl was almost seven, Neil was four and Mark was just six months old. Cheryl and Neil travelled in the back of the wagon surrounded by stuff to keep them occupied on the journey and Mark and I occupied the back seat with Keith in solitary splendour in the front.

After five days of driving with stopovers in Edmundston, Ottawa, some nameless spot between Sudbury and Thunder Bay, Thunder Bay and Kenora we eventually drove into Pinawa at 5.45 p.m. on a Monday evening. Coming up Highway 211, I was beginning to feel as if this place called Pinawa was imaginary – the road seemed endless, then we turned onto Aberdeen to more trees with no habitation in sight. When we eventually got to the corner at Burrows Road, I was thrilled to finally see houses.

Kay and Keith Harvey

We stopped outside of Kelsey House where we were to stay for the first night and Keith went in to get things organized. So, there I was, sitting in the car with three little kids, and the siren went off. I just about needed clean underwear! This was not long after Three Mile Island so nuclear accidents were still in the news. I had no idea this happened every Monday evening at 6 p.m. Needless to say, I won't ever forget my first few minutes in Pinawa!

After the first night we were provided with a furnished house on McGregor until our furniture arrived from Fredericton. When we left New Brunswick it was around 23°C and we were all in T-shirts. A few days after our arrival in Pinawa the temperature was around freezing and it was snowing. Of course, all our winter gear including boots and warm coats was in the moving truck! I remember slipping and sliding down to The Bay (as our store was called in those days) to get supplies for Cheryl's seventh birthday which we celebrated around a tiny table in very tiny kitchen.

Eventually our furniture arrived and we could move into our rental house at 4 Schultz Road. We were really happy to be able to have our own stuff to use again, but, our other car, a VW Beetle, had travelled in the moving truck as well as our household goods. That would have been fine except it made the truck overweight for Manitoba so they just took the car out and left it at the Manitoba border. Keith had a very uncomfortable ride as a passenger in the moving truck back to the border to retrieve the car the next day! He was always convinced afterwards that moving trucks had no shocks and it was just the weight of the contents that kept them on the road!

Once we moved into the house on Schultz we started to look for other household goods. I must have seemed like a complete idiot to the guys at the store when I walked in, looked around and asked where I bought carpets! They very gently explained to me that you ordered them from Sears. After a few other adjustments to living "out in the boonies" I soon realised that this was a truly great place to live, especially if you had young kids. Everyone was very welcoming and friendly and we soon decided we were going to make this our permanent home and started to build our own house. Looking back I can honestly say this was probably one of the best things to happen to our family, and I feel so grateful that my kids grew up here in a safe, healthy environment. As my daughter and son-in-law have now brought their family here I am even more grateful knowing that my grandkids are having the same great childhood my kids had. Thank you, Pinawa!

If the Walls Could Talk – Memories of Kelsey House
By Brenda and Brian Morash and Mac and Shirley Pellow

One of the first experiences most people had when coming to Pinawa in the sixties and seventies was living in Kelsey House.

Kelsey House Staff Hotel was built to house all single employees of AECL, teachers, nurses and Hudson's Bay staff. At that time single staff were not permitted to rent apartments or own homes. The first quarters were trailers that were set up at what is now the site of the Pinawa Motor Inn. Some staff also rented row houses.

Brian and Brenda Morash

The original Kelsey House was built in 1964. In January of 1966 the East Wing was completed. Rooms in the early seventies were rented for about $60 a month. "Bargain basement" rooms (shared accommodation) were available for about $35 per month. At capacity Kelsey House could accommodate about 180 residents. Kitchenettes were available for casual cooking on each floor but a full cafeteria provided three meals a day at reasonable rates. One of the best parts of living in K.H. was daily maid service!

Residents received their mail at the front desk which was staffed by the desk clerks who were also "security" and operated the telephone switchboard—if you weren't in your own room when a call came, they could often find you! Other staff included the resident Assistant Staff house Supervisor whose duties included supervising the maids, desk clerks, and groundskeepers as well as organizing banquets for AECL groups.

Mac and Shirley Pellow

Besides their rooms, staff had access to the Upper and Lower Lounges. The Upper Lounge was the location of many parties and socials. It also had a TV, stereo system and kitchenette and bar area which were used by residents in the evenings. The Lower Lounge was used as a games room.

Other parts of the basement included the laundry area, a workshop, storage area for large equipment such as bikes and sports equipment.

On the main level, there was a V.I.P. and Whiteshell rooms which were used for meetings, socials and special events.

Another area that was an important part of K.H. was the court yard. In its prime, this area was always beautifully maintained as were the flower beds and lawn around K.H. The courtyard was the site of several weddings. This area was used as the "beer garden" during the Birthday dance.

The residents organized themselves into the Kelsey House Staff House Club. This club dealt with resident concerns but more importantly organized many events such as the annual Christmas party, Hallowe'en party, curling bonspiel, baseball team, and ski and canoe trips. The Birthday Weekend always started with a huge party at Kelsey House with two live bands, one in the Upper

Typical Kelsey House Room

Lounge and one in the cafeteria. It was a time when everyone came home and the dance was the place to be to renew acquaintances. At the Saturday Birthday parade, Kelsey House generally entered a contestant in the "Miss Pinawa" contest.

One other important tradition that started in the early years was "Thursday Night Pub Night." When the first K.H. residents came, many of them returned to Winnipeg or home on the weekends so before they went their separate ways on the weekend, Thursday night pub-night was established. The first pub nights involved a trip to Lac du Bonnet until the Pinawa Motor Inn was built.

Kelsey House was a great place to meet people and a result of these "friendships" several couples met their future spouses there. Some of the couples who met in Kelsey House and still live in Pinawa are Greg and Caroline Brady, Dennis and Wendy Chen, Mike and Betty Duclos, Dieter and Dixie Jung, Brian and Brenda McKenzie, Glen and Jackie Snider, Ann and Roy Styles, Dave and Cindy Litke, Ken and Judy Ticknor, Marv and Mary Ryz, Leny and Mitch Ohta, Dave and Marg Smith, Mac and Shirley Pellow, Ralph and Carol Moyer, Gary and Grace Simmons, and Brian and Brenda Morash.

Upper Lounge

In the early seventies, single people were allowed to rent apartments and soon after that could buy their own homes. Life at Kelsey House slowly started to change. The number of residents decreased, the cafeteria was only open part of the day, and some of the rooms were converted into apartments and offices. Kelsey House was privatized in 1997-98 and is now named "Wilderness Edge Resort and Conference Centre."

If the walls could talk, there are many individual stories that could be told (but probably better off, not printed!). Anyone who ever lived in Kelsey House has their own special memories of wonderful times spent there. Kelsey House stories are always a source of lots of laughs and information!

Dominion Catering

Kelsey House – 1970s

Welcome to Pinawa

Pinawa Pioneers at the 25th Anniversary in 1988

The Plunkett Journey to Pinawa
By Louise Daymond

Cec Plunkett joined AECL in 1949, and brought his wife Simone and young family of three from Timmins to Deep River, Ontario. In 1963 he was transferred to Pinawa as Supervisor in the Radiation and Industrial Safety Branch, but he insisted on waiting until the end of the school year. The family of now seven children (Don, Gail, Rick, Jerry, Simone, Louise and Gary) said their goodbyes to friends who were staying behind, packed up their small station wagon and headed to Manitoba, arriving July 4, 1964.

Louise Daymond

The drive took several days, and my parents tried to make it an adventure for their teenaged children, stopping at tourist destinations along the way. Memories of the big Nickel at Sudbury and the Wawa Goose were highlights we remember to this day. There were as many rounds of "Gee Ma, I want to go – back to Ontario" at the top of our lungs for as long as my parents could stand. Many motels and hotels weren't willing to provide lodging to such a large family, so when they were finally released from the cramped car, the boys were eager to let off their energy.

It was quite hot when we finally arrived in Pinawa, and as we drove down the gravel highway to Willis Drive, Dad pointed out the back of our house on McMillan. We thought he was kidding because all we could see was bush and mud. It looked considerably better from the front, but none of the yards had sod, and only a handful of houses on the street were finished. The bi-level house seemed like a mansion to this 6 year old, and the patio stone sidewalk was especially fascinating for some reason.

We didn't have to wait for our furniture to arrive; the van showed up almost immediately after us. I remember them taking my doll's carriage from the truck and discovering that my mom had made a beautiful layette for her as a surprise. I was in heaven.

My oldest sister Gail remembers heading immediately to find the gas station in search of a Coke. It tasted horrible, she recalls. Simone and I headed out to explore and discovered some snakes on the rocks by McDiarmid and Willis. She was horrified and we ran home as fast as we could. It didn't help before we left that we were cautioned to watch out for bears.

Cy and Daisy Seymour hosted our family for dinner that first night. I'm sure Sara and Jamie had never seen so many kids at one time.

The experience of growing up along with your home town, instead of in it, created a bond with our peers that exist to this day. There was no limit to what our imaginations came up with when we had construction materials, hay bales, endless clay, gumbo and bush as our playthings. We built elaborate play towns on rock outcroppings, explored for wildlife and berries in the bush, and learned to swim, fish and boat in the beautiful waters that surrounded us.

Cec Plunkett

We didn't have an abundance of deer in those days, but bears were frequent visitors. We even had a large bear that would sleep in the shade of the willow tree on our lawn while I mowed the grass! Our house was in close proximity to the highway, and one day a large flatbed truck made its way from the bush, down our driveway, then out of town. It contained about ten bears; at seven years old I wasn't sure whether they were tranquilized or dead, but it was the trigger for

Pinawa's first protest. I rallied my friends, made up signs, and protested down by the phone booth at the mall. We couldn't fit 'Save Our Bears' on our cardboard, so we abbreviated it. Our parents must have been so proud to learn our placards read "S.O.B!"

A favourite family pastime was putting the kids in their jammies then driving out to the dump to watch the bears rummaging through the garbage. It wasn't uncommon on a Saturday night to see ten cars in a semi-circle watching an equal number of bears, or more.

One other story that illustrates how growing up here was like nowhere else. My friend and neighbour, Catherine Allwright, and I were exploring in the bush where the crossover to the golf course now sits, where we discovered several large bones we were certain must have come from dinosaurs! We gathered as many as we could, cleaned them up, and asked permission to wear our good shoes to go to the bank. The bank manager was Ed Ingersoll, a wonderful man who went out of his way for his adult clients. To us, he was our friendly neighbour on the cul de sac. We proudly brought him our discovery, and that delightful man very solemnly gave us 10 cents for each one! It wasn't until many years later that I learned the true history of those bones – they were from the animals that hauled away materials when the channel was blasted out.

Of course, we went on to create so many memories during those first months and years of Pinawa's history, and beyond.

My older siblings were involved in some of the earliest teen pranks, which were generally harmless fun. One that is retold often is when the owners of Volkswagen Beetles called the local RCMP to say their car had been switched for an identical one in their driveway. When he left his house to investigate, he discovered that his own driveway had been sodded during the night!

My father's job at the plant was multi-faceted. He taught the New Employees Radiation Safety and Orientation course, which meant that hundreds of new employees attended his classes. His sharp Irish wit, combined with his intellect made for many memorable classes, I am told. He authored a handbook on Radiation Safety, and instructed the health surveyors in the branch. He was one of the employees who monitored both accidents at Chalk River, and was seconded to India for several months to provide training and assistance to the RAPP-1 research reactor project in Rajasthan, India.

Dad retired from AECL in November, 1976; sadly, by July 1977 he had passed away. My brother Jerry and I never left Pinawa; he had a long career with AECL (Operations) until his untimely death in 2001. I also worked at AECL; the last three years in the same branch as my father: Radiation and Industrial Safety. After leaving AECL I enjoyed a 20-year career publishing Pinawa's longest-running independent weekly newspaper The Paper, from 1995 to 2015. It was a true honour and privilege to chronicle the lives and the history of our beautiful community.

Connie Plunkett with Pinawa Life Guards

Pinawa Club and Beach

Stu Iverson

Jay Hawton

Another Pinawa Resident

Trillium Ridge Living – Bill Murray, Todd Meek, Dean Randell, Rick Backer and Bruce Murray

Evelyn and Chuck Vandergraaf

Pinawa Stage Band

Recollections of the Early Pinawa Days
By Marion Goehring

I graduated from Regina General Hospital and had taken a Diploma course at U. of S. in Nursing Administration. I had been Director of Nursing in a rural hospital in Wolseley, SK. and had worked in other small hospitals in SK. and Portage la Prairie, MB. I was working in Calgary in Obstetrics at Calgary General Hospital, when I saw an advertisement in the daily paper for nurses for the hospital and for a nurse at the AECL plant in Pinawa, MB. It looked very interesting. Dr. J. Weeks interviewed me at the Calgary airport. I was hired as the Director of Nursing to start in mid-August 1963. Dr. Weeks painted a picture of the town and hospital as it appeared about 1 ½ years later.

Marion Goehring

I drove out to Pinawa on August 15th, 1963. As I drove east toward Pinawa through the forest, I said to myself 'where am I going?' I finally came to the end of the road and turned right toward some buildings. I saw a sign indicating a post office, so I stopped and went in. I asked the man at the desk 'Where is the centre of town?' He laughed and said 'This is it. You must be one of the nurses we are expecting today.' I said 'Yes, I am.' He said 'I will show you to the rowhouse where you will be living.' Four more nurses soon arrived. We had thought there would be a staff hotel with a cafeteria. We were not prepared to be making our own meals. Because the closest grocery store was in Lac du Bonnet, we drove there to get some groceries. In the meantime some fellows were bringing in the furniture, dishes, pots and pans for our rowhouse unit. The streets were not all complete and houses were under construction, so it was a busy construction site. We were among the first persons to move into town. The men had been living in construction trailers at the plant, while some of the female clerical staff had been in the motel at Whitemouth.

I reported for work to the plant the next morning. Dr. Weeks told us where our hospital would be located. We were to set up a 3 bed hospital in a house and operate that until the 17 bed was finished and ready to be opened.

I was one of the few gals who had a car, so I was often called on for rides. On the weekends I always had a car load headed to Winnipeg.

We set up a nursing station in a rowhouse next to the one we lived in. The nursing station was primarily a doctor's office, where Dr. Beaumont from Lac du Bonnet visited several times per week, until his home was completed and he and his family moved to Pinawa. We had the 3 bed hospital open on October 22/63. In that bi-level house we delivered 45 babies in the next 15 months. Dr. Beaumont delivered most of the babies in that 3 bed, but if he was not available, we called on his wife who was a doctor, or on one of the doctors working in research at the plant. Dr. Abe Petkau was one of the plant doctors who helped us. Dr. Beaumont served Lac du Bonnet and a mining area NE of Lac du Bonnet. Dr. Maggie Beaumont had her baby delivered in the 3 bed.

There was a big change-over in our nursing staff in those early days. There was very little for the general duty staff to do and they felt that this was not for them. Our first staff nurses were: Ann Churchill, Bev J. Degear, Vera McNaughton and Chris MacKay. Ann left Nov 30, 1963. By the time we moved into the 3 bed hospital on January 11, 1964 we had a complete change. The replacements were: Lynn Kobold, Joan (Messerol) Koshuta, Phyllis Hubic, Julie Atamanchuk and Liz Daychuk. Gladys Guthrie and Sis Smith, whose husbands worked at the plant, were our part time nurses. Louise Proven was hired as the plant nurse and had an office at the plant. She called on doctors working in research at the plant for doing physicals, etc.

My time was taken up with planning for the 17 bed hospital and ordering all the supplies that we would need. The 3 bed hospital was open 24 hours a day and 7 days a week, therefore I was on the day shift with one other nurse. Together we looked after our maternity patients and their babes, along with any emergencies that appeared at our door. We also looked after the doctor's office when he was seeing patients. Any trauma patient or seriously ill patient was sent by ambulance to Winnipeg. Minor suture cases we looked after. We ordered the meals on a daily basis from the plant kitchen and they were delivered in time for each meal. The laundry was sent out to be washed.

The first baby born in the 3 bed hospital was born to a Mrs. Ollson from Great Falls, MB. The first baby born to a Pinawa resident was to a Mrs. McAllister. The last baby born in the 3 bed hospital was to a Mrs. Martino. Mother and baby were moved over to the 17 bed and the Martino baby was the first babe in the new hospital nursery. The 17 bed hospital opened on January 11, 1965.

We had our own kitchen. The cook would consult with the nurses re patient diets. Laundry was picked up and sent out for washing. In our Central Supply Room the nurses prepared and sterilized our surgical trays for the case room and for our emergency room. Laboratory services were provided by staff from the plant. Mr. Minton was hired about the time the 17 bed hospital opened. He was an accountant, but was not familiar with hospital workings, so I spent considerable time talking with him regarding the idiosyncrasies of hospital operations. Dr. Opie came to assist with patient care soon after we moved into the 17 bed hospital. Dr. Weeks had visions of hiring a surgeon for the hospital, but this never came about in my time there.

In consultation with the other nursing staff I set up a procedure and policy manual. I ordered all the hospital supplies i.e. medications, dressings, linens and equipment. The hiring of staff was done through Human Resources at the plant, but I also helped with the interview process. We needed nursing aides to help the lone nurse who was on the evening and the night shifts, so we hired aides who had little or no training. I remember teaching them to make beds and do basic nursing care.

The type of patients that we looked after were: maternity patients and their babies, medical patients, emergency patients and pediatrics. Any surgery or seriously ill patient was taken by ambulance to Winnipeg.

The Staff Hotel opened July 22, 1964. All single staff from the hospital and from the plant moved in. There were also rooms for persons visiting at the plant on business. A cafeteria was opened, although a few of us continued to make our own meals in the kitchenette on our floor.

A shopping centre opened, with The Bay being the main store. During the fall of 1965 the bush was being cleared for what is now the golf course. New homes were being constructed all the time.

After the 17 bed was open for just over one year, I decided to move back to Calgary as the new Foothills Hospital was just about to open. I was hired as the head nurse for the first surgical unit that opened the spring of 1966. I had enjoyed my time at Pinawa and had an experience that very few get the opportunity to do, which is to

A beautiful Pinawa day
(Photograph courtesy of Richard Allen Everitt)

organize and assist in the setting up of a hospital from the beginning.

Early Days in Pinawa
By Paul Barnsdale

Once Upon a Time.......in a valley *(Ottawa)* far-far-away, a young couple decided to accept an opportunity for adventure. Roy and Betty Barnsdale, along with several other local valley families, accepted a transfer to the newly established Whiteshell Nuclear Research Establishment (WNRE), located in Manitoba. Roy and several of his fellow Nuclear Reactor Operators from the Chalk River site joined the Whiteshell Reactor 1 (WR-1) Commissioning Team.

The journey began in early August, 1964. They packed their 10 children into their VW Bus, strapped some luggage on the roof, and headed west. Like all great journeys things don't always go as planned. As they neared Thunder Bay, the load and miles traveled proved to be too much for their van. Although much effort was extended to keep the vehicle going, eventually they had to let it go. The remaining journey to Manitoba was completed by train, arriving in Whitemouth on Aug 14, 1964.

An AECL company representative met them at the train station to offer the family a ride to their new community of Pinawa. Although the person had been informed the Barnsdale family was rather large, they were surprised to see so many get off the train. After some discussion and creative thinking, the entire family of 12, along with the driver, managed to squeeze and stack themselves into the Chevy station wagon and travel to Pinawa safe and sound.

Upon arrival the family was informed their household furniture would be late in arriving due to some issues with the moving van. However alternative accommodations were arranged. The company provided two town-houses, which were most appreciated. The older children moved into one house, while the younger children moved into the other, with parents alternating between. Many family members promptly proceeded to catch up with some much needed sleep. Another company rep dropped by to take Roy to the grocery store for supplies. During this shopping trip, the company rep noticed Roy seemed to be loading an unusually large amount of supplies into his cart and felt obliged to inform him that the store was open tomorrow, at which, Roy replied "I know". Roy then informed the fellow of the size of his family and all was understood.

Although the journey to Manitoba was extremely hot and dry, the family recalls 5 days of straight rain in the first week of arrival. It was at this time they were introduced to "Manitoba Gumbo". The children loved it; what child doesn't like playing in the mud. Shortly afterwards they were introduced to the swarms of flying insects. It was about this time Betty recalls wondering if they had made the right decision to relocate, apparently a common thought on the minds of several other early inhabitants of the community. Aside from the mud and the bugs, the majority of the earliest memories were positive. Some of these memories shared by several of the children were:

Barnsdale Children – 1964: Back Row: Tom, Eddie, Danny, Maureen and Roy; Front Row: Glen, Paul, Peter, Walter and Mike; Mark was #11, born in Pinawa in 1965

Having to wear nylon stockings over their head, as protection from the bugs, just to go from house to school.

Horse teams delivering supplies to construction sites.

Lots of bears, wondering unalarmed through the town.

A wilderness wonderland with loads of opportunity for exploring, fishing and hunting.

Building forts (lots of free supplies from construction workers).

Business opportunities such as collecting discarded bottles and collecting return monies *(2 cents/bottle...big money)*, selling cool drinks to work crews *(mobile via a little red wagon)*, laying sod, and general cleanup jobs around construction sites.

Roy and Betty specifically recall a mix of fear and excitement with a strong sense of unity within the community. Pioneers joining together to make each other's experience more enjoyable, while undertaking the grand task of building the foundation of a brand new community. Roy recalls this same environment at the site. Roy, Betty, and a few of their children continue to call Pinawa home and are proud to have been a part of the early pioneer days and continue to look forward to being a part of the future evolution of the community.

Pinawa Club

Our Pinawa Adventure
By Brent Donnelly

The Donnelly family arrived in Pinawa on August 4, 1964. The family had been transferred from Chalk River, Ontario, and Dad Michael (Mickey) continued his career as a reactor operator with AECL. Along with Mickey, the family included his wife Nora, and children Linda, Bobby, Brent, Cathy and Bruce. The

drive in their 1958 Chevy seemed to last forever, particularly for their mother who was 7 months pregnant. Mickey and Nora were both originally from the Ottawa valley, so moving to the west was truly an adventure.

Their first home was at 21 Devonshire Avenue, but they soon moved to a larger home across the street at 22 Devonshire. A healthy Brian Donnelly arrived in November 1964, one of the first babies born in the community hospital, also on McDiarmid.

The Donnelly kids were involved in many sports over the years in Pinawa;

The Donnelly children getting ready for their drive to Pinawa – Brent, Bobby, Cathy, Bruce and Linda

community teams in sports like hockey and softball, all the sports at Pinawa Secondary School, and even for a number of regional sports teams. Many local team photographs since the 1960s have had a Donnelly in the picture.

Out of the original family of eight, six still reside in the area; 5 in Pinawa. Brent married Christine Haugen, whose family came to the community in July, 1965. They had two sons, Adam and Tavis, both born in town. Tavis continues to live in Pinawa with his wife and four children, making it now four generations of Donnellys calling Pinawa home. In fact, the various Donnelly family members have lived in over 10 homes in Pinawa over the years. All of this has been possible because AECL has been a major Donnelly employer, with Mickey, Brent, Cathy, Bruce, Brian and Tavis working for the company.

The Donnelly family came to Pinawa in 1964 sight unseen and chose to make Pinawa their home for the many generations of Donnellys to come. Thank-you Pinawa for the adventure.

Brother Brian born November 1964

2002-03 Pinawa Panthers Midget Team:– Back Row – Dianne Ikeda, Ramsey Aitkenhead, Adam Coleman, Krist Hayes, Trevor Gascoyne, Jeff Krampetz, Joey Enright; Middle Row- Doug Krampetz (coach), Ed Bueckert (coach), Tavis Donnelly, Tyler Malkoske, Walter Bychuk, Wally Bychuk (manager); Front Row – Curtis Graham, Josh Mueller, Troy Miller, Dustin Hiller, Cody Forale, Kenneth Bueckert, Marcus Tomsons
(Photograph courtesy of Kathy Wold)

Mickey Donnelly

Adam Donnelly

Joshua and Jayson Abraham

Cathy Abraham with her mother
Nora Donnelly

World Golf Tournament – June 24, 2000
By Helen and Eddie Olchowy, Bonnie and Doug Edkins, Ann and Fergus Duncan, and Julie and Stuart Halley

The Pinawa Golf Club participated in the World Golf Tournament 2000. All of the participating clubs around the world, teed off at exactly same time. We were lucky that this meant we teed off at 6 pm local time. At the Old Course in St. Andrews, Scotland, it was 12 o'clock midnight. Their original 6 pm start was pushed to midnight as the number of clubs wanting to participate grew.

People dressed in kilts and tartans, enjoyed the piper, Robert Grant from Beausejour, as they registered for the evening, signed an old Pinawa course flag, and picked up their special bag tag under the World Tournament 2000 banner. Ann Duncan and Helen Olchowy included the signed flag with the Pinawa results and pictures that where sent to Scotland to be placed in the time capsule and buried at the Old Course. A certificate for the event, framed by Eddie Olchowy, hangs at the Club.

Using a shot gun start, courtesy of the local RCMP officer, golfers started at all 18 holes in Pinawa. Each team played a 2-ball format and completed 9 holes on either the front or back course, finishing just before darkness. Golf was followed by a social evening of dinner (birdies and salads) and drinks. Julie and Stuart Halley supplied the birdies.

Stuart Halley and Ann Duncan gave out the prizes, participation certificates, target awards and draws. The team of Dennis and Marg Smith, Gerry and Gertie Oliveira and Bev Dougall had the low score. A draw for a tin of Scotch Shortbread was won by Jim Cafferty. A special thank-you was given to Lisa Thomas and her staff for the fine meal.

Pinawa's participation was the result of a visit to Scotland by Eddie, Helen and Tim Olchowy in April, 2000. They visited the Old Course and Helen tore off the last coupon on the bulletin board to register for the tournament. It was a scramble to organize a committee and submit our application and entrance fee. Bonnie Edkins, our Pinawa Club President, became our liaison with the committee in St. Andrews. They kindly accepted Bonnie's personal cheque in Canadian funds for our 100 golfers. We limited our group to 100 as the entrance fee was $500 for each group of 100 golfers. One or 2 golfers over 100 would have been another $500.

Flag Pole at the Pinawa Club

Our committee was Bonnie and Doug Edkins, Stuart and Julie Halley, Fergus and Ann Duncan, and Eddie and Helen Olchowy. Chuck Murphy took videos. The draw was set by Bonnie and she and our golf pro, Brad Poleschuk, tallied the results. Helen and Julie made the banner. Julie, Ann and Sandra Ramsay decorated the club with the lion rampart flag, other tartans and linen scenes from Scotland. Eddie, Fergus, and Stuart made various targets on the course and put up the Canadian and Saltiere flags.

In order to fly the flag of Scotland, we had to first fly the Maple Leaf. The club had no flag or flag pole. We accepted a donation from the Whitemouth Hotel (Alan and Jan Hutchinson) that was used to purchase a Canadian flag. We desperately needed a flag pole and Gerry Dougall, the School Superintendent, offered the one at Lewis School. Immediately, a group of men took it down using the Club tractor and Gerry Smith's trailer. Because of its length, the men walked behind the trailer to the Club. The LGD, Herman Mueller and Dennis Smith established the foundation using the Club backhoe. A front end loader was used to lift and set the pole. Many men, many ropes and great laughter were part of the adventure. Our flag still flies at the club, thanks to simple acts and a willingness by many people to get the job done.

The Ironwood Story
By Dianne Rummery

As the population of Canada ages, the need for seniors housing in safe attractive places, with health care and recreation facilities nearby, increases. Pinawa, Manitoba, a town nestled along the Winnipeg River, has come up with an elegant and efficacious solution, mostly independent of government funding.

Folks were getting older and looking for accommodation without snow to shovel and grass to cut. For some years, finding retirement living meant leaving their hometown and social network to go to other communities. Over the years, various groups worked toward developing more seniors housing in Pinawa but governments were not forthcoming with funding and local people were reluctant to invest. Finally, in 2008, the winds changed and the result was *The Ironwood*, a well-designed and commodious suite residence in Pinawa. The 24 units, all on one floor and with individual patios, are between 860 and 1155 ft^2, with a large common room, flower and vegetable gardens, and a small exercise room. All suites include a den. Interior heated parking is available for a monthly fee. Rents include heat, water, satellite TV and electricity. The project was privately funded through a for–profit corporation, Pinawa Ironwood Investment Limited.

The funding of the Ironwood rests on three legs. The first was an investment of $1 Million by shareholders, mostly from the community. The second was a mortgage from a Credit Union and the third a deposit of $40,000 for each suite put down by the tenant. This deposit earns interest which is paid monthly and is enough to pay for parking. The $40,000 principle is returned to tenants when they leave.

A second part of the Ironwood is the Supportive Housing wing (12 units). The Ironwood owns and operates the facility but admissions, meals and care are provided by the Regional Health Authority. Supportive housing is a relatively new concept in Manitoba and aims to provide an affordable option between Assisted Living and a Personal Care Home. Residents may be frail or have memory or mobility limitations, but are able to care for themselves with some assistance. All meals are provided in the dining room and a "companion" is on site 24 hours a day to ensure that residents take medications, come for meals and generally are in "good heart". The supportive units are smaller, about 500 ft^2, and include a separate bedroom and living area with a microwave. A common patio off the dining room gives residents a chance to tend plants, have outdoor meals and enjoy the sun in good weather.

Honoring the Original Citizens Committee: Jerry Martino, Bill Early, Ray Sochaski, Jay Hawton, Bernice Hawton, Wally Kukurudz, and Mayor Blair Skinner – May 2012 (Photograph courtesy of Stu Iverson)

Part of the capital funding for the supportive wing was provided in the form of a forgivable loan by Manitoba Housing and Renewal Corporation to enable rents to be kept affordable.

How did it all begin?

Building on previous unsuccessful attempts, a group of townspeople including a Councillor and representative of the Pinawa Community Development Corporation, formed a committee that asked for proposals from developers who had built seniors housing complexes in rural Manitoba. Two developers made proposals and Bridge Road Developments had the most inviting bid. They are Mennonites from small-town Manitoba who combine the virtues of honesty, hard work, shrewdness and access to the Steinbach Credit Union, a feature of the west that makes doing business in this area much simpler than dealing with national banks.

Bridge Road and the local committee jointly held open meetings to familiarize residents with the concept and determine if it was possible to raise the necessary investment in the community. Hard work and community enthusiasm resulted in commitments for the necessary $1 Million. Under the Securities Commission of Manitoba rules, requests for such venture capital cannot be advertised so word of mouth was the means of communication. Another dictum was that only 50 investors could be involved.

Some residents of the Ironwood – Christmas 2010
(Photograph courtesy of Stu Iverson)

Several large investments meant that smaller investors could also be included, giving a broad section of the community a stake in the Ironwood. Investors expect dividends from their investment in years to come. An important motivation for most investors was that the town needed such a facility and many were happy to have it available for their own future use. Investors came from outside Pinawa as well, children and grandchildren who had grown up in this extraordinary small town.

Was there enough demand from potential tenants? Again public meetings were held. The developer presented drawings and plans and some 60 to 70% of the required number of tenants came up with a $1,000 refundable deposit to be among the first residents.

With investment capital and tenants in place, the next step was to form a corporation to manage the investment funds. This intrepid group which included a Board of Directors and an Executive "took a deep breath" and, with the approval of shareholders, signed a contract with the Bridge Road Developers. The design, with particular concern for functional kitchens and adequate storage space for tenants, was quickly finalized, land was purchased and construction began.

Another ace Pinawa had in place was a strong team of retired project engineers who were on site during the building with a fine eye for the balance between budget, bottom line and upgraded building features. Experts in finance and real estate also provided their time and skills pro bono.

The 45 shareholders of Pinawa Ironwood Investment Limited have a Board of ten directors. Shareholders meet annually to elect directors and approve a budget and project plan. In the early days the board met monthly but now meets about 4 times year with ongoing informal meetings as required. They in turn hired the manager/caretaker who looks after all day-to-day matters so tenants' needs are met promptly.

The result of the hard work and vision of some determined people is a fine facility, locally owned and managed, that is providing safe and spacious accommodation for many people who made their careers with Atomic Energy of Canada Limited. And yes, there is a mortgage with the Steinbach Credit Union!

The Ironwood - July 18, 2010

Dieter and Hanni Brand at the main entrance of the Ironwood
(Photograph courtesy of Stu Iverson)

Pinawa Players over the years

EMCA Posters

Jeff Long setting ski trails

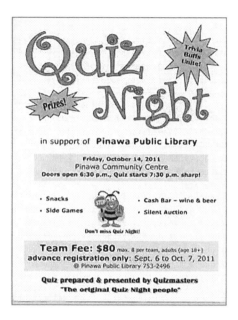

Quiz Night

Trivia Buffs Unite!

Prizes!

in support of **Pinawa Public Library**

Friday, October 14, 2011
Pinawa Community Centre
Doors open 6:30 p.m., Quiz starts 7:30 p.m. sharp!

- Snacks
- Side Games
- Cash Bar – wine & beer
- Silent Auction

Don't miss Quiz Night!

Team Fee: $80 max. 8 per team, adults (age 18+)
advance registration only: Sept. 6 to Oct. 7, 2011
@ Pinawa Public Library 753-2496

**Quiz prepared & presented by Quizmasters
"The original Quiz Night people"**

Ara Mooradian and Brian Wilkins

Ken McCallum cleaning after
first birthday dance

Mayor Blair Skinner

Basement Businesses
By Sandy Murillo, September 1982

Lorna's, a business that began three years ago, is a very personalized craft shop. Mrs. Lorna Truss began her craft work with 4-H, which she belonged to for seven years. 4-H helped to teach Lorna how to sew, knit, and many other handicrafts. "After you learn one craft, - the rest are much easier to learn," replies Lorna. Handiwork is a "natural" for Lorna and her work is very beautifully done, with, great expertise.

Lorna's makes many varieties of macrame hanging planters, yam, weavings, winter hats and mittens, puppets, children's wear, crewel, and petit-point. Making macrame hangings can be very time consuming and intricate work. It can take several hours to complete. If a customer has a particular idea in mind for a macramé hanger, Lorna will try and fill the order.

The majority of kits and supplies are ordered from the Winnipeg and Toronto areas. If a certain pattern or kit is needed by a customer, Lorna will order it for them. If the order is placed to Winnipeg, it usually takes three or four days to receive the merchandise. Lopi wool-yarn is ordered from Montreal. "Lopi is the best true Icelandic wool," answers Lorna.

The handmade pot-holders are very attractive and a good idea to give as gifts. Simple Christmas ornaments made from pipe cleaners and beads have become very popular. "The idea of easy-to-make ornaments is due to the Brownie troop. They are always looking for fun and easy ideas, and these ornaments make nice Christmas gifts," remarks Lorna.

Nice, warm winter sweaters are not too difficult to make. Easy step-by-step directions from some of the 'how to" books Lorna keeps in stock are quite becoming and a lot less expensive.

Lorna will begin knitting classes in October, "I start people with something easy. This way they can take their work home and practice. If they have any problems, they can comeback for help," says Lorna.

Lorna's is located at 15 Lansdowne. The regular working hours are Monday, Wednesday and Friday, 10 am to 4:30 pm; Monday and Wednesday evening, 6:30 pm to 8:30 pm.

The Pinawa Christmas Bird Count
By Peter Taylor

The Christmas Bird Count (CBC) is probably the longest-running "citizen science" project in North America, dating back to 1900 when a few enlightened souls in the northeastern U.S.A. decided to count birds rather than shoot them (as was the tradition) on Christmas Day. Nowadays, several thousand CBCs provide an annual snapshot of winter bird populations across North America. Each count – strictly speaking, a survey rather than a census – is held within a 24-km diameter circle on one day within a two-week Christmas to New Year period.

The first local CBC was held on 2 January 1965 under the leadership of Bruce Stewart. Bruce continued as the coordinator for the first five years, after which the duty rotated for several years. Peter Taylor has filled this role since Christmas 1977, except for two two-year stints when Reto Zach took over. Thus we have an unbroken run of 49 consecutive CBCs – and counting!

Over the years, several hundred people have taken part in the count, some just once but others for 30 years or more. Most participants are from the Pinawa area and Winnipeg, but we have had visitors from as far away as Newfoundland and New York. A major highlight was in 1993, when our 30th count was featured on the popular CBC Manitoba TV show "Coleman and Company" – here the abbreviation CBC has another meaning! Luckily, both birds and birders performed well for the cameras.

This popular event combines a day of good company in the fresh air (often a tad too fresh) and an evening gathering to warm up, fill bellies, compare notes, and combine our group tallies. Typically about 18 to 25 people head out in groups of two to four, each covering a segment of the circle that extends to Lac du Bonnet, Otter Falls, and River Hills. We look forward to our 50th count at the end of Pinawa's anniversary year. Perhaps we'll be lucky enough to add a rarity to our all-time list of just over 80 species; the normal total each year is around 35.

Overall, our local CBC has given a picture of a healthy and fairly stable wintering bird population, with occasional spikes in the numbers of some nomadic species such as Great Gray Owls and White-winged Crossbills. The popularity of bird feeding brought a dramatic rise in numbers of Evening Grosbeaks – for several years, the highest counts in North America – but they have dipped a little in recent years. A few species' winter ranges are edging northward; for example, American Crows, Bald Eagles, and Red-breasted Nuthatches are much more frequent now than in the 1970s. To learn more about Christmas Bird Counts near and far, check out the website at www.bsc-eoc.org/volunteer/cbc.

Every Christmas Bird Count we hope for at least one sighting of Manitoba's provincial bird, the Great Gray Owl

Rowing at dusk

216

Pinawa Bridge – History of Design and Construction
By R.O. Sochaski, P. Eng.

Reason for the Bridge

The Pinawa Land Development Group, under the chair of Marsha Sheppard, felt they required a bridge across the Pinawa Channel in the vicinity of the Pinawa Cemetery to provide a closed walking loop around the town of Pinawa. The time period was about 1996-97. The proposed loop included the Ironwood trail located along the Winnipeg River on the South side of town, then West along Willis Drive to Highway 211, across the highway to the Pinawa cemetery, then over the proposed bridge just North of the cemetery, and along the North shore of the Pinawa Channel to the Diversion Dam. From the Diversion Dam the trail would follow Highway 211 to the first town entrance, along the first hole of the golf course, and rejoin the Ironwood trail behind the tennis courts and swimming pool. At the time, it was hoped the trail would become part of the Trans-Canada Walking Trail.

Bridge Design

In late summer of 1996, Marsha Sheppard invited me to undertake the design of a bridge to meet the Pinawa Land Development Group requirements. In the fall of 1996, on the advice of Barrie Burnett (a local hobby surveyor), a site was selected about 200 m north of the Pinawa Cemetery. It had granite outcropping on both sides of the channel which was ideal for bridge footings and anchors, and the span across the channel was narrow, about 50 m. Surveys were conducted to establish the bridge centre line, centre line elevations and by using triangulation, the exact distance across the Channel.

During the winter of 96/97, much preliminary design work was completed; most of it on Vancouver Island, at Qualicum Beach, during winter vacations. The design considered two suspension bridge types, one with a horizontal deck held in place by two cables positioned above the deck. The other design had the deck attached directly to the lower suspension cables. The biggest disadvantage with the horizontal deck bridge was its cost. The simpler catenary deck bridge was finally selected because of its lower cost, the desire, by some, to make the bridge a swinging bridge with wooden decking instead of the proposed open metallic grating deck used on the other design. It was also thought that wood would blend more naturally with the surrounding forest.

Bridge Specifications
Distance between towers - 50 m
Distance between anchors - 67.5m
Sag - 3.4 m
Minimum height above water - 3m
East tower height - 6.5m
West tower height - 2.8m
Decking - wood with expanded metal anti-slip walkway
Cable diameter - 25mm
Number of cables used - 4
Bridge commissioned - Oct 1998
Official Opening - May 24, 1999
Bridge cost - $25,000, excluding volunteer labour costs.
Bridge design - Ray Sochaski
Rock Mechanic - Peter Baumgartner
Surveying - Barrie Burnett
Rock Drilling - Allan Hampton
Anchor Grouting - Larry Rolleston

Approvals

Approvals to build the bridge were required from several government agencies. These included:

- Local Government District of Pinawa
- Manitoba Land Titles Office
- Manitoba Natural Resources
- Fisheries and Oceans Canada

Two sources of funding were made available for the construction of the bridge; the major source was a grant from the Manitoba Sustainable Development Innovation Fund. The other source came from the sale of plaques for each of the boards in the bridge decking.

Procurement of Materials

A quantity of used mine cable was provided by Tanco. Gravel was provided by Meisner Limited and LGD of Pinawa. Atomic Energy of Canada Ltd. (AECL) provided us with the use of a boat, a welder, and rock drilling equipment, such as a compressor, air lines to span the channel, drills, winches and many other miscellaneous items.

Volunteers

Over 60 people put their hands on some piece of the bridge project. Without them, the project would not have happened. Just some of these volunteers included Ray Sochaski, Peter Baumgartner, Larry Rolleston, Allan Hampton, Kirk Haugen, Gerry Hampton, Larry Gauthier, Marsha Sheppard, Steve Sheppard, Metro Dmytriw, Lynn Ewing, Tony Wiewel, Pinawa Lions, John Westdal, Vince Lopata, Mike Motycka, Heinz Ehlers, Bill Murray, Wally Kukurudz, Dale Lidfors, and the Limit Group.

Pinawa Suspension Bridge in the Early Morning
(Photograph courtesy of Stu Iverson)

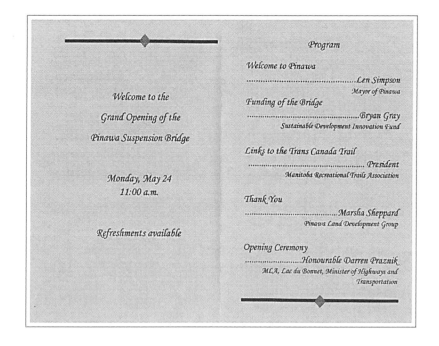

Welcome to the

Grand Opening of the

Pinawa Suspension Bridge

Monday, May 24
11:00 a.m.

Refreshments available

Program

Welcome to Pinawa
....Len Simpson
Mayor of Pinawa

Funding of the Bridge
....Bryan Gray
Sustainable Development Innovation Fund

Links to the Trans Canada Trail
.... President
Manitoba Recreational Trails Association

Thank You
....Marsha Sheppard
Pinawa Land Development Group

Opening Ceremony
....Honourable Darren Praznik
MLA, Lac du Bonnet, Minister of Highways and
Transportation

Pinawa Heritage Sundial
By Carl Sabanski

A sundial is a fascinating instrument. Just imagine. The tip of any vertical object can be used to tell the time. As the sun passes, the tip of the shadow traces the hours throughout the day; spring, summer, autumn and winter. Sundials date back to about 1500 BC when L-shaped sundials were used in Egypt. There are a variety of types and sizes ranging from ring to pocket to very large. Sundials built over the ages demonstrate great skill in workmanship and many are works of art.

Carl Sabanski

The Pinawa Heritage Sundial was built to mark the new millennium through the expression of a variety of themes: art, science, and heritage. It was a community project supported by the LGD of Pinawa. The project's importance extends beyond the borders of Pinawa. The Pinawa Heritage Sundial was a project that brought form and function together to illustrate the history of the region of Eastern Manitoba.

Form: the beauty of the sundial creation through the efforts of local area artists sharing their talents with all who wish to see.

Function: the science of understanding the relationship between the earth and sun in the construction of a timepiece with unique characteristics for each and every location on the earth.

The Pinawa Heritage Sundial is a horizontal dial stretching 10 m square, with a gnomon 5 m high. It consists of two dials. The outer portion of the sundial indicates local apparent time while the inner portion indicates the time corrected for the longitude of the sundial's location. Forming an integral part of the sundial are 12 heritage icons depicting the Eastman region and includes themes of the First Peoples, La Vérendrye, the fur trade, the development of hydroelectric power, industry, research, as well as others. These icons illustrate the history of the region and its people.

Interpretive Display

The site for the Pinawa Heritage Sundial is a small park in the centre of town near the marina. The park creates a restful spot overlooking the Winnipeg River and offers visitors an opportunity to discover a new interpretation of heritage in this area. The site was selected because it is a meeting place where trails, roads, and waterways converge in the region.

Through funding assistance from Manitoba Culture, Heritage and Tourism as well as assistance from the LGD of Pinawa, AECL Underground Research Laboratory (URL), AECL Whiteshell Laboratories and numerous volunteers, an impressive interpretive display was constructed in 2003 to help guests get the most from a visit. The interpretive display consists of seven polished granite tablets. The tablets were mounted on a concrete display located at the north end of the sundial. The tablets give a general description of the sundial, how to use the sundial and short descriptions of the icons. A memorial supplier sandblasted the polished granite tablets which came from a local granite quarry. The granite was the same as that used on the sundial base. The concrete pad that was required for the concrete display base was built by the LGD, URL personnel Larry Rolleston and Glen Snider and volunteers Wilson Tiede, Harry Noel and Carl Sabanski.

The concrete base was constructed and assembled by URL personnel and donated to the project. The following volunteers participated in this phase of the project: Dennis Bilinsky, Darcy Dooley, Paul Gombar, Kirk Haugen, Glen Karklin, Shawn Keith, Clifford Kohle, Larry Rolleston and Glen Snider. The base was built at the URL and moved to the sundial site for assembly. This help was greatly appreciated. Reassembly of the base on-site involved volunteers Gib Drynan and Carl Sabanski.

Entrance Stone

The granite tablets were transported from the quarry to the sandblaster and then to the sundial site by the LGD of Pinawa.

At the sundial entrance is a grey piece of limestone (Tyndall stone), displaying the location of the sundial as well as the site motto. Below the tablet is a stainless steel pamphlet holder that was made by Ervin Hemminger and Glenn Graham.

The design and construction of the sundial involved a great deal of volunteer effort. We were very fortunate to have received funding through grants and the donations of numerous individuals and businesses to aid in the project. We also developed a number of fundraising activities. The first fundraising event was a raffle for a brass sundial specifically designed and constructed for the place where the winner lived. The winner of the dial was Brenda McKenzie, an artist and teacher residing in Pinawa.

Pinawa Sundial

Sara Coleman

Sujin Wren

Cheryl Lidfors

Shannon Lidfors

Heather Stanley

Holley Stanley and Tim Olchowy

Were you a figure skater?

Back Row Kathy Gauthier, Laurie MacLean, Holly Stanley; Front Row – Brenda Williams, Joanne Kelly, Lee Olchowy, Linda Truss, Cindy Serkes, and Kathy Kelly
(Photograph courtesy of Larry Gauthier)

Patrick Woodbeck and Pam Tymko

Do you remember broomball or jam can curling?

Or Red Rock Camp?

Pickleball Anyone?

One Church, Many Faiths
Pinawa models multidenominational approach
By: Brenda Suderman, Winnipeg Free Press, July 20, 2013

PINAWA - They sing from the United Church hymnbook, practise communion according to Anglican traditions, organize themselves according to Mennonite sensibilities and are served by a Presbyterian minister. For half a century, the folks at Pinawa Christian Fellowship - PCF for short - have been happily multidenominational, and they have no plans to change their ecumenical ways.

"It works this way because we've done it for 50 years," says retired scientist Roger Dutton, an Anglican member of PCF for 45 years. "We wanted it to work. I think people aren't as hidebound now about what their denomination does," adds Marion Stewart, a United Church member at PCF since 1963.

The congregation celebrates its 50th anniversary with a joint worship service 10 a.m., Sunday, July 21 in the gym of F. W. Gilbert Elementary School, the worship place of the congregation since 1963.

Conceived by Atomic Energy of Canada Limited employees in Deep River before the Whiteshell Laboratories near Pinawa opened in 1963, the church was always intended to accommodate multiple denominations, says church convenor

Long-time members of Pinawa Christian Fellowship: Ken Reddig, Marion Stewart, Roger Dutton, Thelma Boase and Chuck Vandergraaf

Chuck Vandergraaf, a retired AECL scientist of Presbyterian stock. He says the idea was to have one church for the Roman Catholics, and one for all the others, so people who worked together would worship together. "It was always understood if this town would continue to grow to 5,000 people, each denomination would split off because we would have enough critical mass," he explains.

With only 1,500 residents in Pinawa, that split won't happen any time soon for the congregation that's officially affiliated with the Anglicans, Presbyterians, United Church, and Mennonite Church Manitoba. The town is also home to Lutheran and Alliance churches. As one church represented by many denominations -- adherents also come from Lutheran, Baptist, Greek Orthodox, Roman Catholic, and Daoist background; PCF could be a model for other communities with declining church membership.

Although the congregation owns property in this scenic community along the Winnipeg River about 110 kilometres northeast of Winnipeg, and went as far as drawing up blueprints, they're committed to not owning a dedicated church building, preferring to rent office space for their minister, Rev. Robert Murray, and transforming the school gym into worship space each week. "The backdrops are rolled down from the ceiling, the pulpit is wheeled in, the font is wheeled in, the stalls are wheeled in," Dutton said about the regular Sunday morning preparations. "The school is very adaptable and works with us in this."

Structures and practices are worked out by a general committee, which has representatives from each denomination. Baptisms are administered according to denominational practices but worship is unique to PCF. The group takes communion following the Anglican tradition, sings from the United Church hymnal, and follows the lectionary reading for each Sunday. "There's a breadth in the diversity. There's a wideness in understanding. We learn from each other," explains Ken Reddig, one of three Mennonites in the 150 member congregation.

Christians across Canada could learn from this made-in-Pinawa model of ecumenical co-operation, suggests the general secretary of the Canadian Council of Churches, which represents all the denominations officially part of PCF.

Justin Trudeau meets Doug Platford

Pinawa Players carolling in the mall

All Things Pinawa Information Meeting –
October, 2009

Good morning Pinawa!

Good morning to you!

Justin Trudeau meets Pinawa students

My Recollections
By John (Jock) Guthrie

Our Arrival in Pinawa

Following a three day journey from Deep River, Ontario, Gladys and Jock, daughters Patricia and Beth, and last but not least "Buster" the family dog, arrived in Pinawa on 1963 August 7. The humans in this group

were ordinary. The same can't be said for Buster. His mother was a pedigree spaniel which had been indiscreet with a beagle hound. The resulting litter reflected the mother's spaniel characteristics. Not Buster! He had to be different, he was of beagle persuasion. Regrettably the veterinarian who docked the pups' tails did not realize this. Buster's tail was duly docked after the fashion of spaniels. The consequence of which was his lack of caudal appendage would haunt him for life. Said life ended one mid-winter. Buster was "laid to rest" in a WNRE Waste Management area tile hole where his remains may be an enigma for some future anthropologist.

Back to our arrival in Pinawa. The furniture van had not arrived as promised. Thanks to Bill McKeown and Ed Lundman who found sleeping bags for us, we slept on the floor of one of the upstairs bedrooms of 8 McDiarmid Road. In due course our furniture arrived and we settled in. Yes, we still live at 8 McDiarmid - we never changed houses.

Jock Guthrie

Mud!!

The stories of Pinawa's mud are legion. In the early days before the roads were paved, cars were parked out by Highway 211. Gum boots were essential equipment. The ladies carried more dressy shoes for wear when they got to pavement. Their nearest source of "Oh Be Joyful" was Lac du Bonnet. Only once did Gladys and other wives who travelled together to procure comestibles, etc., buy beer for their husbands. They didn't appreciate the whistles they provoked after repeated entrances to the beer parlour, mistaking the entrance for the door in to the Vendors!

Volunteer Firefighters

In the early days, please forgive the frequent use of that term; the town fire truck was manned by unpaid volunteers. There were few telephones in town which explains the following - let us say mix up. Ben Banham the fire chief had been lacking sleep for several nights because of insomnia. The night he gave in and took a sleeping pill - you guessed it - there was a fire. Scrap building material behind new construction on McMillan Place caught fire and threatened the houses being built. Ben, because of the lack of telephones, had to rouse the duty crew by calling at their homes. He roused the crew chief (for want of a better term), and a second member who lived next door. But by the time he arrived at the home of the third member the sleeping pill was taking effect. Said member's response was "Go home Banham - you're drunk." Wife to the rescue! Hearing the sound of a heavy truck she concluded it was for real and persuaded hubby to go forth and do his duty. Said hubby was halfway to the Plant when he realized he didn't know where the fire was! Nevertheless all the crew assembled in time to join in extinguishing the flames before any damage to property was done.

Then there was the adventure of the furnace fire! During working hours the LGD boys manned the fire truck. The lady of a house realizing all was not well with her furnace called in an alarm, then proceeded to put it out with a fire extinguisher. Just as well! The "boys" duly assembled outside her house and joined in a general debate. The gist of which was "I thought you were bringing the fire truck!"

The Hospital Next Door

Pinawa's second hospital was at No. 6 McDiarmid Road; the first was a clinic in one of the row houses. It was a convenient location for Gladys Guthrie, a part time nurse, since we lived next door. Pinawa's first baby, a girl, was born there. Father Hugh McAllister was a technician in the Environmental Control group of the Health and Safety Branch. This temporary hospital was closed and converted for occupation as a dwelling when the present Pinawa hospital was opened. For several years the house was the manse for PCF ministers, the Revs. Gilbertson, Barker and Corman.

One Saturday afternoon Dr. Henry knocked on the door and promptly entered as was his custom. "Do you have any 2x4's?" he asked. Hearing I did he commanded, "Get down to your workbench Jock; I want you to construct a frame to fit over the baby crib in the hospital." He had admitted a young baby with a dislocated hip and required a crib frame to put the child in traction.

Wild Life

The first time Jock went to see his future home in Pinawa the structure was closed in but lacked windows and doors. Approaching the open doorway he was greeted by a large bear coming up the make shift stairs from the basement. House inspection was deferred - a prompt retreat being in order.

Bears were not uncommon in the early days of Pinawa! The Guthries acquired a new plastic garbage can. Early one summer morning Jock heard the familiar sound of a bear at his new garbage can. He ran to the back door and hollered at the animal which quickly took off over the rock outcrop with the can. Jock gave chase, all the while throwing stones at the thief. He was determined not to lose his new garbage can! The bear dropped the can and disappeared from view. While standing on the outcrop with the garbage can congratulating himself, three incidents occurred: the bear returned to contest possession of the can; the night nurse on duty appeared at the back door of the hospital to see what the ruckus was about; and the cord holding up his pyjamas let go. I wonder if Lynne Kobald remembers the incident!

Another bear encounter. While out practicing connecting and laying hose with the fire engine Jock and his jolly crew got bored with the exercise. A bear appeared on the edge on the nearby bush. Now for some fun to liven up the practice. The fire hydrant was turned on and the bear was duly hosed. Said bear was supposed to run for cover in the bush. Regrettably the bear was not briefed. It charged! The dauntless crew beat a hasty retreat. Too bad they didn't disconnect the hose first. About 200 feet streamed off the retreating fire truck. Fire Chief Tom Lamb was not amused!

Entertainment

The bear-hosing fire engine crew was also involved in some of the entertainments put on in the early days of town. One of their skits, sung in commendable harmony I'll have you know, recounted some of the adventures and mis-adventures of the volunteer fire brigade. The town's resident administrator at the time was not entertained.

The Pinawa Christian Fellowship

What became the Pinawa Christian Fellowship (PCF) was conceived in Deep River, Ontario. CRNL employees had been designated for the Whiteshell Nuclear Research Establishment which would be situated in Manitoba. Plans had been made for laboratories, nuclear reactors, houses, schools, to name only a few items. Nothing had been planned for Christian worship. Bob Robertson, Jim Putnam and Jock Guthrie called a meeting of those designated to go to Manitoba. "We are going to be working together, living together, why not worship together?" Those attending the meeting appointed them to contact several denominations about establishing worship in the town which would be called Pinawa. It was stipulated that no commitment should be made until a meeting could be held in Pinawa, in order that new AECL employees could be present to express their views. The proposal to form a multi-denominational congregation was subsequently approved, and supported by the Anglican, Baptist Conference of Western

Canada, Lutheran, Mennonite Conference, Presbyterian and United Church denominations. The most enthusiastic supporter of the new concept for Christian witness was the late Very Rev. H.E. Hives, Bishop of Keewatin. The name Pinawa Christian Fellowship was suggested by Dr. Abram Petkau. Church School began in the elementary school at the end of October, 1963. Harry Allen was the first superintendent. The first worship was held the first Sunday in November. It was thought at the time that the PCF might endure for five, possibly ten years. The congregation continues to thrive 45 years later!

Recollections – 1963
By Gladys Guthrie

We were living in Deep River, Ontario. When I first learned about returning to Manitoba I was excited thinking of being closer to family. But on the other hand I was sorry to leave friends we made in Ontario. We had lived in different places which I loved and all the people we associated with. In those ten years this prairie girl was very comfortable living in the East. But another move, reminiscent of the days spent as an army wife, was exciting too.

Gladys Guthrie

We arrived in Pinawa early in the day, as we had spent the previous night at West Hawk Lake in a rustic cabin. Surprise as we approached No. 8 McDiarmid Road! There was a front-end loader parked on the bare earth (no grass) in the front yard. Jock has described how we spent our first night in Pinawa sleeping on the floor. The moving van pulled in the next day. What a lot of dirt and gravel was tracked in on the floors!

At first there was no shopping in town. We took turns with friends driving to Lac du Bonnet to buy the week's groceries. If you forgot something you borrowed, or did without until the next week's trip. Highway #211 was dreadful, gravel composed of large stones and potholes too numerous to count. That Fall the first Hudson Bay store was opened on Athlone Crescent. Cal Jewison was the manager and his garage was the store. He was great and did his best to fulfill all requests for food items. But we still made trips out for clothing, etc. and gas. There was no gas station in town. On returning from Winnipeg, it was prudent to fill up at Benny's (Seig's) corner.

Street lights had still to be installed. No telephones except those assigned to the Fire Chief and RCMP constable. To give a message to a neighbour meant going for a visit and, of course, coffee. What might have been a ten minute phone call was perhaps a two hour plus visit.

The Winnipeg gumbo was discouraging! I soon acquired my first ever rubber boots; I had grown up on a farm. We dried laundry on ropes strung between trees, wearing our rubber boots of course. Lots of whistles and hellos from construction workers building more houses for families which were yet to arrive, was not unpleasant accompaniment to wash day.

Room #15 in the elementary school was the town's community meeting centre. Pinawa's teachers were Inez Streimer, Joyce (Brown) Tabe, Bob Woods. The principal was Peter Thiessen. We had recreation director, Jim Spencer who filled many shoes (and wore many hats). School trips were organized. Grades 7 and 8 were taken on a school trip to Winnipeg. Jim Spencer was the navigator, guiding Dorothy Robertson and I around the city. The first stop was the Legislature Building. The students tumbled out of the cars and promptly began rolling on the green grass! No grass in Pinawa at that time.

October, 1963 was a lovely month with warm temperatures and little rain. Non-native Manitobans thought it was a great climate they had come to. Then came November and Manitoba settled into a normal pattern of snow and cold.

Initially, Dr. Henry Beaumont had office hours in a row house on McGregor Crescent. A split-level home at 6 McDiarmid Road was converted for our first hospital. The main floor had a delivery room, nursery and three wards. The lower level was doctor's office, examining room, waiting area and storage. The patients' meals were delivered from the Plant site. Dr. Beaumont was the only doctor on 24 hour call. He also had office hours in Lac du Bonnet and Pointe du Bois. At least once a month he travelled to Werner Lake, a mining community, to conduct medical examinations and see patients. Otherwise, the patients had to make the trip to Pinawa over a mining road, giving way to many ore trucks on route. Dr. Maggie Beaumont took care of maternity cases when Henry was out-of-town. Drs. Petkau and Weeks took some weekend calls. Our present hospital opened in late 1964. These are a few of many memories of our early days in Pinawa.

Office of the
Prime Minister

Cabinet du
Premier ministre

Ottawa. Canada K1A 0A2

Release

Date: October 5, 2009

For immediate release

PRIME MINISTER STEPHEN HARPER HONOURS OUTSTANDING LOCAL TEACHER FOR HER CONTRIBUTION TO CANADA'S FUTURE

OTTAWA — Prime Minister Stephen Harper today presented Jacquelyn Sturton of Pinawa Cooperative Nursery School, in Pinawa, Manitoba, with a 2009 Prime Minister's Award for Excellence in Early Childhood Education. The Award was presented at a ceremony in Ottawa marking the celebration of World Teachers' Day.

"A good teacher inspires a thirst for learning that lasts a lifetime," said Prime Minister Harper. "The outstanding teachers honoured today are an inspiration to us all. They play an invaluable role in our children's development and in the future success of our country."

This year, the Prime Minister presented 84 awards to educators from across Canada, including Certificates of Excellence and Certificates of Achievement for teaching excellence at all grade levels, from preschool through to secondary school. All recipients have been recognized by parents and fellow educators as innovative leaders who have helped students excel.

Canada

Pinawa Pioneers
Residents of Pinawa in 1963 through 2012

1. Fjola Davidson
2. Harley Davidson
3. Gerry Smith
4. Ed Wuschke
5. Marion Stewart
6. Barb Jones

7. Ruth Dobbin
8. May Dunford
9. Mari-ann Weeks
10. Isabel Acres
11. Jay Hawton
12. Grant Bailey

13. Bonnie Bailey
14. Fran Booth
15. Dave Booth
16. Lyn Grant
17. Jock Guthrie
18. Lori Robb

19. Helen Tomlinson
20. Fay Sochaski
21. Lynn Patterson
22. Joyce Tabe
23. Ray Kirkham
24. Ron MacLean

25. Doris Sawatzky
26. Jane Petkau
27. Sylvia Bjornson
28. Mike Tomlinson
29. Ray Sochaski

Photograph taken September 13, 2012 by Stu Iverson

Pinawa Residents – First Year
Residents of Pinawa in 1963-64 through 2012

1. Fjola Davidson
2. Harley Davidson
3. Gerry Smith
4. Ed Wuschke
5. Marion Stewart
6. Barb Jones
7. Ruth Dobbin
8. May Dunford
9. Mari-ann Weeks
10. Isabel Acres
11. Jay Hawton
12. Grant Bailey
13. Bonnie Bailey

14. Fran Booth
15. Dave Booth
16. Lyn Grant
17. Sylvia Wilkins
18. Pat Williamson
19. Margaret Williamson
20. Helen Tomlinson
21. Fay Sochaski
22. Lynn Patterson
23. Joyce Tabe
24. Ray Kirkham
25. Ron MacLean
26. Doris Sawatzky

27. Jane Petkau
28. Sylvia Bjornson
29. Marilyn Berry
30. Cathy Abraham
31. Maureen Bychuk
32. Betty Barnsdale
33. Roy Barnsdale
34. Michael Tomlinson
35. Ray Sochaski
36. Jerry Martino
37. Sheila Martino
38. Pat Lucas
39. Tom Tabe

40. Brian Wilkins
41. Fay Campbell
42. Wilf Campbell
43. Harry Backer
44. Doreen Backer
45. Lori Robb
46. Barb Remington
47. Pam Meeker
48. Doreen Legall
49. Annette Gauthier
50. Frank Oravec
51. Ann Oravec
52. Mary Ryz

53. Louise Daymond
54. Jock Guthrie
55. Al Nelson
56. Shirley Nelson
57. Doug Legall
58. Larry Gauthier
59. Lloyd Rattai
60. Lloyd Dreger
61. Bill Chelack
62. Mike Berry
63. Suzanne Rueckert
64. Stephen Berry

Photograph taken September 13, 2012 by Stu Iverson

Pinawa Home Comers

Many of the students who attended Pinawa schools, then stayed or returned to raise their families and retire. This is by no means the entire group of Home Comers; only the ones who were available for the photo (Photograph courtesy of Stu Iverson)

Front row: Myrna Tiede, Cathy Abraham, Pam Meeker, Fjola Davidson, Holly Parcey, Lynn Patterson, Lori Robb, Louise Daymond; *2nd row:* Carol Sandul, Kirk Edwards, Dennis Graham, Lori Graham, Suzanne Rueckert, Tara Fitzmaurice, Michelle Orvis, Stacy Clark, Jenny Crosthwaite; *3rd row:* Susan Barnett, Kara Bissonnette, Tammy Murray, Cheryl Michaluk, Rhonwen Mikkelson, Tamara Tinant, Joye Platford, Brad Holmlund, Kristen Ticknor, Wendy Berry; *4th row:* Rachel Dutton, Maureen Bychuk, Chris Reimer, Gertie Oliveira, David Bilsky, Brent Stokes, Paul Greber, Todd Berry, Kyle Wilken, Kevin Ticknor, Mike Stanley; *5th row:* Shawn Elcock, Paul Chambers, Daryl Woodbeck, Jennifer James-Thiessen, Connie Plunkett, Susan Clarke; *Back row:* Kim Reimer, Rob Gowryluk, Terry Reimer, Scott Suski, Ryan Bilinsky, Bill Murray, Kevin Borgford, Myles Drynan, Stu Hughes, Mike Berry, Stephen Berry.

Pinawa – Twelve Years Later
By Len Simpson
Published in the Canadian nuclear Society Bulletin- Volume 29, No. 3, 2008

Whiteshell To Close!

"Pinawa waits for the worst!" This was one of the many front page headlines in the Winnipeg Free Press during the month of November, 1995. What followed were weeks of confusion, panic, demonstrations, and denials by AECL that a decision to close Whiteshell had been made. However, when the dust finally settled, it was confirmed that AECL would be discontinuing support for the Nuclear Waste Management Program, and moving Reactor Safety Research, and other core programs supporting the CANDU product, to Chalk River. This began a long period of anxiety, rumours and false anticipations.

The History

Pinawa was established in 1963 as a bedroom community for the employees of AECL's second research laboratory, named the Whiteshell Nuclear Research Establishment (WNRE). The Labs were located on the east shore of the Winnipeg River about 100 Km north east of Winnipeg. Pinawa was located 12 Km to the east of the lab at the end of a highway. While the location was fantastic in terms of the natural beauty and recreation potential, it was off the beaten track and visitors rarely came to town unless they had business there. Pinawa's isolation was not a concern since AECL's vision was that it would grow to a population of 5000 with the anticipated expansion of the lab (one early model of the site showed four reactors, WR1 to WR4). The community actually grew to a population of about 2200 and WNRE did thrive while developing the organic-cooled reactor, studying other reactor concepts and researching reactor safety issues. Because of the early success of the Pickering reactors, AECL's interest in the organic-cooled concept waned, but emerging concerns about spent fuel disposal spawned the Nuclear Waste Management Program (NWMP). By the mid-nineties, the NWMP and the Reactor Safety Research Program were the main programs at the site, employing over 1000 employees. However there were clouds on the horizon. In 1995, because the nuclear industry was out of favour with the Liberal government of the time, AECL was instructed to cut back. A decision was made that AECL would consolidate core R&D (supporting CANDU) at Chalk River and attempt to commercialize the remaining programs, including the NWMP, at Whiteshell.

Until this time, Pinawa had been a true company town. There was only one general store, a drug store and a bank. A special school district was established, to ensure that the AECL employees would have control over the educational choices of their children, and a Local Government District (LGD) was established that dealt with municipal needs of the community. AECL provided the capital infrastructure of the LGD, including schools, a municipal office, a shopping mall, a community centre, a nine hole golf course and a well-equipped town yard. In later years, AECL also provided a hockey rink and an outdoor swimming pool. The operation of the town was covered by municipal taxes and a large grant-in-lieu from AECL. Obviously, it was a very comfortable life, especially for those raising families. Winnipeg was only 90 minutes away if one wished to partake of the cultural events or visit shops. Little thought was given, either by the Pinawa citizens or AECL, to diversify the economy of the town. Initially, nearly all employees rented houses from AECL, but in the seventies employees were encouraged by AECL to buy their homes. With home ownership residents began to improve their properties. In spite of that the market prices stayed low relative to the surrounding communities. Because Pinawa was still seen as an AECL town, there was not much interest in moving there, unless you worked for AECL or one of the few town businesses.

Early Events

In February 1996 the federal government set up the Whiteshell Task Force under the chairmanship of Peter Siemens, a successful Manitoba businessman, to recommend ways to commercialize the site. In July, the task force report was submitted to natural Resources Canada (now NRCan) recommending the establishment of an authority to proceed with commercialization. Finally, after another six months, the federal and provincial governments created the Economic Development Authority of Whiteshell (EDAW) under the directorship of Peter Siemens, whose mandate was to find new tenants for the site and employment for laid off AECL employees. A loan fund of $20 million was established to help entrepreneurs start new businesses in town, and in April 1997 NRCan invited a consortium led by British Nuclear Fuels Ltd. (BNFL), to negotiate taking over the site, bringing in their own businesses, and taking over the Nuclear Waste Management Program (NWMP). A Senior Vice President from BNFL was sent to work in Pinawa for as long as it took to come to an agreement with AECL to transfer facilities.

In 1998, a federal fund of $3.5 million was established, to be distributed to Pinawa and the surrounding communities to help start new projects that would provide jobs. This was known as the Community Adjustment Fund (CAF) and was administered by a committee made up of local reeves and mayors, a representative from the Pinawa Community Development Corporation (PCDC), Peter Siemens of the EDAW and a representative from the Western Economic Diversification Office.

The three years from 1996 to 1998 were filled with confusion and mixed messages. AECL was anxious to commence downsizing, but layoffs were frozen by NRCan pending possible commercialization. While members of the core programs were under pressure to complete research for licensing CANDU reactors, the NWMP employees were neglected by the executive, and their programs had been cut. Some staff in both programs began leaving AECL for jobs abroad or in other industries. Also, some members of the core program who did not want to transfer to Chalk River were talking to Peter Siemens about privatizing their programs at Whiteshell, and also to BNFL about joining their project. There was considerable conflict between Siemens and AECL because of this. At least one division director forbade his staff to talk to EDAW and BNFL, an instruction that was mostly ignored.

In April 1998, frustrated by an inability to engage AECL in serious negotiations, the BNFL group pulled out. By November 1998, AECL announced they were proceeding to close the site and move core programs to Chalk River.

Because of the relatively low expectation of selling one's house at a reasonable price, AECL launched a program that would pay the difference between an employee's selling price and the assessed value. This applied to those employees being transferred to Chalk River or those laid off and moving out of town. During this period, property values in Pinawa crashed.

Many people declined the offer to move to Chalk River and took a lay-off or retirement package. Moving to Chalk River was not welcomed by many as Chalk River's prospects for surviving the political climate were not thought to be much better than Pinawa's, and real estate there was two to three times the cost in Pinawa. Some of the best and brightest moved to the USA or Europe if they were young enough to restart their career. My position as Director of Reactor Safety Research was moved to Chalk River and I was offered a retirement package if I declined to go. It was an offer I couldn't refuse. Most of those of my age took the same path. Some started new businesses, some consulted, some took courses and started new endeavours and some just retired. No one wanted to leave this paradise called Pinawa. Of those called to Chalk River less than 50% accepted the transfer.

The Mysterious Israelis

The $20 million EDAW loan was established to help entrepreneurs start businesses in Pinawa but whenever government funding is available, all sorts of people turn up including what Peter Siemens referred to as bottom feeders. One day, a group claiming to represent an Israeli development company dropped into Peter's office. They had a plan to make Pinawa the "only five diamond resort between Toronto and Lake Louise", starting with the AECL staff hotel. In a town meeting they flabbergasted the citizens with their grandiose plan. Peter Siemens put them in touch with AECL and negotiations began to sell the staff hotel, the Pinawa marina area and several parcels of land in town. The staff hotel was offered to the town first, but the council of the time turned this down as the maintenance would have been a huge financial burden. AECL sold the property for one dollar to this group even though, two weeks earlier, information from Israel suggested this group was misrepresenting themselves.

It soon became clear that they had no money of their own to invest, apart from a Scotiabank loan based on their business plan, which was subsequently rejected by EDAW. They managed to run the staff hotel for only a few months before going into receivership in the spring of 1999. By then I was Mayor of Pinawa, and one day a few months after the receivership, we were visited in the Council office by two investigators from the Israeli government, who were searching for Israeli government funds that had been released to the same group during a project in Israel. We assured them that they had brought no funds to Pinawa and we spent the rest of the day sharing stories of our incredible experiences with these people.

Council Takes Action

In October 1998 there was an election for Pinawa Council. I was elected mayor and three new councillors were elected along with one member of the previous council. The election turnout was about 80%, extremely high for a municipal election. The people of Pinawa wanted action. I immediately met with Darren Praznik, our MLA, to discuss AECL's announcement to close Whiteshell. We decided to form a Leader's Group, consisting of four provincial ministers and the reeves and mayors of the communities affected by AECL's action. We met monthly to develop a unified approach to deal with AECL's decision and wrote a report on the impacts to the communities, including economic effect, the environment, and the fact that Manitoba would no longer be receiving its fair share of federal research dollars. Darren and several municipal leaders took the Leader's Report to Ottawa and met with several ministries, AECL and the Auditor General's Office. We expressed our concerns about the delays in commercialization of Whiteshell, and also the emerging inadequate decommissioning plans which were being prepared for the site. The Leader's Group united about seven local municipalities to a common cause. The group lives on, now expanded to include all of the northeast Manitoba municipalities, working together on economic issues and sharing resources.

Up until the municipal election in December 1998, the high level discussions that affected our future were carried out by EDAW, the federal government, AECL and the various companies that were interested in the site. The new council, supported by the general population, were determined to get more involved in our future. In a community workshop, we established that Pinawa needed to lessen our strong dependence on AECL and to do this, the community had to grow. We decided not to wait for outcomes that may arise from EDAW's efforts to bring new businesses to the AECL site, but to act in areas where we had total control. We recognized that Pinawa was already becoming a popular place for retirees, and many people from Winnipeg were purchasing Pinawa houses as recreational properties. However a complete town needs young working families and we decided to focus on attracting new businesses to our town.

EDAW had assisted in helping a number of small businesses spin out of AECL. The loan fund was helpful in a few cases, but several entrepreneurs found it very bureaucratic. The PCDC purchased the vacant elementary school to accommodate new businesses and renamed it the Lewis Centre. Darren Praznik placed the North Eastman Health Authority's head office in the centre and they are still the major tenant occupying about half the building. Other occupants include EcoMatters, now employing about a dozen people formerly in the NWMP, Granite Internet, which has grown into an internet service provider for the Eastman region and other small businesses. EcoMatters has a world-wide business providing advice to nuclear agencies in Sweden, France, the UK and Canada, investigating disposal of greenhouse gases for Canadian oil and coal industries, and modeling agricultural impacts across Canada. Space was rented at the AECL site for Acsion Industries, which offers irradiation services and composite materials for specialized uses. This is a spin-off from AECL'S Radiation Applications Branch. One of their products is a fibre-composite panel cured by radiation for Air Canada. They are also developing a course in radiation safety with the University of Winnipeg. Channel Technologies, another spun-out business, offers hardware for monitoring spent fuel bays in nuclear reactors to prevent nuclear proliferation, and does software development for AECL.

It was clear from day one that AECL's original plan to close the site and leave it with a skeleton staff, deferring major decommissioning for decades was unacceptable, a position shared by the Manitoba government. We also felt that the Whiteshell site was a valuable resource and every effort should be made to bring in another federal program, as they had done in similar situations elsewhere. With the establishment of the Leader's Group, we had built a strong relationship with the Province and maintained this when Gary Doer's NDP government won power in September, 1999. Following our first visit to Ottawa with Daren Praznik, I continued to lobby Ottawa on an annual basis, taking advantage of the annual CNA conference each year in Ottawa to meet with federal ministers, the nuclear regulator and AECL executives. We reminded the federal government at every opportunity that they had an obligation to leave Pinawa in a stable condition. We never approached them empty handed, but came with detailed proposals for locating anticipated new federal programs to the site. One of these suggested programs was a centre for climate change studies, where we had developed a concept with a Winnipeg consulting firm using funds from both the federal government and the province. While well received by government bureaucrats, our study now appears to be gathering dust somewhere on a shelf in Ottawa.

Decommissioning was a serious issue. Shortly after becoming mayor, EDAW identified decommissioning as a potential new industry for Whiteshell to develop. Up until then it appeared that AECL viewed decommissioning as cursory decontamination and mothballing a facility until proper disposal facilities were built to take care of the decommissioning wastes. It apparently was not part of their mission to provide such facilities so we went after NRCan to provide them. Even though NRCan's motto at the time was "polluter pays", there was an extended period of buck passing over who had the financial responsibility.

As I was visiting Paris in the spring of 1999, I invited Peter Siemens and the Assistant Deputy Minister of Manitoba Environment (Dave Wotton) to meet me in the UK and visit several sites where they could witness serious decommissioning in progress. Our first stop was the UK Atomic Energy Authority site at Harwell near Oxford. We saw an entire building of hot cells undergoing full dismantling, and active laboratory buildings being decontaminated so they could be released from the nuclear license. Through their privatization project, they were successfully attracting new businesses to the site and commercializing some of their old ones. This was basically what we were trying to do in Pinawa, but so far with little success. We saw similar things happening in Winfrith, the site of the Steam Generating Heavy Water Reactor, where they proudly showed us their spent-fuel bay that was now so clean that they actually served a lunch there when the decommissioning job was complete. Our final visit was to Sellafield, in the English Lake District, where we visited the British national site for low level waste disposal (Drigg), and toured the recently completed Thorpe reprocessing plant. Thorpe was an impressive sight, especially its cleanliness, but even more amazing was the simultaneous decommissioning of surrounding buildings, some clearly badly contaminated. Our visits made us realize the value of a site licensed for nuclear activities. They didn't just discard a site when they had no use for it, but were ready to bring in new nuclear activities to a community that is comfortable with the nuclear business.

At Harwell we were greeted by the UKAEA Chief Executive, Dr. John McKeown, who met with us for an hour and drove us to lunch later that day. We were treated to well-prepared presentations by senior people at all three sites. Dr. McKeown explained to us the importance of maintaining good relations with the local population, and stated that he personally spent one or two days a month in the communities explaining UKAEA activities to the local citizens. At this time, AECL senior executives showed little interest in communicating with the Pinawa residents. Being a politician also allowed me easy access to government ministers on my trips to Ottawa and Winnipeg, and also to talk to other community leaders in Eastern Manitoba.

We returned to Pinawa envious of what other countries were doing and frustrated with our own nuclear industry. Dave Wotton and I each wrote trip reports. Soon after, when AECL presented its Decommissioning plan to the Canadian Nuclear Regulator in November 2002, we both made Powerpoint presentations protesting the plan to defer decommissioning. We stressed the safety issue of deferring decommissioning and losing the expertise of workers familiar with the site, and the moral issue of deferring the decommissioning costs to future generations.

About the same time, I was invited to make a presentation at an OECD Nuclear Energy Agency workshop in Ottawa. The theme of the workshop was the relationship between the nuclear industry and the communities hosting that industry. Most countries boasted of strong industry relationships with their local communities but, at that time, AECL was clearly bound to get out of Pinawa as cheaply and as quickly as possible. I said some unkind things about our treatment by AECL and the federal government and was later reprimanded by one of AECL's public affairs staff for criticizing AECL in an international forum. However, I had no choice. I was no longer an AECL employee but was there speaking for the people of Pinawa, and I was expressing their views on the conference theme.

Later, I began to notice subtle changes in AECL's attitude to decommissioning and changes to AECL's relationship with the town. The Liberal government in Ottawa still had not responded to our many proposals, but in the summer of 2006 following a change in federal government, the new minister of NRCan, Gary Lunn, announced a five year budget of over $500 million to address Canada's nuclear legacies. One quarter of that money was targeted for Whiteshell decommissioning. AECL now employs about 300 persons in Pinawa and expects to be continuously decommissioning for the next 20 or more years. We will never know exactly how much our lobbying led to this decision, but we had certainly stayed in the face of the federal government, and with the Conservatives coming to power we made sure our new MP, Vic Toews, was well aware of our situation.

Demise of the EDAW

In March of 1999 Peter Siemens resigned as Executive Director of EDAW. His relations with AECL were never good, primarily because there was a conflict of interest between AECL's strategy and the goals of EDAW. AECL's first goal, apparently, was to prevent any new occupant at Whiteshell from using the nuclear facilities in competition with them. They had also removed most of the equipment from the site that could have been used even by non-threatening businesses such as mechanical testing. After several attempts to get something going at the site, Peter finally had had enough and resigned. He was replaced by Pat Haney, another Winnipeg businessman. The focus by then was on the creation of an employee-owned business formed out of the Waste Management group, or what was left of it. With a consultant from Ottawa and assistance from AECL, a business plan was developed for spinning out the NWMP. Then in the summer of 2001, AECL decided that the NWMP would stay with AECL and become part of their new Waste Management and Decommissioning program. The board of Directors of the EDAW all resigned in protest and the EDAW was dissolved. Bob van Adel had become CEO of AECL in February of 2001, had cleaned house and installed a completely new executive except for Dave Torgerson and Gary Kugler.

With the end of EDAW, Pinawa's future became totally in our control and in hindsight that was a good thing. It put us in direct communication with AECL (we were never included in meetings between AECL and EDAW even though it was us they were talking about). Things began to improve after that. At a meeting between Council and Bob van Adel we agreed to put the past behind us and move forward. When our community centre needed a new heating system and roof, Dave Torgerson, who was then in charge of the research sites, contributed $800 thousand. The Economic Development Committee of Council merged with the PCDC and, following some strategic planning sessions, set out to market the community as a good place to live and work. Success was slow but steady. Real estate values increased. The first $100 thousand house sale occurred and a year later one sold for over $300,000. Today the market is mostly between $150 and $250 thousand. At the time of AECL's assistance plan, they were selling for $40 to $70 thousand.

Every year sees an increase in building permit purchases, not just for new houses, but also for property improvements as people see the value of their property rise.

For years, people wishing to move to Pinawa had to buy one of the few houses on the market or build. Builders were reluctant to come to Pinawa because of the boom in Winnipeg. To address the shortage of houses for sale, PCDC recently formed the Pinawa Housing Corporation to provide new houses for sale. The first one, a ready-to- move (RTM) house, was sold two weeks after delivery to site. Two more are now under construction using a local contractor and labour. We now also have a Pinawa entrepreneur who just brought in three RTMs and has already sold two. Potential residents do not want the headache of building, but will readily buy a new house already in place. Thus by building houses ourselves we are meeting a demand.

Over a decade ago, Rick Backer built an RV campsite just west of town on the Winnipeg River. It quickly became popular with nearly all the sites becoming seasonal. It now increases our summertime population by about 400 and brings more business to our modernized deli-supermarket, now known as the Solo Store, and other local businesses. Several campsite residents have purchased lots or houses in Pinawa or are building new homes. Having camped here they now want to live here year round. We have other residents moving here from across Canada and even Europe.

After the bankruptcy of the former Kelsey House, the building and some waterfront property was purchased from the receiver (for real money) by an eastern Manitoba company and turned into the Wilderness Edge Resort. It specializes in organizing retreats for a variety of groups, including church groups, provincial cabinet meetings, companies and government organizations. They are now operating close to capacity and are considering expansion, plus a sixty unit luxury condo complex. The Kelsey House experience with the Israelis taught us one golden rule. Never sell property for a dollar based on promises from a developer!

Our world-wide public relations campaign to attract homebased entrepreneurs is slowly starting to bear fruit. We advertise Pinawa as a safe environment in an area of natural beauty with all the necessary amenities of a large urban centre, including two providers of high-speed internet. Our website "Pinawa.com" is the centre of our marketing campaign and was developed with the help of funding from the Community Adjustment Fund.

AECL continues to be a vital part of our community. They are hiring again and expect to be decommissioning the Whiteshell site for at least the next twenty years. The relationship between the company and the town is solid again, but we are no longer seen as being a company town. AECL is once again participating in town events such as the Pinawa parade and sponsoring our website. It remains our goal to diversify further and grow to lessen our dependence on a single company. We believe that having a site that is licensed for nuclear activities and situated on a transmission line corridor to Winnipeg is a real asset, especially with the nuclear renaissance in progress and the interest in Western Canada in going nuclear. For the past three years or so we have been meeting with Manitoba Hydro and the Provincial Government to get them to consider a nuclear power plant at the Whiteshell site, instead of relying on northern rivers with their need for billion dollar transmission lines to the markets of Winnipeg, Western Canada and the northern states. We feel we are beginning to make some progress here.

Pinawa – The Secret Discovered

It has been an incredible experience to live in Pinawa during the past decade. The early years were frustrating but with the strong support of the Filmon and Doer provincial governments we survived that period and learned many lessons. The EDAW concept seemed like a good idea at the time, but required the cooperation of two levels of government (at least two ministries on the federal side) and AECL, and the goals were not always focused on the same outcome. Accessing the loan fund was incredibly complex and negotiations were difficult. The absence of the town from the top-level meetings left us unable to bring our desires directly to the table. The demise of the EDAW left the council fully in control of our future and we took control with a passion.

Our community's greatest asset is its volunteers. Early on they designed and built the Pinawa Suspension Bridge across the Pinawa Channel.

It was part of the Pinawa section of the Trans Canada Trail, the first section to be completed in Manitoba. At the town centre, they designed and erected the Pinawa Heritage Sundial, which has become our most familiar landmark and is a must-see for visitors to Pinawa. They also organize our annual events such as the Manitoba Loppet, the Pinawa Triathlon, Art in the Garden and the Pinawa Birthday Celebrations, all of which attract outside visitors and participants.

The one government program that was very useful was the Community Adjustment Fund. The $3.5 million was controlled by a committee of local council members and overseen by Western Economic Diversification. About half of the money came to Pinawa projects with the rest going to nearby communities that were also affected by AECL's downsize. Projects funded in Pinawa included the purchase of the Lewis School and converting it to a business centre, a business incubator program, several economic development initiatives, and a grant for the Pinawa Housing Corporation for pre-apprentice training during their building projects. The CAF committee worked together and disagreement was very rare even though several different communities were involved.

What was once seen as a company town located at the end of a 12 km road is changed forever. In 1998 we took over the AECL highway signs and developed the slogan "Discover the Secret". We now have a growing and diverse population, and an expanding business community. The future looks bright. We have recently changed our slogan to "Imagine Yourself in a Place". The secret has been discovered and Pinawa is on the map.

Pinawa's Ironwood Trail

Pinawa's Unlikely Rebirth
By: Margo Goodhand, Winnipeg Free Press – February 2, 2013

PINAWA - The little town of Pinawa celebrates its 50th birthday this summer -- an unusual milestone for a place that was actually born in 1903, died in the 1950s, and reincarnated down the road in 1963. But then Pinawa is an unusual little town.

Not many communities of 1,444 boast their own public swimming pool and beachfront, marina, rowing and sailing club, tennis courts, softball pitch and one of the province's top 18-hole golf courses. In the winter, there's hockey, curling, figure skating and more than 40 kilometres of groomed cross-country ski trails winding through the boreal forest, alongside frozen waterways, up and down the Precambrian Shield.

A community this small would consider itself lucky to have its hospital, schools, community centre and shopping mall. Pinawa offers year-round recreation in some of the prettiest real estate in the country.

Pinawa Mayor Blair Skinner said he came for a summer job in 1980, and "I'm still here," calling the move "the best fluke of my life."

Plans for the big 5-0 July 20 got a boost last month when world-renowned Lund Boats announced it would bring its fifth annual Lund Mania fishing tournament to Canada for the first time. So now on top of the day's fireworks, music and parade, there's a whole lot of walleye fishing. Top three fishers win Lund boats, engines and trailers.

Former and current residents alike can hardly wait for the party.

The town's unusual claim to two birthdays and only one funeral so far is a powerful tale of, well, power.

Pinawa was first built in 1903 as the province's first big power project, the Pinawa Dam, 110 kilometres northeast of Winnipeg at what is now the northwest tip of Whiteshell Provincial Park. But the old Pinawa petered out after a bigger hydro-electric station was built downstream at Seven Sisters. In 1963, when Atomic Energy of Canada Limited came shopping for a nuclear-research facility site, they picked a place less than 10 kilometres from the old dam, designed a perfect little town for its workers, with all the amenities, and called it Pinawa.

Pinawa.2 flourished in the 70s and 80s, with the feds employing some 900 people in its heyday. AECL also built a controversial $40-million underground research laboratory there in 1985 to see whether nuclear waste could be safely stored under the Canadian Shield.

When it decided to decommission the facility in 1995, and then closed the underground lab in 2010, many thought that was the end of Pinawa. Again.

Only this time, the town didn't die.

Four hundred townsfolk still work at AECL, according to Skinner. Apparently, cleaning up a radioactive research facility takes decades (one might not want to rush the job). Some former workers chose to stay and create home-based businesses. And healthy retirees began flocking to Pinawa for its lifestyle -- at least, until U.S. real estate prices took a dive and made hot spots like Arizona and Florida cheaper.

Skinner knows they need to diversify their economy and bring in young families. Pinawa has lost about 50 people since the 2007 census. Its facilities are aging and so is its population.

That's another unusual fact about Pinawa: Its average age is almost 54. Those who move for the lifestyle tend to stick around, said Elaine Greenfield, president of the Whiteshell Cross Country Ski Club. "Lots of people have grown old in town."

The former Realtor has her own reasons for admiring Pinawa. It was designed to desegregate the rich and the poor, with big and little houses built together on its streets. "And the entire waterfront is public land," she said. "You can walk, swim, bike along it. That's a very unusual concept."

Pinawa's motto is Live, Work and Play. And play they do.

The average 54-year-old Pinawanian could probably outskate or ski the average 44-year-old Winnipegger. It's an active population, with a particularly enthusiastic old-timers' hockey league. Unusual Pinawa fact No. 5, if you're keeping track: More Pinawa residents (12.7 per cent) walk or cycle to work than the average Manitoban (8.9), according to a StatsCan database compiled by city-data.com.

Even the mayor has taken up cross-country skiing. Kind of.

Asked to open up a new warming hut last year on the 10-kilometre Orange Trail, Skinner had too much pride to allow him to accept a snowmobile ride to the ribbon-cutting. Instead, he dug up some skis of his own and he and his wife practised on the undulating Pinawa golf course trail before making the trek out to the woods. It was a start.

Skinner is still practising and claims to enjoy the sport despite a recent thrill on a hill. "I was going down, and I could see I just wasn't going to make this corner at the end," he confessed. "So I reached out and grabbed onto the softest-looking tree I could find to stop from falling." My son said, 'So, dad, I guess that officially makes you a tree-hugger.' "

A tree-hugging mayor in a town built on radioactive research. Only in Pinawa.

Welcome Home!

Chapter 8
Appendix

PINAWA EXCHANGE

DIRECTORY LIST

of

Subscribers Connected to the

Pinawa Exchange

SPECIAL NOTICE

This revised directory is issued in view of the changes and additional
subscribers services installed on the Pinawa Exchange.

MANITOBA TELEPHONE SYSTEM

JULY, 1964

How To Use
THE DIAL TELEPHONE

(1) Consult directory for correct number.

(2) REMOVE HAND-SET (RECEIVER) before operating dial.

(3) LISTEN FOR THE DIAL TONE. A steady humming sound indicates your line is ready to receive your call. If you do not hear dial tone, hang up and call later.

(4) DIAL THE NUMBER, by inserting index finger in the dial opening of each digit of the number in succession, rotating dial until the finger reaches the stop, and then removing finger to allow dial to return UNAIDED. If your finger slips or you make a mistake, replace the receiver for a few seconds, and begin again.

(5) LISTEN with hand-set (receiver) for called party to answer.

(6) A slow intermittent burring sound will be heard if the called party's bell is ringing.

(7) A rapid succession of sounds, "Buzz-Buzz-Buzz", will indicate that the called party's line is busy. If this is heard, replace hand-set and try again later.

PINAWA

Business Office - 412 Main St, Selkirk

EMERGENCY CALLS
For direct connection to emergency services please dial the number listed below.
FIRE 753-2585
POLICE 753-2919
HOSPITAL 753-2334

BUSINESS OFFICE
Call Operator and ask for Zenith 56000
ASSISTANCE
INFORMATION } **CALL OPERATOR**
LONG DISTANCE
REPAIR SERVICE
Call Operator and ask for Repair Service

Telephone Accounts may be paid to the following Authorized Agent: Pinawa Pharmacy, Pinawa.

For inquiries regarding accounts please contact the Business Office.

Acres O 30 McDiarmid Rd 753-2540	Bjornson B 2 Tweedsmuir Pl 753-2593
Allan M G 21 McDiarmid Rd 753-2723	Booth D 17 McDiarmid rd 753-2578
Allen J H 10 McDiarmid Rd 753-2630	Boulton J 7 Burrows Rd 753-2550
Allwright W 5 Devonshire 753-2638	Breti A 27 Athlone Cres 753-2680
Archinuk R E 7 McMillan Pl 753-2279	Caldwell D G 47 Alexander 753-2537
Atomic Energy of Canada	Cameron C G 13 Alexander.............753-2271
Medical Bldg—Plant Site 753-2311	Campbell Don 11 Athlone Cres 753-2268
Guest House—29 McGregor Cres 753-2732	Central Mortgage & Housing Corporation
Townsite Office—10 McGregor Cres 753-2992	9 McGregor Cres 753-2737
Nurse's Residence—12 McGregor Cres ..753-2763	Chelack Wm 49 Alexander 753-2263
Staff Hostel—Burrows Rd 753-2321	Dalby K 11 McDiarmid rd 753-2973
Badger D 52 Alexander 753-2529	Davidson H J 27 Devonshire 753-2650
Bailey G 6 McWilliams Pl 753-2233	Day R C 31 McGregor Cres 753-2553
Banham Ben 2 Tupper Pl 753-2548	Deroche L 45 Alexander 753-2636
Bank of Montreal	Dobbin Everet 25 Devonshire Pl 753-2251
General Office—	Dobflaw J 13 McGregor Cres 753-2500
Shopping Centre Burrows Rd 753-2643	Dunlop I H 19 Alexander 753-2629
Manager's Office 753-2903	Eaton's of Canada—Winnipeg
Banks B 12 Alexander 753-2565	Call Long Distance (No Toll Charge) and
Beaumont Dr H W 12 McDiarmid Rd 753-2506	ask for ....Zenith 12300
Belinski Brian 38 Alexander 753-2730	English A 34 Alexander 753-2740
Bell David 1 Tweedsmuir Pl 753-2555	Ennis P C 25 Athlone Cres 753-2613
Birnie T M 4 McWilliams Pl 753-2966	Fenton J H 32 McGregor Cres 753-2664
	Finlay B A 4 McDiarmid Rd 753-2564

FIRE	753-2585
Fitzsimmons D 4 Tupper Pl	753-2503
French D J 1 McGregor Cres	753-2531
From Milton 36 Alexander	753-2770
Futcher A M 36 McDiarmid rd	753-2684
Gibson George M 2 McGregor Cres	753-2681
Gilbert Fred 2 Devonshire	753-2557
Gille C B 3 McGregor Cres	753-2533
Gilmour H 38 McDiarmid rd	753-2222
Godschalk C E 9 Athlone Cres	753-2257
Graham D 17 Athlone Cres	753-2510
Grant Ed 11 McGregor Cres	753-2546
Grant G R 48 Alexander	753-2933
Green Don 4 Devonshire	753-2951
Guthrie J E 8 McDiarmid rd	753-2622
Hannam Marvin 13 Athlone Cres	753-2219
Hatcher S R 1 Burrows rd	753-2245
Hawton J 3 Devonshire	753-2782
Hlus Zenith 7 Athlone Cres	753-2216
Hollies R 27 McGregor Cres	753-2658
Horn L 16 McDiarmid rd	753-2771
Hudson's Bay Co	
General Office—Shopping Centre Burrows Rd	753-2697
Retail Section	753-2944
Imperial Construction Ltd 60 Alexander	753-2525
Irvin's Electric—Lac du Bonnet	
Call Long Distance (No Toll Charge) and ask for	Zenith 11300
Iveson L 25 McDiarmid rd	753-2795
Jennings J J 28 McDiarmid rd	753-2666
Jewison C 4 Athlone Cres	753-2709
Johnson Leslie A 17 Burrows rd	753-2695
Jones R W 3 McWilliams Pl	753-2618
Keith Wilfred 51 Alexander	753-2275
Kingston P F 4 Minto Pl	753-2513
Kirkham T R 10 McWilliams Pl	753-2677
Koshuta E R 31 Devonshire	753-2228
Lamb Tom 17 Alexander	753-2208
Legall Doug 1 18 Alexander	753-2590
Litvinsky W 14 Devonshire	753-2214
Lundman E 1 Alexander	753-2646
Luxton C W 13 McDiarmid Rd	753-2734
MacLean R H 13 Devonshire	753-2236
Malcom Construction Plant Site	753-2276
MANITOBA TELEPHONE SYSTEM	
Business Office—	
Call operator and ask for	Zenith 56000
For assistance in making a call	
For numbers not listed in Directory	Call Operator
To call out-of-town points	
To report telephones out of order—	
Call Operator and ask for Repair Service	
McAllister H 8 McWilliams Pl	753-2544
McConnachie R 5 McGregor Cres	753-2693
McFarland A R 62 Alexander	753-2247
McIntyre A K 23 Devonshire	753-2243
McKeown W A 11 Devonshire	753-2757
Minton R J 4 Burrows Rd	753-2669
Morgan D 23 McDiarmid Rd	753-2712
Nerbas D W 6 Athlone Cres	753-2631
Olson H 9 McDiarmid Rd	753-2230
Penner A K & Sons Vanier	753-2530
Perth's Cleaners & Launderers	
Shopping Centre Burrows Rd	753-2969

Petkau Dr A 27 McDiarmid Rd	753-2249
Pinawa Barbers Shopping Centre Burrows Rd	753-2953
Pinawa Beautician	
Shopping Centre Burrows Rd	753-2609

PINAWA PHARMACY

PRESCRIPTIONS

PHOTO SUPPLIES - GIFTS

Shopping Centre Burrows Rd	753-2582

Pinawa Service Centre	
Burrows Rd & Vanier	753-2777
Pinawa Town of	
Fire—Burrows Rd	753-2585
Police—Burrows Rd	753-2919
Hospital—Vanier	753-2334
Local Gov't District Office—Burrows Rd	753-2331
Dept of Public Works	
Water Treatment Plant—Willis Dr	753-2542
If no answer call	753-2331
Emergency Calls	
D Green res	753-2951
A Gille res	753-2533
Poulin P C 11 Alexander	753-2587
Pratt Barry N 10 Alexander	753-2602
Putnam J 6 Tweedsmuir Pl	753-2702
Randell Robert 50 Alexander	753-2504
Rankin J 46 Alexander	753-2753
Robertson R F 6 Tupper Pl	753-2259
Rosser A 2 McWilliams Pl	753-2717
Russell Ray 6 Burrows Rd	753-2675
Sawatzky A 5 Tupper Pl	753-2573
Schwartz W 18 McDiarmid Rd	753-2539
Searle N 12 Devonshire	753-2767
Seymour C G 10 Devonshire	753-2616
Shawinigan Engineering Co Ltd Plant Site	753-2311
Smith Gerald D 19 Burrows Rd	753-2266
Smith H V 9 McWilliams Pl	753-2604
Smith Roger 7 McWilliams Pl	753-2655
Sochaski R O 13 Burrows Rd	753-2662
Spencer J 15 Athlone Cres	753-2648
Stannard E J 9 Burrows Rd	753-2755
Stewart R B 1 McWilliams Pl	753-2611
Stone C 31 Alexander	753-2640
Striemer I 23 Burrows Rd	753-2900
Stromberg T R 44 Alexander	753-2920
Swiddle J 2 Minto Pl	753-2595
Thiessen P 15 Alexander	753-2626
Thompson Don A 33 Devonshire	753-2607
Tomlinson M 2 McMillan Pl	753-2253
Tymko R R 1 Connaught Pl	753-2987
Universal Electric Plant Site	753-2517
Wallace R J 21 McGregor Cres	753-2788
Wardrop W L & Associates Ltd	
10 McGregor Cres	753-2923
Weeks Dr J L 54 Alexander	753-2745
Whiteshell School District No 2408	
McDiarmid Rd	753-2559
Williams G P L 10 McMillan Pl	753-2690
Williamson J P 23 McGregor Cres	753-2265
Wood R 32 McDiarmid Rd	753-2576
Wuschke E 5 McMillan Pl	753-2706
Zacharias E 34 McDiarmid Rd	753-2225

Temperature:	Jan	Feb	Mar	Apr	May	Jun	Jul	Aug	Sep	Oct	Nov	Dec	Year	Code
Daily Average (°C)	-18.1	-13.7	-6.2	3.4	11.4	16.2	18.9	17.7	11.8	5.1	-4.9	-14.5	2.3	A
Standard Deviation	3.8	4.3	3.3	2.5	2.4	1.7	1.4	1.7	1.4	1.6	3.1	4	1.2	A
Daily Maximum (°C)	-12.6	-7.8	-0.4	9.7	18.1	22.2	24.8	23.7	17.3	9.8	-1.3	-9.8	7.8	A
Daily Minimum (°C)	-23.5	-19.5	-12	-2.9	4.7	10.1	12.9	11.6	6.3	0.4	-8.5	-19	-3.3	A
Extreme Maximum (°C)	8	12	20	32.5	34.5	**37.5**	35	35.5	36	27.2	23.3	10		
Date (yyyy/dd)	1986/11	2000/23	1967/30	1980/21	1980/21	**1995/17**	1975/30+	1983/04+	1983/02	1964/14	1975/05	1969/01		
Extreme Minimum (°C)	-43.9	**-47.8**	-39.4	-28.9	-13.9	-3.9	-0.6	-1.5	-6.7	-15.5	-34.5	-40		
Date (yyyy/dd)	1974/01	**1966/19**	1974/24	1979/06	1966/01	1964/01	1972/03	1982/28	1965/25	1991/31	1985/30	1984/31+		
Precipitation:														
Rainfall (mm)	0.3	2	8.3	22	58.1	94.5	78.3	71.5	63.5	37.3	8.7	1.2	445.5	A
Snowfall (cm)	21.4	14.9	19	9.9	1.4	0	0	0	0.6	8.3	21.9	22.5	119.8	A
Precipitation (mm)	21.7	16.9	27.3	31.9	59.5	94.5	78.3	71.5	64.1	45.5	30.6	23.7	565.3	A
Average Snow Depth (cm)					0	0	0	0	0	0				B
Median Snow Depth (cm)					0	0	0	0	0	0				B
Snow Depth at Month-end (cm)	34	36	24	2	0	0	0	0	0	3	14	22		B
Extreme Daily Rainfall (mm)	5.1	19.2	17.4	32	65	**168.4**	60	77.2	75.2	56.5	21.2	17.6		
Date (yyyy/dd)	1964/02	2000/25	1983/06	1964/12	1974/19	**1973/14**	1988/05	1995/18	1977/08	1994/06	2000/01	1982/01		
Extreme Daily Snowfall (cm)	23.9	15.7	23.9	**48**	9.9	0	0	0	4	36.8	20.8	14.5		
Date (yyyy/dd)	1974/25	1977/24	1996/29	**1997/04**	1979/10	1964/01+	1964/01+	1964/01+	1981/30	1971/30	1977/20	1966/05		
Extreme Daily Precipitation (mm)	23.9	19.2	23.9	48	65	**168.4**	60	77.2	75.2	56.5	21.2	17.6		
Date (yyyy/dd)	1974/25	1998/25+	1996/29	1997/04	1974/19	**1973/14**	1988/05	1995/18	1977/08	1994/06	2000/01	1982/01		
Extreme Snow Depth (cm)	66	75	85	**90**	3	0	0	0	0	30	43	57		
Date (yyyy/dd)	1974/29+	1997/17	1997/25	**1997/07**	1997/13	1964/01+	1964/01+	1964/01+	1964/01+	1971/31	1965/27	1996/13		

Pinawa Weather Records

INDEX

Note:

1. The bolded names are contributors to this book.

2. Names in picture captions have not been included in this index.

72967567R00141

Made in the USA
Columbia, SC
03 July 2017